Hermann Everts

A Complete and Comprehensive History of the Ninth Regiment New Jersey Volunteer Infantry

From its first Organization to its Final Muster Out

Hermann Everts

A Complete and Comprehensive History of the Ninth Regiment New Jersey Volunteer Infantry
From its first Organization to its Final Muster Out

ISBN/EAN: 9783337402105

Printed in Europe, USA, Canada, Australia, Japan

Cover: Foto ©ninafisch / pixelio.de

More available books at **www.hansebooks.com**

A COMPLETE AND COMPREHENSIVE

HISTORY

OF THE

Ninth Regiment New Jersey Vols.

INFANTRY.

FROM ITS FIRST ORGANIZATION TO ITS FINAL MUSTER OUT.

BY HERMANN EVERTS.

NEWARK, N. J. .

A. STEPHEN HOLBROOK, PRINTER,

No. 3 Mechanic Street.

1865.

PREFACE.

In presenting the following history to the members and friends of the Regiment, and the public generally, the Author would state that the utmost accuracy has been observed in relation to marches, scouts, skirmishes, and camp life; the names of men and officers with remarks, and the list of diseases, have been taken from company-rolls, regimental and medical records, and the greatest care and fidelity paid thereto.

The history comprises the name, place of birth, year of enlistment, and date of re-enlistment of every man who has ever been connected with the regiment; the location and nature of wounds; when and where received; when, where, and why discharged; date, place, and cause of death; place of burial; promotion and resignation-table of officers, with full remarks; mile-table, giving distances traveled by water, railroad, and marches; consolidated table of all additional changes and transfers to and from the regiment; tabular list of diseases, with general summary thereto; sketches of the lives of Gen. Heckmann and Col. Zabriskie; every day's occurrences; interesting reminiscences; humorous anecdotes; regimental and general orders of interest and importance, together with much information of interest to the general reader.

The writer takes this opportunity to express his sincere gratitude to all officers and men who have either contributed towards his work, or assisted him in any information wanted.

First Regimental Muster at Trenton, New Jersey,

October 8th, 1861.

FIELD AND STAFF OFFICERS.

JOSEPH WARNER ALLEN, - - COLONEL.

. C. A. HECKMANN, - - - - - MAJOR.

F. W. WELLER, - - - - - SURGEON.

LOUIS BRAUN, - - - ASSISTANT SURGEON.

ABRAM ZABRISKIE, - - - - ADJUTANT.

SAMUEL KEYES, - - - QUARTERMASTER.

THOMAS DRUMM, - - - - CHAPLAIN.

NON-COMMISSIONED STAFF.

ARMSTEADT GULICK, - SERGEANT MAJOR.

JOHN W. LEWIS, - - HOSPITAL STEWARD.

JOHN BAMFORD, - QUARTERMASTER SERGEANT.

SHMIDT BILDERBECK, - COMMISSARY SERGEANT.

First Roll shows aggregate of 1142 : twelve Companies, from A to M, inclusive, encamped at Camp Olden, near Trenton, N. J.

Company A.

HERMANN RUMPF, Captain.

CHARLES HAYES, 1st Lieut.   PHILIP SPEAR, 2d Lieut.

Enlisted Men.

Friedrich Folger, discharged for promotion, Oct. 25, 1861.
E. Willburn,   "   "   "   Dec. 5, 1861.
George Muller,   "   "   "   June 24, 1862.
James Hand, Rahway, N. J., disch. at Camp Olden, being under age.
Peter Hermes, disch. at Camp Olden, for wounds received previous to enlistment.
John Pelar, John Heidecker, William Musket, John Lauterbach, John Ernst, A. Muttenzee, deserted before leaving Camp Olden, 1861.
William Geist, Thomas Braun, Friedr. Rappa, Chr. Fuchs, F. Eberle, were left behind at Washington, D. C., 1861.
—— Peterman, deserted at Annapolis, Md., 1861.
F. Muller, Newark, N. J., wounded in both legs at Roanoke Island, February 8, 1862; legs amputated; died at Roanoke.
John Eckel, wounded at Roanoke Island, February 8, 1862; died at Roanoke.
A. Meiss, died at Roanoke, March 16, 1862; typhoid fever.
John Scheriff, died on board hospital-boat, near Newbern, March, 1862.
Henry Weitzell, killed in action near Newbern, March 14, 1862.
William Muller, wounded at Newbern, N. C., March 14, 1862; died of wounds received, March 19, 1862.
F. Tuschmann, wounded at Newbern, March 14. 1862; died of wounds received, when home on furlough.
John Konig, discharged at Newbern.
C. Heinrich, H. Daring, deserted at Newport Barracks, N. C., 1862.
D. Knobble, M. Scheill, F. Schultz, S. Stout, H. Fricke, T. Baumann, A. Hannapal, discharged at Newport Barracks, N. C., for general disability and rheumatism.
L. Kumps, P. Gassen, C. Goss, —— Hockenjoss, O. Jordan, Wm. Kuhn, John Frank, B. Nittinger, J. Spitznagle, F. Kroter, A. Kummich, Grauss and Young, discharged at Morehead City, 1862, for general disability.
John Eckert, discharged at Washington, D. C., 1862, for general disability.

REMARKS.—The old companies A. and L. were consolidated into the other ten companies, in November, 1862. The names of men so transferred are marked either A. or L.
If the statements of the above are not entirely correct, it will be attributed that the old company records have been partly lost in action at Roanoke and Newbern.

Company B.

CORNELIUS CASTNER, Captain.

H. BARTHELMEW, 1st. Lieut.   C. H. SOFIELD, 2d Lieut.

Enlisted Men.

Philipp Acker, Middlesex, N. J., wounded at Newbern, March 14, 1862; discharged at Newark, N. J., September 6, 1862.

C. S. Abrams, Greene Co., N. Y., had a furlough; sent in a certificate as being under age and deranged, and was discharged.

Thomas Burnett, Ireland, discharged for promotion, June 11, 1862.

John Butterworth, England, discharged at Newbern, May 30, 1863; hæmophitis.

Thomas Buckley, England, discharged at Morehead City, November 6, 1862; dropsy.

John F. Benjamin, Suffolk, N. Y., discharged at Morehead City, November 19, 1862; disease of the heart.

Phineas Bloodgood, Middlesex, N. J., accidentally wounded; discharged, Morehead City, October 23, 1862.

Henry Brecce, Middlesex, N. J., discharged at Morehead City, November 18, 1863; mephritis.

William B. Boudinot, New Brunswick, N. J., discharged at Camp Olden, November 2, 1861; hemorrhoids.

E. J. Boream, Washington, N. J., discharged at Camp Olden, November 1, 1861; rheumatism.

D. C. Bradford, Middlesex, N. J., taken prisoner while on picket, April 7, 1862; exchanged, returned to regiment, and deserted.

Thomas Birney, Ireland, wounded in knee at Newbern, March 14, 1862, deserted while home on furlough, February, 1864.

John H. Caster, Monmouth, N. J., discharged at Newbern, May 30, 1863; rheumatism.

Edward Cury, England, received a furlough at Newbern hospital, and deserted at New Brunswick, N. J., November 5, 1863.

C. A. Coburn, Middlesex, N. J., deserted April, 1863; was arrested 27th of July, 1864, and confined in Fort Columbus.

Deserted at Camp Olden, 1861.

Wm. Collins, New Brunswick.	William Sharlow.
M. Daily, Waterford, Ireland.	M. Houton.
G. Demot.	John Vanderwater.
P. H. Munslow, England.	C. Irwin King.
M. Jackson.	Wm. H. Newman, Hudson.

Discharged at expiration of time of service, at Trenton. N. J.,
December 7, 1864.

James Crawford, Union.
D. W. D. Gray, Somerset.
B. V. Nevius, "
John Clerkin, Middlesex.
D. Haggerty, "
R. Vanderhoff, "
R. N. Gould, Suffolk.

John H. Shmidt, Hunterdon.
James McClay, Philadelphia.
F. Cahill, Ireland.
John Sheehan, Ireland.
Peter Lawless, "
H. Headley, England.
John Myers, Hungary.

D. Cosgrove, Ireland, Theodore De Hart, Union, Th. V. Hughes, Middlesex, taken prisoners while on picket near Newport Barracks, N. C., April 7, 1862; returned when the regiment returned from South Carolina, and discharged at the expiration of time of service, December 7, 1864.

James Dunham, Middlesex, N. J., discharged at Carolina City, May 28, 1863; hemorrhoids.

H. M. Danberry, Hunterdon, wounded in left leg, at Newbern, March 14, 1862, and discharged when home on furlough, October 18, 1862.

William Danberry, Middlesex, discharged at Annapolis, December 28, 1861.

Edwin Dow, Suffolk, N. J., discharged at Newport Barracks, Aug. 4, 1862; general disability.

Isaac Dye, New Brunswick, transferred to 4th Reg't New Jersey Vols., for insubordination, October 21, 1861, at Camp Olden.

Ferdinand Distrow, New York, wounded in arm, at Roanoke, February 8, 1862; arm amputated; died at Roanoke hospital, March 19, 1862.

John Dadey, New York, missing at Drury's Bluff, Va., May 16, '64.

Joseph Fowler, Middlesex, discharged November 22, 1863, at Newbern; disability.

Isaac L. Jordan, Suffolk, discharged at Morehead City, Nov 6, '62; disability.

Ethelbert Hubbs, New York, discharged for promotion, Dec. 29, '62.

J. Hoffmann, Germany, transferred from Company A; discharged at Newbern, May 12, 1863; disability.

E. M. Hayes, Middlesex, N. J., drowned while home on furlough, October 10, 1863, at the foot of Barclay street, New York.

C. Irwin, England, discharged at Newbern, June 23, 1862; disability.

D. G. Knowles, Beaver Co., Pa., discharged at Newbern, June 23, 1862; disability.

James Loughlin, Kings Co., New York, wounded in head, at Whitehall, December 16, 1862; re-enlisted November 26, 1863; discharged for promotion, March 14, 1864.

W. W. Labone, Middlesex, N. J., wounded; lost fore-finger right hand, at Roanoke, February 8, 1862; discharged at Morehead City, November 18, 1862.

John Lawrence, Germany, discharged at Beaufort, N. C., October 22, 1862; disability.

P. Lalley, Galloway, discharged at Newbern, March 1, 1863; varicose veins of legs.

C. DL. oper, Suffolk, New York, died at Newbern, Aug. 19, 1863; typhoid fever.

James Murphy, Wexford, taken prisoner while on picket, 1862; exchanged, went home on furlough, and deserted.

Martin Moore, Ireland, wounded in the leg at Newbern, March 14, 1862; leg amputated; died at Newbern hospital.

S. Nicolas, Suffolk, N. Y., discharged November 22, 1862; disability.

John L. Pierson, Union, discharged at St. Helena Island, March 28, 1863; disability.

J. R. Penny, Suffolk, N. Y., discharged at Newbern, May 7, 1863; disability.

J. Reynolds, Ireland, discharged at Morehead City, November 18, 1862; deafness.

Christian Reiss, Monrovia, accidentally shot at Williamston, N. C., November 3, 1862: buried at Plymouth, N. C.

E. Roe, Ireland, died on transport Cossack, on the passage from Roanoke to Newbern, April 18, 1862; consumption.

Bergen Silcox, Somerset, wounded in the mouth at Kinston, Dec. 14, 1862; discharged at Newport News, Va., Nov. 19, 1863.

Benjamin Selah, Suffolk, N. Y., deserted at Newbern, Dec., 1863.

Yoakim Skillmann, Kingston, deserted at Annapolis, Md., January 7, 1862; was arrested and returned to the regiment, Aug. '64.

Henry Tutenberg, Germany, taken prisoner while on picket, at Newport Barracks, April 7, 1862; returned and deserted.

W. W. Sweesy, Suffolk, wounded in body while on picket, at Newport Barracks, April 7, 1862; discharged at expiration of service, December 7, 1864.

D. C. Voorhees, Middlesex, discharged at Newbern, June 23, '62; Thos. Egan, Ireland, E. F. Roscomon, Ireland, Peter Sherry, Ireland, disability.

Re-Enlisted November 26, 1864.

John Bennett, Union, discharged for promotion, April 26, 1865.

Jacob Bonnett, Pennyslvania, died at Chesapeake hospital, June 17, 1864; disease, cerebritis.

C. Dennis, Suffolk, New York, killed; ball entered neck, cutting jugular vein—exit throat, before Petersburg, Va., July 10, '64.

James Van Buskirk, Hudson, and R. H. White, Suffolk, N. Y., went as scouts when in front of Petersburg, Va., May 22, '64, by order of Major-General Smith; they were taken prisoners; returned March, 1865.

William Cisko, Warren, N, J., wounded in breast, Minnie, at Drury's Bluff, May 15, 1864; dropped on Co. roll as killed in action.

William Johnson, Mercer, N. J., wounded, slight, Cold Harbor, July 10, 1864.

E. F. Bond.
D. Dennis, Suffolk, New York.
G. W. Church, Middlesex.
E. Hall, England.
William H. Moore, New York.
Peter Meagher, Ireland.
J. Danberry, Hunterdon.

Re-Enlisted December 20, 1863.

Abram Doch, Monmouth, wounded in leg at Young's Cross Roads, July 27, 1863.

William Morris, Virginia, taken prisoner while on picket at Newport Barracks, April 7, '62; returned; deserted at New York, February 8, '63; was arrested; came back to company May 20, '63; wounded in left arm, April 7, '62, when on picket; again in left toe and right side, July 6, '63, and again at Drury's Bluff, May 16, '64.

Charles Hild, Germany, transferred from Co. A.
A. Hunt, Middlesex, N. J.

Re-Enlisted January 18, 1864.

M. C. Blackney, New York, taken prisoner while on picket at Newport Barracks, N. C., April 7, 1862; returned when regiment returned from South Carolina.

S. B. Strong, Suffolk, N. Y., missing at Drury's Bluff, May 16, 1864, never heard from, and reported as killed in action.

C. Bough, Germany, missing at Drury's Bluff, May 16, 1864.

J. B. Gibney, Ireland, deserted April 20, 1864.(?)

S. R. Hubbart, Suffolk, N. Y., wounded in finger of right hand, at Wise's Fork, March 8, 1865.

Joseph Haas, Swiss, transferred from Co. A; wounded in right hand and left leg, before Petersburg, July 30, 1864.

Thomas B. Moore, Middlesex, missing, May 16, 1864, at Drury's Bluff; never heard from, and reported as killed in action.

Y. S. Tayne, Suffolk, N. Y., wounded in back at Wise's Fork, March 8, 1865.

J. C. Youngs, Hunterdon, wounded in left arm at Gardener's Bridge, December 8, 1864.

A. Streit, Germany, transferred from Co. A; wounded, contusion of left leg, at Wise's Fork, March 8, 1865.

John Scheibele, Germany, transferred from Co. A; wounded at Drury's Bluff, May 16, 1864, died at Whitehall hospital, Pa., January 21, 1865.

Transferred from Company A.

James Prall, Middlesex.
J. B. Bender, Somerset.
Isaac Dock,   "
John Lowton, London.
William Lair, Hunterdon.
Wm. H. Strycker, Hunterdon.
William Rule, New York.
John Hoff, Germany.
F. Hague, Bohemia.

Recruits received 1862.

R. C. Cogan, Newark, discharged for promotion, Sept. 29, 1864.

M. Garabrant, " wounded; contusion of right thigh, at Cold Harbor, Va., June 3, 1864; mustered out, June 14, 1865.

Levi Bolton, Pa., discharged at Newport News, Va., November 19, 1863; rheumatism.

Thomas J. Putnam, Newark, wounded in left shoulder-blade, penetrating lung; died at field-hospital before Petersburg, July 14, 1864.

John Logas, Hanover, wounded at Port Walthall, May 7, 1864; mustered out June 14, 1865.

J. J. Nicholson, Glasgow, deserted April 20, 1864.

Walter Dye, Cranberry, wounded in mouth at Whitehall, December 16, 1862; discharged when home November 19, 1863.

Mustered out June 14, 1865.

Thomas H. Brown, Newark.	Thomas C. Gardener, Newark.
G. A. Larter, "	M. Gerstenmeyer, "
Fr. Prager, "	G. W. Henyon, New York.
M. Yoemann, "	J. P. Heary, Ireland.
Walter S. Thompson, "	F. Owens, "
Wm. Taylor, "	George Smith, Germany.
Thomas V. Virtue, "	J. J. Putnam, Plainfield.

Valentine Eckart, Philadelphia.

Recruits received 1863.

George Givenwein, Germany.	J. Coymann, Belleville.
G. Groff, "	D. O'Connor.

The last two are missing since the battle of Drury's Bluff, May 16, 1864, and have not been heard from; Groff is reported killed.

Recruits received 1864.

Allen McAndrew, wounded in great finger of right hand at Petersburg, July 2, 1864.

James Lidgett, Ireland, died June 14, 1865, at Greensboro', of the heart disease.

Francis Acker, N. Y., wounded in left shoulder at Walthall, May 6, 1864.

Francis Montaloo, New Brunswick, discharged for disability, at Newark, October 5, 1864.

Albert Cook, Spotswood, killed, ball entered breast, Drury's Bluff, May 14, 1864.

Reuben Hall, Kingland, wounded in foot at Drury's Bluff, May 16, 1864.

George Lowton, England, wounded at Cold Harbor, June 3, 1864.

V. Runyon Giles, Somerset.	Thomas James, Kingland.
S. Barnes, Gilson.	Daniel Buckley, Ireland.
Beverley Clayton, N Brunsw'k.	Francis Kenyon, New York.

Garrit Piermann, New York. Robert Schafer, Germany.
August Bonet, Bethlehem, Pa. Francis Jerome, New York.
M. O'Rourke, Ireland. John H. Voorhees, New York.
Patrick Carilon, Ireland.

Mustered Out June 14, 1865.

Thomas Anderson, Ireland. M. Bunspeck, Germany.
W. D. Hanyon, " Theodore Jacobs, Germany.
William Brennan, " Thomas Monahan, "
H. J. Ryno, New Brunswick. William Johnson, "
J. R. Jurgens, New York. John Hammon, "
S. F. Hopkins, New Jersey. Charles Krumm, "
Charles Lamair, Germany.

Recruits received 1865.

Louis Roeser, Gloucester. Joseph Barth, Germany.
James McCallum, Ireland. Jacob Beickel, "
John Foughy, " G. Paul, Philadelphia.
Owen Riley, " William Thompson, England.
P. McCloskey, " C. C. Osborn, "
J. J. Burns, " William Devitt, Liverpool.
E. Miller, Somerset. John P. Jones, Wales.
C. C. Denton, New Jersey. J. Harrison, New York.
Wm. Greathead. New Jersey. James Burns, Delaware, Pa.
Wm. Garrison, " " Wesley Parson, New York.
C. E. Williams, " " Charles Brown, Newark.
Jacob Wagoner, " " Thomas Caldwell, Hudson.
Wm. Howell, " " John S. Stout, New Jersey.

Company C.

CHARLES HOPKINSON, Captain.

E. S. HARRIS, 1st Lieut.   J. W. CLEFT, 2d Lieut.

Enlisted Men.

John Atkinson, Burlington, N. J., died at Newport Barracks, N. C., June 2, 1862.

A. B. Brown, Monmouth, N. J., discharged for promotion, March 8, 1862.

John W. Blackfan, Berks, Pa., discharged to be promoted Assistant Surgeon 1st N. J. Cavalry, March 16, 1863.

C. W. Barber, Burlington, discharged Nov. 25, 1862, to be transferred to Co. E, U. S. Artillery.

John R. Bourbon, Liverpool, wounded at Kinston, N. C., December 14, 1862; missing at Drury's Bluff, May 16, 1864.

Gustav Bender, Germany, transferred from Co. L; discharged at Newark, N. J., August 26, 1864, for general disability.

Benjamin Clinton, Hunterdon, wounded at Roanoke Island, Feb. 8, 1862; discharged August 11, 1862, at Newport Barracks.

D. J. Caster, Cardington, Pa., discharged September 1, 1862, at Newport Barracks, for disability.

A. B. Clyne, Bordentown, wounded at Kinston, December 14, 1862; discharged at Washington, September 24, 1864.

Discharged at expiration of time of service, December 7, 1864, at Trenton, N. J.

J. F. Craig, Salem.	E. C. Rodgers, Camden.
C. Hiser, Middlesex.	C. H. Thompson, Mercer.
W. N. Lanagan, Burlington.	E. Vanhise, Ocean.
W. R. Trout, "	W. H. Stout, Easton, Pa.
Thos. J. Wood, "	W. M. Wendell, Easton, Pa.
William Myer, Sussex.	Thomas J. Hibbs, Bucks, Pa.
Thomas Ricker, Passaic.	J. H. A. Jacobus, New York.
W. W. Stagg, "	Jacob Hesley, " "

D. B. Gerroe, Passaic, N. J.; G. Hoyer, A. Konig, H. Tinitus, Herman Werner, Germany; transferred from Co. L Nov. 18, 1862, were discharged at Trenton, December 7, 1864, for expiration of time of service.

A. Chewitz, Sweden, transferred from Co. L, died at Carolina City, June 13, 1863.

S. Donaldson, Monmouth, discharged at Newport Barracks, Sept. 16, 1862; disability.

James Herber, Burlington, killed at Roanoke Island, Feb. 8, '62.

John P. Heckman, Easton, Pa., discharged for promotion, March 8, 1862.

John H. Hiers, Burlington, discharged at Washington, August 11, 1862; disability.

Thomas Hutton, Lisbon, Portugal, discharged at Beaufort, March 29, 1863; disability.

E. W. Hand, Cape May, wounded in hand at Kinston, December, 14, 1862; discharged December 7, 1864, expiration of time of service.

J. Heritage, Gloucester, wounded in thigh, at Roanoke Island, February 8, 1862; discharged December 7, 1864, expiration of time of service.

C. Humburg, Germany, transferred from Co. L; wounded at Kinston, December 14, 1862; discharged at Trenton, Mar. 18, '63.

Israel Johnson, Burlington, killed at Kinston, December 14, '62.

Joseph Klein, Burlington, wounded in hand at Kinston, December 14, 1862; discharged for disability, May 28, 1863.

John Keyser, Germany, transferred from Co. L; discharged at St. Helena Island, S. C., March 7, 1863; disability.

P. Kirchgassner, Germany, transferred from Co. L, and discharged March 24, '63, at Fort Monroe, for wounds received in action.

C. Klapproth, Germany, transferred from Co. L; discharged at Newbern, March 4, 1863; disability.

J. D. Long, Boston, Mass.

C. Leming, Mercer, wounded while on picket, at Newport Barracks, ——, 1862; discharged December 7, 1864, expiration of time of service.

A. Lowe, Germany, transferred from Co. L; discharged at Beaufort, November 25, 1862; disability.

F. T. Machii, Trenton, died at Newbern hospital, May 31, 1862.

Theodore Myers, Sussex, died February 26, 1862.

F. T. Mitchell, Bucks, Pa., was left on schooner Horace Brown, when the regiment marched to Newbern; drowned in the Neuse river March 13, 1862.

Wm. M. Morrison, Philadelphia.

J. Muller, Germany, transferred from Co. L; discharged November 25, 1862.

G. Nelson, Mercer, discharged at Washington, January 21, 1862; disability.

C. Oberst, Germany, transferred from Co. L; discharged May 28, 1863.

Thomas Pratsch, Germany, transferred from Co. L; mustered out November 19, 1862.

S. Page, Burlington, wounded in the month, at Kinston, Dec. 14, 1862; discharged Dec. 7, 1864, expiration time of service.

B. McCoy, New York, discharged at Beaufort, January 17, 1863; disability.

C. C. Rudranff, Philadelphia, discharged at Newport Barracks, June 10, 1862; disability.

W. D. Rodgers, Camden, wounded in right side, at the Goldsboro' Expedition, 1862; discharged for promotion, April 13, 1863.

A. Rodney, Luzerne, Pa , mustered out at Washington, November 17, 1862.

J. R. Sickles, Philadelphia, discharged at Newbern, May 12, '62; disability.

J. R. Stockes, Philadelphia, discharged at Newbern, May 12, '62; disability.

B. Schafer, Germany, transferred from Co. L; wounded at Whitehall, December 16, 1862; discharged November 20, 1863.

J. Watson, New York, died at Newbern, N. C., April 11, 1862.

J. H. Williams, Burlington, discharged at Newport Barracks, September 1, 1862; disability.

Wm. C. Zayne, Gloucester, discharged at Beaufort, N. C., Nov. 23, 1862; disability.

Re-Enlisted November 24, 1863.

C. Drost, Somerset, transferred at his own request to Co. F.

J. W. Backeley, Camden, missing at Drury's Bluff, May 16, '64.

E. B. Smith, New York, killed in the trenches before Petersburg, June 22, 1864.

John Corcoran, Ireland.   J. E. Poppey, Mercer.

J. B. Cunningham, Warren.   Wm. Van Brunt, Mercer.

John Garrigan, Burlington.

Re-Enlisted December 19, 1863.

Daniel Hendrickson, Burlington, wounded in hand, on Goldsboro' Expedition.

J. W. Hudnutt, Detroit, Mich., missing, Drury's Bluff, May 16, '64.

L. Forbes, Burlington.   G. C. Gould, Passaic.

R. Heritage, Gloucester.

C. Knespel, Germany, transferred from Co. L.

Re-Enlisted January 18, 1864.

W. W. Hooper, Burlington, wounded at Newbern, May 14, 1862.

John Keller,   "   transferred at his own request to Co. D.

S. Lauer, Germany, transferred from Co. L, at his own request to Co. K.

D. D. Burch, Egg Harbor, wounded in the hand at Kinston, Dec. 14, 1862.

D. R. Cooperthwaite, Burlington, wounded through penis; both thighs grazed; at Drury's Bluff, Va., May 16, 1864; died at Hampton hospital, June 16, 1864.

H. C. Cooper, Passaic, wounded in side, at Kinston, Dec. 14, '62.

John Conway, Ireland, transferred at his own request to Co. A.

James Dougherty, Sussex, missing, Drury's Bluff, May 16, 1864, and dropped on Co. rolls as died in rebel prison.

E. H. Estlack, Gloucester, wounded at Drury's Bluff, May 16, '64.

A. Garwood, Burlington, wounded, contusion of right shoulder, at Drury's Bluff, May 14, 1864.

J. Hoffmann, Essex, missing, Drury's Bluff, May 16, 1864, and dropped on Co. rolls as died in rebel prison.

P. H. McDonnell, Burlington, missing, Drury's Bluff, May 16, '64; returned to regiment, June, 1865.

Alfred Rose, Mercer, wounded in right arm, on Goldsboro' Exp'n.

J. H. Roberts, Burlington, missing, at Drury's Bluff, May 16, '64.

August Spaulding, Gloucester, wounded in right arm, at Drury's Bluff, May 16, 1864.

Charles Keyser, Germany, transferred from Co. L; missing at Drury's Bluff, May 16, 1864.

H. Voorhees, Passaic.	G. M. Backeley, Camden.
J. L. S. Clark, Gloucester.	S. D. Corsan, Cape May.
J. W. Dennis, Ireland.	G. Hawk, Germany.
Wesley Thorn, Burlington.	B. Manning, New York.
J. Garrigan, "	R. Williams, Donegal.

J. Schmitz, Germany, transferred from Co. L.

Ch. Koch, Germany, transferred from Co. L; taken prisoner near Hamilton, N. C., December 12, 1864; died in rebel prison at Salisbury, N. C.

Adam Weinreich, Germany, transferred from Co. L; missing at Drury's Bluff, May 16, 1864; died in rebel prison.·

Recruits received 1862.

John Kramer, Germany, transferred from Co. L; discharged at Carolina City, June 28, 1863; disability.

Wm. Long, Newark, deserted April 1, 1865, at Newark; returned to regiment June 4, 1865; mustered out June 14, 1865.

Recruits received 1863.

M. Shannon, Ireland; Wm. Fischer, London; P. Taylor, Bristol; Thomas McGinn, Ireland, transferred from Co. L; missing, Drury's Bluff, May 16, 1864, and died in rebel prison.

B. B. Garrison, Cape May, died at Division hospital, Greensboro', N. C., May 17, 1865; typhoid fever.

C. Strudel, Germany	S. Voighten, Newport.
J. Voighten, "	A. Pool, Montgomery, N. C.

Recruits received 1864.

J. Kahn, Burlington, died at Washington, June 24, '64; typhoid fever.

F. Gurtner, Swiss, missing, Drury's Bluff, May 16, 1864.

Wm. Wegle, Germany, wounded in thigh, at Cold Harbor, June 4, 1864.

J. Backley, Camden, sent to Fort Macon for repeated desertion.

D. Brewer, Ocean, wounded in right arm, at Cold Harbor, June 9, 1864; discharged at U. S. Army General hospital.

J. Murphy, Ireland, wounded left hand, Drury's Bluff, May 16, '64.

J. Robinson, New Brunswick, wounded left leg, before Petersburg, Aug. 19, '64; died at 18th Army Corps hospital, Aug. 19, '64.

Isaac Mosher, Orange, fracture of wrist from fall by night marching.

George Hano, Portsville, Pa., died at 18th Army Corps hospital. before Petersburg, Va., July 21, 1864 ; pneumonia.

William Ball, Germany.	S. V. Norcross, Ocean.
L. Kumps, "	S. Worth, "
J. W. Drake, Somerville.	Wm. H. Moore, "
John D. Long, Boston, Mass.	Wm. F. Johnson, Ocean.
Joseph Dennis, New Jersey.	D. E. Ely, "
B. H. Todd, Camden.	G. Collins, "
C. Budding, Columbus.	M. Lightcap, "
H. A. Clevinger, Burlington.	B. B. Camburn, Wantown.
F. Salvens, Flemington.	F. E. Camburn, "
F. Simmons, "	J. F. McKilbey, Tom's River.
F. Dotson, Newburg.	F. McCullough, Philadelphia.

Jeremiah Garrison, Cape May.

Recruits received 1865.

John M. Clark, Chester, died at Mansfield general hospital, Morehead City, April 25, 1865 ; typhoid fever.

Virgil Vanderwarter, dropped as deserter, May 11, 1865.

Charles Schmidt, Germany.	Timothy Meyer, Ireland.
Charles Brown, "	Lewis Osborn, "
R. Harrison, "	Henry Lewis, "
C. Baumann, "	Joseph Sackville, "
Charles Miller, "	John Bradley, "
Theodor Spintel, "	Robert Graham, "
Frank Habich, "	Isaac Yiles, Boundbrook.
Leander Habich, "	H. McFarron, "
Hermann Pflum, "	James H. Stockley, Sussex.
John Scherz, "	C. P. Angle, Gloucester.
H. L. Brown, Burlington.	N. D. Ledden, "
Wm. M. Johnson, Burlington.	Sam'l Ledden, "
John S. Doolin, "	D. R. Smith, Cumberland.
J. J. Hoffmann, Glassboro'.	A. Bonnefoy, France.
Francis Kelly, New Jersey.	E. W. Brick, Camden.
M. C. Crane, "	John B. Brown, Newark.
Geo. G. Elsdone, "	L. Chappius, Swiss.
E. F. Avery, New York.	John O. Garrison, Schuyler.
Wm. M. Morrisson, Philadelphia.	J. J. Floch, New York.
Wm. Busch, Berks, Pa.	Isaac Henry, Delaware.
James Yoder, Chester	Thomas S. Hancock, Ocean.

G. Taylor, Ocean.

William Van Brunt, V. V., discharged for promotion, May 14, '65.

3

Company D.

THOMAS W. MIDDLETON, Captain.

G. G. IRONS, 1st Lieut.   EDGAR KISSAM, 2d Lieut.

Enlisted Men.

Joseph Atlerson, wounded at Roanoke Island, February 8, '62; died May 12, '62.

E. G. Aschton, Atlantic, died at Carolina City, Sept. 16, '63; typhoid fever.

J. Ackermann, Isaac Cranmar, William Johnson, and Orlando Imley, deserted at Camp Olden, 1861.

G. Benner, Germany, transferred from Co. L; discharged at Newbern; disability.

G. Beathy, Ocean, discharged Carolina City, May, '63; disability.

J. W. Barklay, Burlington, discharged at Beaufort, June 1, '63; disability.

Discharged at expiration of time of service, at Trenton, N. J.,
December 7, 1864.

C. Brandt, Germany, transferred from Co. L.

P. Thier, France,   "   "   " A.

William Braun, Philadelphia.	H. Erickson, Ocean.
Jesse M. Wilkins, "	William Gregory, Ocean.
C. P. Cambern, Ocean.	N. E. Jeffrey, "
H. A. Cambern, "	Joseph Loveless, "
John Cornelius, "	C. M. Levy, "

C. Brindley, Germany, discharged at Trenton, Oct. 23, '61; rupture.

M. Balst, Germany, transferred from Co. A; missing at Drury's Bluff, May 16, '64; died in rebel prison, July 15, '64.

J. W. Cranmar, Ocean, wounded at Whitehall, Dec. 16, '62; discharged at Trenton, August 10, '64; disability.

Wm. B. Clayton, Ocean, discharged at Beaufort, June 1, '63; disability.

Ezra Cranmar, Ocean, died at Newbern hospital, April 12, '62; typhoid fever.

Joseph Ellern, England, transferred to Invalid Corps, January 21, '64, by order of Major General Fry, Provost Marshal.

William A. Gulick, Philadelphia, discharged at Roanoke Island, September 8, '62; disability.

Wm. H. Hurley, Ocean, wounded in shoulder, at Newbern, March 14, '62; discharged at Hilton Head, S. C., March 29, '63.

Wm. Horner, Ocean, deserted at Carolina City, May, 1863.

C. Hufty, Philadelphia, discharged for promotion, Sept. 5, '63.

D. A. Johnson, wounded at Roanoke Island, February 8, '62; discharged Dec. 7, '64, at expiration of time of service.

B. Johnson, Ocean, discharged Newbern, May 12, '63; disability.

B. Jones, Chester, Pa., discharged at Newport Barracks, June, '62; disability.

Isaac M. Inmann, Ocean, wounded in left shoulder-blade, before Petersburg, July 1, '64; discharged Dec. 7, '64, at expiration of time of service.

James Johnson, Ocean, transferred to Invalid Corps, by order of Major General Fry, Provost Marshal.

O. P. Inmann, Ocean, discharged at Hilton Head, S. C., March 29, '63; disability.

H. B. Kraft, Philadelphia, discharged at Carolina City, May 29, 1863; disability.

H. Lacher, Swiss, killed at Newbern, March 14, '62.

W. B. Norcross, Burlington, discharged at Newbern, May, 1863; disability.

S. Osborn, Ocean, died at Newport Barracks, June 8, '62; consumption.

Thomas D. Randolph, Ocean, wounded in feet, at Cold Harbor, June, 1864; discharged at Newark hospital.

O. J. Rulong, Ocean, died at Newbern hospital, July, 1862.

J. H. Robinson, New Brunswick, discharged at Beaufort, March 29, '63; disability.

Louis Southard, tried by regimental court-martial, at Trenton.

William Philipps, Ocean, wounded in head at Roanoke Island, February 8, '62; died at Beaufort hospital, January 20, '63.

John R. Steelman, Atlantic, wounded at Newbern, March 14, '62; died at Newbern, April 16, '62.

John Trautwein, Germany, transferred from Co. A; wounded at Newbern, March 14, '62; discharged at Newark, May 23, '63.

James Truax, Ocean, discharged at Newbern, June, '62; disability.

John W. Perrine, Ocean, transferred to Invalid Corps, by order of Major General Fry, Provost Marshal, January 24, '63.

G. R. Worth, Ocean, wounded at Roanoke, February 8, '62; discharged at Newbern, September 8, '62; disability.

Jacob Yenney, Swiss, wounded at Newbern, March 14, '62; discharged at Newport Barracks, July 19, '62; disability.

Andrew Elberthson, Ocean, discharged for promotion, Dec. 1862.

F. Westermann, Germany, transferred from Co. A; wounded during the N. Y. city raid, July, 1863; transferred to Invalid Corps.

M. Ullrich, Germany, transferred from Co. A; died at Fort Monroe, September 9, '64.

Re-Enlisted November 25, 1863.

C. Archer, Ocean, missing, Drury's Bluff, May 16, '64; **returned** May 20, '65.

J. L. Bennett, Ocean, missing, Drury's Bluff, May 16, '64; died
in rebel prison, October 29, '64.

B. Homann, Wayne Co., N. Y., missing, Drury's Bluff, May 16, '64.

F. C. Beathy, Ocean, transferred to the Navy Department, May
3, '64, by order of Major General Butler.

J. Erickson, Ocean, wounded, right wrist, Newbern, March 14, '62.

N. P. Fithian, Philadelphia, wounded accidentally, in right hand,
pistol-shot, before Petersburg, August 24, '64.

G. V. Hyer, Ocean, wounded, left leg, before Petersburg, July 1, '64.

Joel Hulse. Ocean, wounded at Deep Creek, March 1, '64; died
at Balfour hospital, Portsmouth, Va., March 8, '64.

Albert Nutt, Burlington, killed at Deep Creek, March 1, '64;
buried at Gettysville Station.

W. B. Conklin, Ocean.   James Hulse, Ocean.
William Dennis,   "   G. Hyers,   "
D. C. Hamkins, Burlington.   C. P. Robinson, Newport city.
            E. Vantilburg, Bucks Co., Pa.

Re-Enlisted December 20, 1863.

Jesse L. Hulsart. Ocean, missing, at Drury's Bluff, May 16, '64;
returned to regiment, April 23, '65.

A. L. Johnson, Ocean, missing at Drury's Bluff, May 16, '64;
dropped as died in rebel prison, May 1, '65

C. P. Chaffey, Ocean, accidental fracture of rib.

J. Clark, Ireland, wounded in right arm, May 19, '64.

John M. Clayton, Ocean.   F. N. Petit, Ocean.
            N. Champion, Atlantic.

Re-Enlisted January 18, '64.

Caleb Mount, Ocean, wounded at Newbern, March 14, '62; missing,
Drury's Bluff, May 16, '64; died in rebel prison, Sept. 1, '64.

C. P. Shmidt, Ocean, killed, ball entering chest and penetrating
right lung, before Petersburg, August 15, '64.

E. Shinn, Ocean, was reported and tried for desertion and over
twelve months' absence, but acquitted by general court-martial, approved of by Major General Butler.

David Riley, Trenton, missing at Drury's Bluff, May 16, '64;
reported as a paroled prisoner.

A. Reed, Ocean, missing at Drury's Bluff, May 16, '64; died in
rebel prison, September 1, '64.

David McKilbey, Ocean, deserted March 20, '62, at Roanoke;
was arrested, acquitted, and returned to duty Dec. 6 '63.

Thomas Hazelton, Ocean, taken prisoner at Drury's Bluff, May
16, '64; returned to regiment May 20, '65.

Joseph Ockerson, Ocean, wounded in arm at Roanoke, Feb. 8, '62.

H. H. Hewitt, Ocean, transferred to Navy Department, May 3, '64,
by order of Major General Butler.

John Zimmerlin, Swiss, transferred from Co. A.

John Keller, Burlington, transferred from Co. C.

N. P. Penn, Philadelphia, wounded in thigh at Walthall, May 7, '64.

J. L. Cranmar, Ocean.   Wm. H. Peck, Burlington.

H. G. W. Rogers, Ocean.   C. A. Johnson, Ocean.

Wm. Sharp,   "   Jos. Johnson,   "

C. W. Truax,   "   E. A. Crane,   "

           B. A. Rogers, Ocean.

Recruits received 1862.

B. V. Gale, Union, missing, Drury's Bluff, May 16, '64; died in rebel prison, October 2, '64.

C. Fuchs, Germany, transferred from Co. A; missing at Drury's Bluff, May 16, '64; returned, and mustered out June 14, '65.

E. Tindell, Ocean, died at White House landing, June 12, '64; typhoid fever.

M. Zipfel, Germany, wounded in head by shell, at Kinston, Dec. 14, '62; mustered out June 14, '65.

Knox Bechler, Germany, transferred from Co. A; wounded in left foot, at Petersburg, Aug. 6, '64; mustered out June 14, '65.

Ernst Biehl, Germany, wounded in right arm, before Petersburg, August 6, '64; arm amputated; mustered out June 14, '65.

F. Schilling, Germany, died Point of Rocks, July 27, '64; diarrhœa.

S. Goodfellow, Lambertsville, mustered out June 14, '65.

H. Schleicher, Germany, transferred from Co. A; mustered out June 14, '65.

E. Troudt, Germany, transferred from Co. A; mustered out June 14, 1865.

John Siegel, France, transferred from Co. A; mustered out June 14, 1865.

Charles Sepp, Newark, transferred from Co. A; mustered out June 14, '65.

Recruits received 1863.

S. Geimer, Williamsburg, transferred from Co. A.

J. R. Chadwick, Barnegat, transferred to Navy Department, May 3, '64, by order of Major General Butler.

Recruits received 1864.

J. R. Johnson, Ocean, died at Fort Monroe, Aug. 29, '64; diarrhœa.

W. H. Rodgers, Ocean, died at Kinston, March 29, '65; diarrhœa.

Thos. P. Johnson, Tom's River, died at Portsmouth, April 6, '64; congestive fever.

H. W. Polhemus, Ocean, missing, Drury's Bluff, May 16, '64; died in rebel prison, September 28, '64.

J. J. Streit, Ocean, missing, Drury's Bluff, May 16, '64; died in rebel prison, September 1, '64.

Joel H. Gant, Ocean, missing, Drury's Bluff, May 16, '64; died in rebel prison, August 20, '64.

George Beathy, Ocean, missing, at Drury's Bluff, May 16, '64; returned to regiment April 28, '65.

S. Brindley, Ocean, missing, Drury's Bluff, May 16, '64; exchanged.

John Johnson, Ocean, discharged April 10, '65, at New York; disability.

Robert Crossley, Trenton, substitute in the 37th N. J. 100 days' Vols.; deserted from his regiment on the 23d of May; was arrested, tried by court-martial, and sentenced to be transferred to the 9th N. J. Vols., to make good time lost by desertion (80 days), and to forfeit to the United States twelve dollars per month of his pay for that time; discharged at Newbern, February 10, '65.

Charles Philipps, Newark, deserted from the 37th Reg't., 100 days Vols.; was arrested at Pittsburg, Pa., tried by court-martial, and sentenced to be transferred to the 9th N. J. Vols., to make good his time lost by desertion (90 days); discharged at Goldsboro', N. C.

J. F. Matthew, Monmouth, mustered out, June 14, '65.
John Vantilburg, Kingston,   "   "   "   "
W. H. H. Bunnell, Ocean,   "   "   "   "
Jacob Walter, Germany,   "   "   "   "
William Armstrong, Phila.,   "   "   "   "
Jacob Wirtz, Germany,   "   "   "   "

W. W. Martin, Readington, wounded in breast, exit scapula, at Drury's Bluff, May 14, '64.

A. J. Johnson, Ocean.	S. Huls, Middlesex.
Wallace Irons, "	Th. C. Joslin, Atlantic.
W. L. Truax, "	James Parmer, Canada.
S. R. Gant, "	John A. Clayton, Ocean.
H. H. Gant, "	O. P. Inmann, "
John S. McKilvey, Ocean.	J. Oakerson, "
John W. McKilvey, "	S. R. Penn, "
C. L. Tildon, "	P. Clark, Ireland.

Recruits received 1865.

F. B. Erickson, Ocean, accidentally wounded in knee, at Greensboro', May 4, '65.

Paul Bowers, Gloucester.	Charles Dennis, Ocean.
Wm. McIlwaine, "	S. W. Hankins, "
Daniel Westcott, Camden.	Cornelius Grover, "
Jesaiah Norcross, "	J. Willburn, "
Fr. Springer, Springfield.	C. H. Gaston, Camden.
John Cameron, Burlington.	Joseph M. Smith, Mercer.
Henry Clayhill, Atlantic.	S. Day, Newark.
Isaac Collins, Mansfield.	A. Kuerthner, Newark.
Walter Simpkins, New Jersey.	C. W. Roll, New York.
David Terry, "	F. E. Mailley, England.
James Neal, Philadelphia.	James Simpson, Scotland.
William Hyder, Pennsylvania.	N. Bohr, Germany,
J. Cavanagh, Indiana.	Emil Frank, Germany.
Francis Fagan, Indiana.	Timothy Driscoll, Ireland.

E. W. Savage, Ohio.

Company E.

WILLIAM DEHART, Captain.

W. H. ABEL, 1st Lieut.   A. B. BEACH, 2d Lieut.

Enlisted Men.

I. B. Brown, Passaic, wounded at Newbern, March 14, '62; discharged at Beaufort, N. C., June 1, '63.

R. A. Burris, Orange, wounded at Newbern, March 14, '62; discharged November 18, '62.

C. F. Banney, Litchfield, Conn.; discharged for promotion Dec. '62.

John Bell, transferred to Co. C.

James McClelland, Scotland, discharged at Newbern, Feb. 28, '63; disability.

F. Bergenkemper, Germany, discharged at Newbern, Aug. 12, '63; disability.

S. S. Crowell, Orange, discharged at Newbern, June 7, '63; disability.

Samuel Castmore, Morris, discharged at Newbern, March 31, '63; disability.

R. V. Duffort, Morris, discharged at Newbern, Aug. 17, '62; disability.

John Gehring, Swiss, transferred from Co. A; discharged at Newbern, June 15, '63; disability.

H. Havens, Morris, discharged at Newbern, May 29, '63; disability.

P. Lappin, Ireland, discharged at Newbern, August 5, '62; disability.

Isaac Morrill, Kings Co., New York, discharged at Newbern, June, 1863; disability.

Cornelius Ryerson, Passaic, discharged at Newbern, Aug. 12, '62; disability.

S. C. Suydam, Sussex, discharged at Newbern, November 18, '62; disability.

R. M. Smith, Passaic, discharged at Newbern, March 29, '63; scrotal hernia.

L. Turce, Bergen, died at Newbern, April 17, '62; black tongue fever.

Joseph Van Etten, Sussex, discharged at Newbern, Nov. 18, '62.

F. G. Coyte, Kings Co., New York, discharged for promotion, September 23, '63.

A. Cole, Passaic, wounded in arm at Drury's Bluff, May 16, '64; discharged at expiration of time of service, Dec. 7, '64.

John Degelmann, New York, transferred from Co. A; discharged at Beaufort, N. C., January 17, '63.

Enoch Dunkerly, England, wounded, Drury's Bluff, May 16, '64; discharged at expiration of time, December 7, '64.

T. Ebly, Baden, transferred from Co. A; discharged at Beaufort, N. C., January 2, '63; disability.

Delany Finthon, Ireland, died at Craven Street hospital, Newbern, April 29, '62; hæmorrhage of bowels.

J. B. Goldshmidt, Orange, discharged to be promoted 2d Lieut. Battery E, 1st Reg't N. J. Vol. Artillery.

G. M. Gilliam, Bergen, wounded in leg, at Walthall, Va., May 6, '64; discharged.

J. M. Gilliam, Bergen, wounded in arm, Whitehall, Dec. 16, '62; discharged at expiration of time of service, Dec. 7, '64.

Jacob Graber, Germany, transferred from Co. A; wounded in leg and hand, on Goldsboro' Expedition, 1862; discharged at expiration of time of service, December 7, '64.

B. W. Hopper, Bergen, discharged for promotion, Dec. 22, '62.

J. Heckmann, England, wounded in hand, at Roanoke, Feb. 8, '62; discharged at expiration of time of service, Dec. 7, '64.

Th. J. Hallowell, England, wounded in arm, at Kinston, Dec. 14, '62; discharged at expiration of time of service, Dec. 7, '64.

M. King, New York, wounded at Kinston, Dec. 14, '62; discharged at Newbern, March 31, '63.

David Kimball, Morris, wounded in leg, at Kinston, Dec. 14, '62; discharged at Newbern, March 31, '63.

Valentin Keiler, Germany, transferred from Co. A; wounded at Drury's Bluff, Va., May 16, '64; discharged at expiration of time of service, December 7, '64.

J. Lyons, Morris, died at Hatteras Inlet, March 4, '62; typhoid fever.

John H. Lennox, New York, wounded in hand, at Kinston, Dec. 14, '62; discharged at expiration of time of service, December 7, '64.

J. O. Maxwell, Sussex, died at Hatteras Inlet, Feb. 22, '62.

F. W. Meiss, Germany, transferred from Co. A; wounded in leg, at Walthall, Va., May 6, '64; leg amputated; discharged.

William Reed, Sussex, wounded in side, at Kinston, Dec. 14, '62; discharged at Newark, March 15, '64; disability.

G. Simons, Warren, wounded in side, at Kinston, Dec. 14, '62; discharged at expiration of time of service, Dec. 7, '64.

A. Scheidemantel, Germany, transferred from Co. A; died at Newark hospital, October, 1863; apoplexy.

D. Valentine, Passaic, wounded in arm at Whitehall, Dec 16, '64; arm amputated; discharged at Newport News, Jan. 14, '64.

U. D. Vorhees, Middlesex, discharged at Beaufort, June 1, '63; disability.

Hampton Whitehead, Morris, wounded by Minnie ball, in breast and lungs, at Newbern, March 14, '62; died March 17, '62.

E. Wishard, Germany, transferred from Co. A; drowned on transport Albany, December 20, '62.

D. E. Westbrook, Sussex, wounded in arm, Kinston, Dec. 14, '62; discharged at expiration of time of service, Dec. 7, '64.

Robert Wood, New York, wounded at Petersburg, June 24, '64; discharged at expiration of time of service, Dec. 7, '64.

A. Hundershot, Bergen.   E. King, Passaic.

E. Walmsby, Rockland, New York, deserted at Camp Olden, near Trenton.

B. W. Hunt, Sussex.   J. H. Osborn, Bergen.

Johnson Pierson, Sussex.   R. Rogers, Sussex.

Discharged at expiration of time of service, December 7, 1864, at Trenton, N. J.

Morris Breslin, Ireland.   R. Post, Passaic.
J. Collins,   "   Wm. P. Normann, Sussex.
L. D. Cummings, Sussex.   A. H. Rose, Newton.
Thomas Fredenburgh, Sussex.   H. Post, Passaic.
J. D. Huftellin, Essex.   John Skill, Camden.
J. D. Jennings, Morris.   D. J. Senior, Passaic.
D. Keefe,   "   John Tierce,   "
M. Lyons, Rockland.   Ira Weaver, Morris.
Wm. L. Munson, Sussex.   James Williams, Essex.
William Prentice, Passaic.   John Winter, Passaic.
John Prentice,   "   J. N. Elmer, Sussex.

Re-Enlisted November 30, 1863.

Hiram Gray, Caledonia, Vt., killed; Minnie ball entered chest, exit right shoulder-blade, before Petersburg, June 25, '64.

A. A. Busch, Bergen, wounded in arm, at Cold Harbor, June 4, '64.

G. Cooper. Sussex, wounded in abdomen, at Drury's Bluff, May 16, '64; reported on Co. rolls as died on the battle-field.

Wm. J. Van Riper, Essex.

Re-Enlisted December 20, 1863.

H. M. Van Schaick, appointed Sergeant-Major, Dec. 24, '63.

Wm. P. Amermann, Hunterdon.

Re-Enlisted January 18, 1864

G. Love, Morris, died at Newton, N. J., when home on veteran furlough, February 24, '64; intemperance.

Oscar Van Houten, Bergen, appointed Quartermaster-Sergeant, December, 1863.

R. J. Berdan, Bergen, wounded at Whitehall, Dec. 16, '62; discharged for promotion, Sept. 8, '64.

George Myers, Michigan, wounded at Drury's Bluff, May 16, '64; discharged at Greensboro', N. C., May 10, '65; debility.

J. H. Huff, Sussex, wounded at Petersburg, June 30, '64; discharged March 26, '65.

H. Hopper, Morris, wounded in head, Drury's Bluff, May 16, '64; discharged for promotion, March 7, '65.

William Lemons, Sussex, wounded at Drury's Bluff, May 16, '64; discharged at Philadelphia, May 15, '65; debility.

J. Monsch, France, killed at Walthall, May 6, '64; Minnie ball through head.

William Moore, England, failed to report on expiration of veteran furlough, March 7, '64.

J. E. Sickles, Warren, wounded; ball entered left gluteal region, exit over right pubis, Walthall, May 6, '64; died at Hampton hospital, June 1. '64.

M. Ward, Ireland, wounded in back, at Cold Harbor, June 4, '64; transferred to Veteran Reserve Corps, September 30, '64, by order of War Department.

W. H. Somers, England; William Castmore, Morris; taken prisoners at Wise's Fork, N. C., March 8, '65; returned to regiment, April, 1865.

J. Kent, Sussex, wounded at Walthall, May 6, '64.

J. Rankin, Scotland, wounded in hand, at Kinston, Dec. 14, '62.

R. E. Sasson, Ireland, wounded in neck, Drury's Bluff, Mar. 16, '64.

E. M. Ward, Warren,   "   "   "   "

C. B. Wear, Morris,   "   "   "   "

J. Ralph, Passaic, wounded in right buttock, at Drury's Bluff, March 16, '64.

J. N. Carlough, Bergen.   J. June, Ocean.

William Reid, Passaic.   H. Raber, Sussex.

A. Rice, Ireland.   E. C. Tuttle, Sussex.

W. H. King, Passaic.

William Fricke, Germany, transferred from Co. A.

Recruits received 1862.

Th. Predmore, Morris, died at Balfour hospital, Portsmouth, Va., August 2, '64; chronic diarrhœa.

J. G. Cole, Morris, discharged at Beaufort, N. C., June 1, '63; disability.

S. H. Cole, Morris, discharged at Beaufort, N. C., Dec. 9, '63; disability.

J. Newmann, Bergen, transferred from Co. A; taken prisoner at Wise's Fork, N. C., March 8, '65; returned to regiment April, 1865; mustered out, June 14, '65.

William B. Maines, Newton, mustered out June 14, '65.

J. C. Gordon, Morris,   "   "   "

Recruits received 1864.

J. B. Dolde, Germany, wounded in chest, Walthall, May 6, '64; transferred to Veteran Reserve Corps, by order of War Department, September 30, '64.

C. Ribble, Warren, died at Fort Monroe, Sept. 24, '64; typhoid pneumonia.

G. B. Dixon, Burlington, wounded in abdomen, at Drury's Bluff, May 16, '64; died in Philadelphia, September 23, '64.

Thomas Sales, Liverpool, killed, Minnie ball through body, at Walthall, May 6, '64.

J. Wilson, New York, deserted at Portsmouth, Va., April, 1864.

Th. Chepmann, England, deserted at Carolina City, Nov. 20, '64.

Wm. Griffin, Canada,   "   and dropped from Co. rolls.

R. Haling, England,   "   at Carolina City, Nov. 20, '64.

C. H. Street, Germany,   "   "   "   "

James Smith, Canada,   "   "   "   "

John Burke, Ireland,   "   "   "   "

Wm. Butler,   "   "   "   "   "

H. Campbell, Ireland, deserted at Carolina City, Nov. 20, '64; mustered out June 14, '65.

A. Decker, New Jersey.   P. Kinnley, England.
J. Campbell, Sussex.   J. M. Pflum, Germany.
Wm. Ellison, Canada.   J. Nan,   "
Joseph Murphy, Ireland   Otto Schnabel,   "
Wm. Parker,   "   Jos. Wagoner,   "
Thomas Owens,   "   J. H. Smith, New Jersey.
A. Higgins,   "   Wm. Robbins,   "
J. Dent,   "   M. Pharo,   "
R. Cass,   "   James O'Brien, Canada.
W. K. Brennan, Africa.   J. Giltfather,   "
J. Brown, Jamaica.   Th. Bixby,   "
J. C. Brown, England.   Wm. J. Brown, England.

The following men were taken prisoners at Wise's Fork, N. C., March 8, '65; returned April, 1865; mustered out June 14, '65:

J. Gross, Germany.   E. Politz, Germany.
Wm. Matthew, Germany.   Otto Schliffka, Germany.
C. Neuhauser,   "   John Seefried,   "
Otto Plesch,   "   Fred. Marshall,   "

William Canar, Ireland; J. Saville, England; taken prisoners at Wise's Fork, N. C., March 8, '65; paroled and exchanged; did not return to the regiment.

G. Gunther, Germany, wounded, Minnie ball, shoulder-blade, at Wise's Fork, March 8, '65; mustered out June 14, '65.

James Slaven, Ireland, sent to Fort Macon, Feb. 13, '65; sentence of General Court-martial, for desertion

Taylor Wainwright, Ocean, wounded in hand, at Drury's Bluff, May 16, '64.

N. S. Applegate, Tom's River, wounded, contusion of head, Drury's Bluff, May 16, '64.

C. G. Banta, West Milford, taken prisoner March 8, '65; returned to regiment May, 1865.

A. S. Emery, Franklin, Pa., wounded in side, at Drury's Bluff, May 16, '64.

N. Reed, Sussex, wounded in arm, at Petersburg, Aug. 22, '64.

C. D. Wallace, Pennsylvania.
C. T. Barren, Bucks, Pa.
Tilgham Barren, Franklin, Pa.
Thomas B. Hardy, Hunterdon.
A. J. Steelmann, Atlantic.
Henry Nickle, Germany.
Aaron Moss, West Milford.
Wm. Amery, Franklin, Pa.
G. M. Decker, Sussex.
C. K. Castmore, Morris.
E. Applegate, Tom's River.
David Kent, New Jersey.
Wm. H. Sales, Liverpool.

Recruits received 1865.

G. Walters, Hoboken, taken prisoner at Wise's Fork, March 8, '65; returned May, 1865.

Wm. Randall, Providence, taken prisoner at Wise's Fork, March 8, '65; returned May, 1865.

H. Reinhard, Germany.
Henry Schick, "
D. D. Ackermann, New Jersey.
A. Brooke, "
John L. Jordon, "
Jenkins Fayette, "
J. H. Peterson, "
Henry Andrew, Greenville.
C. W. Barker, New York.
C. Deforest. "
H. H. Small, "
Frank Huwitt, Preston, Conn.
J. S. Lee, St. John's, N. B.
R. M. Russell, Vermont.
John Schmitz, Massachusetts.
John Peter Schmidt, Mass.
Jacob Whitemore, France.
C. F. Weatherby, Gloucester.
Wm. L. Taggart, "
Jacob Keissler, Passaic.
Simon Keissler, "
P. G. Speer, Acquia Creek.
John Sindle, "
James Steward, Paterson.
M. Breslin, Ireland.
Morris Cody, "
John Kilf, "
P. Kerrigan, Ireland.
P. Lynch, "
James McClay, "
R. McDonald, "
John McDonald, Ireland.
P. Powers, "
R. Roberts, "
A. Maxwell, Massachusetts.

Company F.

WILLIAM B. CURLIES, Captain.

AUGUST THOMPSON, 1st Lieut.   JAS. W. GIBSON, 2d Lieut.

Enlisted Men.

M. M. Auten, Somerville, deserted at Philadelphia, Dec. 3, '61.

A. Aubick, Philadelphia, discharged May 28, '63; disability.

Edwin Acten, Ireland, killed; Minnie ball entered forehead, at Cold Harbor, Va., June 4, '64.

C. E. Blackwell, Princeton, discharged Oct. 22, '62; disability.

D. S. Baily, Pennington, mustered out Nov. 17, '62.

R. S. Baldwin, Mercer, discharged Nov. 18, '62; disability.

J. V. D. Blackwell, Princeton, killed at Roanoke, Feb. 8, '62.

M. Boyle, Philadelphia, wounded at Newbern, March 14, '62; died March 15, '62.

S. L. Blake, Somerset, wounded at Roanoke, Feb. 8, '62; died February, 1862.

E. Schanon, Elizabeth, wounded in arm, Newbern, March 14, '62; arm amputated; discharged at Philadelphia, May 10, '62.

John Craig, England, died at Beaufort, August 24, '62.

C. M. Ford, Hightstown, discharged June 19, '63; disability.

C. W. Hurt, Trenton, discharged at Camp Olden, 1861, under age.

Wm. H. Hussell, Hunterdon, died on board brigantine "Dragoon," March 27, '62; fever.

John Kennedy, Ireland, wounded in second finger of right hand, on Goldsboro' Expedition, 1862; died at Newbern, Aug. 8, '63.

J. McNeal, Ireland, deserted at Trenton, Nov. 7, '61.

J. Mitchell, Ireland, discharged May 12, '63; disability.

H. McLarkin, Cherryville, accidental loss of finger; discharged at Trenton, 1862.

D. B. McCrady, Hudson, died at Newbern, July 17, '62; jaundice and fever.

H. Nelson, Hudson, died at Newbern, May 4, '62; fever.

M. C. Runyon, Morris, discharged for promotion, May 18, '62.

J. Richmond, Cumberland, died on board brigantine "Dragoon," March 23, '62; fever.

Joseph Sailor, Lambertsville, discharged at Camp Olden, 1861; epilepsy.

W. G. Smith, East Hadden, Conn., discharged Nov. 18, '61; disability.

Jonathan Schmidt, Mercer, discharged Oct. 22, '62; disability.

Henry Simskins, Cumberland, joined regular service Nov. 25, '62.
Joel Seals, Hunterdon, wounded at Whitehall, Dec. 16, '62; died
    at Kinston, N. C., December 19, '62.
L. D. Shephard, Cumberland, discharged for promotion, Jan. 8, '63.
J. Van Sickle, Readington, discharged May 30, '63; disability.
J. O. Van Fleet, Michigan; mustered out January 17, '62.
S. Webster, Sussex, discharged March 16, '63; disability.

Discharged at expiration of time of service, December 7, 1864, at Trenton, N. J.

C. N. Burroughs, Mercer.	L. L. Cronce, Hunterdon.
J. Finan, Ireland.	P. R. Cronce, "
G. J. Hall, Pennington.	H. O. Lowe, Mercer.
Wm. H. Hendershot, Hunterd'n.	Wm. M. Metz, Philadelphia.
Ph. Hendershot, "	James Mailiff, Kings Co., N. Y.
B. Y. Saily, Mercer.	A. B. Thomas, Princeton.
Joseph Thompson, Bordentown.	Th. W. Tooker, Elizabeth.
H. V. D. Van Nest, Mechanic.	H. G. Vorhees, Middlesex.
W. L. Vanderwater, Princeton.	G. W. H. Weaver, Hunterdon.

Re-Enlisted November 25, 1863.

Cornelius Drost, Somerset, transferred at his own request to Co. C.
F. Blizzard, Meggs, died at Morehead City, Nov. 28, '64; syphilis.
A. H. Evans, Pennington, discharged for promotion June 18. '64.
J. D. Nymaster, Hunterdon, killed; shot through head at Cold
    Harbor, June 3, '64.
J. Osborn, Woodville, died at Newbern, Oct. 12, '64; yellow fever.
William Suydam, Sussex, wounded in arm, at Drury's Bluff, May
    16, '64; died at Drury's Bluff, May 16, '64.
J. N. Smith, Metuchin, killed at Drury's Bluff, May 16, '64.
A. A. Brown, Monmouth, wounded in shoulder, at Walthall, Va.,
    May 7, '64.
C. Gerry, Mercer, wounded in leg, at Drury's Bluff, May 16, '64;
    wounded in back, at Cold Harbor, June 3, '64.
J. Hellinger, Burlington, wounded in hand, at Cold Harbor, June
    7, '64.
J. Johnson, Warren, missing, Drury's Bluff, May 16, '64; died in
    rebel prison.
John Kitchen, Hunterdon, wounded in leg, at Drury's Bluff, May
    16, '64; wounded in foot, at Cold Harbor, June 4, '64.
C. W. Mitchell, Yardleyville, wounded in back, at Drury's Bluff,
    May 16, '64.
J. E. French, Cumberland, wounded in the second joint of second
    finger of right hand, Minnie, at Wise's Fork, March 8, '65.

C. Buckelew, Pennington.	J. Black, Somerset.
W. S. Klein, Hunterdon.	J. P. Scudder, Mercer.

Re-Enlisted December 19, 1863.

James Johnson, Phila., wounded in shoulder, at Drury's Bluff,
    May 16, '64; died July 13, '65, near Danville; typhoid fever.

W. F. Larue, Bucks, Pa., wounded in left foot, at Petersburg,
August 21, '64.

H. B. Lenning, Pennington, discharged for promotion, Nov. 4, '64.

Re-Enlisted January 18, 1864.

William Harmann, Mercer, wounded in elbow, at Walthall, May
7, '64; died at Hampton hospital, July 20, '64.

R. M. Hall, Mercer, died at Beaufort, N. C., Nov. 17, '64; yellow
fever.

G. E. Emmons, Hunterdon, deserted at Trenton, December 1, '61;
returned to company August 6, '62.

Edward Carlees, New York, wounded, Drury's Bluff, May 16, '64.

J. Wood, Mercer, wounded in scrotum, Cold Harbor, June 6, '64.

John McGregor, Easton, wounded, at   "   "   June 3, '64.

J. V. Sutphen, New Brunswick, wounded in right leg, before
Petersburg, August 19, '64.

G. S. Titus, Mercer, blinded by a shell, at Cold Harbor, June 3, '64;
wounded, Minnie, calf of left leg.

F. H. Benjamin, New York.	S. R. Mills, Cumberland.
J. P. Baily, Somerset.	C. M. Preston, Greenwich.
J. Bauer, Salem.	W. J. Parker, Kinston.
J. Clark, Southwick.	J. R. Reading, Hunterdon.
J. E. Dalrymple, Hunterdon.	R. G. Shephard, Cumberland.
Simon Hughes, Sandtown.	S. Suydam, Mercer.
B. Higgins, Hunterdon.	Wm. J. Thompson, Monmouth.
D. Johnson, Princeton.	J. W. Tindell, Princeton.
J. Knowles, New York.	A. Vanderwater, Kinston.
R. H. Leaming, Cumberland.	Jacob Viat, Germany.

Justus Woodhull, Sussex, wounded in thigh, Walthall, May 7, '64.

Recruits received 1862.

Thomas Horn, Lamberton, mustered out June 14, '65.

J. J. Rooks, Lambertsville,   "   "

Recruits received 1863.

L. S. Hough, Martinsburg, discharged January 26, '65.

B. Morrisson, Ireland, wounded in right arm, before Petersburg,
June 24, '64.

J. Sheridan, Ireland, wounded in left scapular region, at Drury's
Bluff, May 15, '64.

A. L. Spangenberg, wounded in left hand, Minnie, at Petersburg,
July 30, '65.

H. W. Hopkins, Haddonfield.	J. Tumith, Ireland.
Joseph Little, Sussex.	Oscar Kays, Sussex.

Recruits received 1864.

W. Buckelew, Mercer, died at Newark hospital, June 20, '64;
chronic diarrhœa.

N. G. Smith, London, missing, Drury's Bluff, May 16, '64; died
in rebel prison.

P. J. Low, Somerset, missing, Drury's Bluff, May 16, '64; died in rebel prison.

J. W. Hulziger, Warren, wounded in left arm, before Petersburg, July 13, '64.

R. H. Kitchen, Bethlehem, wounded in left toe, at Drury's Bluff, May 14, '64.

R. King, Ireland, wounded in head, Drury's Bluff, May 16, '64.

S. Allkire, Bridgetown, wounded, foot, Drury's Bluff, May 16, '64.

B. Cain, Bordentown, wounded in arm, Swift Creek, Sept. 10, '64.

B. A. Osborn, Sussex, wounded under mascular region, before Petersburg, July 15, '64.

A. Sergeant, Flemington, wounded, foot, Drury's Bluff, May 16, '64.

A. Strycker, Hunterdon,   "   arm,   "   "

J. V. D. Drost, Flagtown, deserted, White House landing, June 2, '64; returned to company May 8, '65.

J. Sheridan, called the second, England, deserted at Carolina City, November 2, '64.

Joseph Price, Sussex.	A. P. Hoagland, Mercer.
E. Berrit, Clifford.	J. S. Ames, Bridgeton.
J. C. S. Berrit, Bridgeport, Conn.	T. G. Claussen, Newark.
M. Gray, Burlington.	A. M. Conover, Hunterdon.
P. Cyphers, Belvidere.	C. M. Fitzgerald, New York.
J. M. Low, Hunterdon.	Wm. Vanacker, Mercer.
David Williams, England.	R. Wackefield, England.

Mustered Out June 14, 1865.

C. Boyd, New York.	E. Murat, France.
G. Conover, Mercer.	J. Smith, Germany.
G. P. Baily, Somerset.	J. Steele, "

Recruits received 1865.

Jacob Bradfield, Gloucester.	Jacob Koch, Germany.
Long Benjamin, Ireland.	Isaac Little, Sussex.
Wm. Benton, Boston.	Pierre Lafont, France.
James Couchmann, England.	A. Liesengang, Germany.
W. H. Kraft, Camden.	Philipp Lonst, "
D. S. Carter, Gloucester.	G. W. Matlock, "
Wm. T. Carr, "	Wm. Meyer, "
William Dunn, Jersey City.	F. Quincey, "
James Darling, England.	G. Sylvester, "
Benjamin Fagan, Ireland.	Timothy Titus, Trenton.
Hugh Galligher, "	John Waters, England.
S. Huth, Germany.	Daniel Waters, "

Company G.

JOHN PETER RITTER, Captain.

WM. ZIMMERMAN, 1st Lieut. WM. BENTON, 2d Lieut.

Enlisted Men.

James H. Agens, Orange, transferred to Invalid Corps, 1864.

George Asch, England, discharged November 23, '62, at Newbern; rheumatism.

William Brondstetter, Sr., Germany, discharged June 17, '62; disability.

William Brondstetter, Jr., Germany, wounded with shell, in leg, at Goldsboro', Dec. 17, '62; leg amputated; discharged at Newark, June 29, '63.

S. Beathy, Glasgow, Scotland, wounded at Newbern, March 14, '62; received a furlough; did not return; reported as a deserter, by order of the War Department, Aug. 18, '62; apprehended; sent to U. S. general hospital, Newark; discharged.

Frederick Brander, Germany, transferred from Co. A; wounded in arm, at Walthall, May 6, '64; discharged at expiration of time of service, December 7, '64.

Frederick Brand, Germany, transferred from Co. A; discharged at expiration of time of service, September 24, '64.

George Brown, Germany, transferred from Co. A; wounded in head, at Walthall, June 6, '64; discharged at expiration of time of service, December 7, '64.

P. Comeford, Ireland, wounded in shoulder, at Whitehall, Dec. 16, '62; died at Newbern, January 3, '63.

J. Crowley, Ireland, wounded at Newbern, March 14, '62; went home on furlough; did not return; reported as a deserter, by order of the War Department, August 18, '62; apprehended, and discharged at Alexandria, Va.

M. Dolan, Ireland, killed at Newbern, N. C., March 14, '62.

A. Dickert, Germany, discharged at Newbern, Oct. 15, '63; disability.

C. A. Faczeck, Elizabeth, discharged at Trenton, March 17, '63; disability.

Thomas Fitzpatrick, Ireland, discharged at Newbern, June 29, '63; disability.

James Hand, Rahway, disch. at Trenton, Nov. 26, '61; under age.

H. Happ, Germany, transferred to Invalid Corps at the Douglas hospital, Washington, D. C.

5

F. Hobart, Elizabeth, wounded in car, at Roanoke Island, Feb. 8, '62; discharged for promotion, July 1, '62.

Joseph Hogg, Germany, transferred from Co. A; missing, Drury's Bluff, May 16, '64; died in rebel prison, at Andersonville, October, 1864.

M. Kunkel, Germany, transferred from Co. A; discharged at Newbern, March 26, '63; hernia.

William Lodesson, Newark, transferred from Co. A; wounded at Whitehall, Dec. 16, '62; transferred to Invalid Corps, Newark hospital, September 30, '63.

Henry Loetzsch, Germany, wounded in leg, at Whitehall, Dec. 16, '62; leg amputated; died at Newbern, January 31, '63.

Timothy Mulvey, Ireland, wounded at Newbern, March 14, '62; died at Newbern, March 29, '62.

J. McCloskey, New Brunswick, deserted at Annapolis, Md., January 15, '62.

William Mills, Bristol, transferred from Co. A; discharged at Newbern hospital, December 12, '63.

P. McBride, Ireland, discharged at Newbern, March 7, '63; disability.

P. Moran, Ireland, discharged at Newbern, June 24, '63; disability.

S. Neuhofer, Germany, missing, Drury's Bluff, May 16, '64; died in rebel prison.

Henry Ott, Germany, killed at Roanoke Island, Feb. 8, '62.

F. Porepp, Germany, discharged at Morehead City, Nov. 21, '62; rupture.

M. Row, Ireland, discharged at Beaufort, March 30, '63; disability.

B. Riedinger, Germany, wounded severely, in mouth, at Roanoke Island, February 8, '62; discharged at expiration of time of service, December 7, 64.

J. Rannard, England, discharged at Newbern, April 1, '63; disability.

Terence Riley, Ireland, discharged at Newbern, July 10, '62; disability.

C. Scheller, Germany, discharged at Beaufort, June 1, '63; disability.

S. Simon, Swiss, discharged at Beaufort, June 1, '63; disability.

Edward Stockmann, Dublin, deserted at Camp Olden, Oct. 29, '61.

Joseph Schnetzer, Swiss, slightly wounded at Newbern, March 14, '62; discharged for promotion, December 29, '62.

William M. Smith, New York, died at Mansfield general hospital, Morehead City, October 10, '64; yellow fever.

J. P. Saland, Germany, discharged at Newbern, June 17, '62; disability.

Jacob Sauerbrunn, Elizabeth, discharged at Morehead City, November 21, '62; disability.

Philipp Schweitzer, Germany, transferred from Co. A; missing, Drury's Bluff, May 16, '64; died in rebel prison, at Andersonville, Georgia.

John Thiele, transferred from Co. A; discharged at Newbern, June 23, '63; disability.

G. V. Tylee, New York, discharged at Newbern, June 17, '62; disability.

Cornelius Van Nest, Somerset, wounded mortally, in head, at Walthall, May 6, '64; died in 18th Army Corps hospital, at Point of Rocks, Va., May 8, '64.

V. Williamson, Ireland, wounded at Roanoke Island, Feb. 8, '62; discharged at Newbern, June 23, '63.

James Wall, Ireland, wounded in leg, at Whitehall, Dec. 16, '62; discharged at expiration of time of service, Sept. 16, '64.

John Welscher, Germany, died at Beaufort, N. C., Jan. 4, '63; dropsy.

T. Whittemore, England, deserted at Trenton, Nov. 10, '62.

J. J. Waters, Plainfield, missing, Drury's Bluff, May 16, '64; died in rebel prison.

Thomas Ford, Newark, sentenced Dec. 9, '63, by general court-martial, to serve the rest of his time at the Rip Raps; charges: drunkenness, and striking his superior officer; discharged at expiration of time of service, December 7, '64.

Valentine Gessler, Germany, transferred from Co. A; discharged June 15, '63.

A. Grienich, Germany, transferred from Co. A; died at U. S. general army hospital, Fort Monroe, Sept. 17, '64; diarrhœa.

S. Hurst, Germany, wounded at Whitehall, Dec. 16, '62; discharged at Newark, March 15, '64.

Discharged at expiration of time of service, at Trenton, N. J., December 7, 1864.

Henry Baumann, Swiss.	George Lee, England.
Jacob Bopp, Germany.	Patrick Lee, Ireland.
Thomas Byrnes, Ireland.	Philipp Meyer, Germany.
D. Dimmler, Germany.	D. McCandless, Ireland.
S. K. Doty, Martinsville.	James McCree, "
John Fritz, Germany.	M. Supple, "
C. Garthwaite, Union.	A. B. Stites, Warren.
P. Hindes, Elizabeth.	Valentine Schardien, Germany.

Henry Knaben, Elizabeth.

Re-Enlisted November 26, 1863.

Thomas McGinn, Ireland, transferred at his own request to Co. C.

J. Schulders, Germany, deserted May 30, '64, from N. Y. hospital.

J. H. Fatty, Elizabeth, missing, at Drury's Bluff, May 16, '64; returned to regiment May, 1865.

G. Seidel, Germany, wounded in finger of right hand, at Drury's Bluff, May 16, '64.

William Ward, Rahway, wounded, abdomen, Walthall, May 6, '64.

Paul Engel, Germany.   Racy Evans, Ireland.

Stephen Mahony, Ireland.

Re-Enlisted January 18, 1864.

E. Dillon, Ireland, missing, Drury's Bluff, May 16, '64; died in rebel prison, at Andersonville.

John Mueller, Germany, missing, Drury's Bluff, May 16, '64; died in rebel prison, at Florence.

Robert Sloan, Ireland, wounded at Walthall, May 7, '64; wounded at Drury's Bluff, May 16, '64; killed, Minnie ball entering right and exit left temple, before Petersburg, July 1, '64.

S. Luterbeck, France, killed at Walthall, May 6, '64.

Patrick Dawns, Ireland, did not return from veteran furlough; reported as deserter.

Philipp Eckerson, Elizabeth, wounded, leg, on Goldsboro' Expedition, December 16, '62.

F. Rosenbauer, New York, accidentally wounded in leg, Drury's Bluff, May 12, '64.

George Peters, Elizabeth, received commission as 2d Lieutenant of Co. G, April 29, '64, at Yorktown, Va.

William Godfrey, England.   Ch. Zimmermann, Elizabeth.
Thomas Keenan, Ireland.   Wm. Zimmermann,   "
S. Murray.   "   William Terrell, Newark.
M. Sanders,   "   Charles Ward, Rahway.

            Morris Welsch, Philadelphia.

Anthony Rang, France, re enlisted February 29, '64; missing, at Drury's Bluff, May 16, '64; died in rebel prison, Sept. 20, '64.

Re-Enlisted March 13, 1864.

James McMullen, Ireland, missing, Drury's Bluff, May 16, '64; paroled, exchanged, and discharged, June 19, '65, at Trenton; disability.

Robert Dickey, Ireland.   Beaumont Brook, England.

Recruits received 1862.

Franz Basch, Germany, discharged at expiration of time of service, May 28, '65.

Friedrich Fessel, Germany, discharged; disability.

Adam Seeger, Trenton, discharged at Hilton Head, S. C., May 11, '63; disability.

G. Naumann, Germany, transferred to Invalid Corps, by order of Brigadier General Palmer.

Chr. Huber, Germany, missing, Drury's Bluff, May 16, '64; shot while in rebel prison, at Andersonville, for stepping on the so-called Death-line, Minnie-ball passing in right breast.

H. J. Ball, Germany, transferred from Co. A; missing, at Drury's Bluff, May 16, '65; returned May, '65; mustered out June 2, '65.

Philipp Beck, Germany, died at Morehead City, Nov. 5, '62; typhoid fever.

John Knapp, Germany, discharged at Newark, May 26, '64; disability; mustered out June 14, '64.

William Biermann, Germany.   Edwin Somet, Heckstown.

Hermann Everts, Germany.   G. Smith, Frenchtown.
Theodor Stubener,   "   J. A. Raymond, New York.

Recruits received 1863.

Th. Thompson, Liverpool, killed, Minnie-ball through heart, at Cold Harbor, Va , June 4, '64.

C. Shmidt, Germany, missing, Drury's Bluff, May 16, '64; died in rebel prison.

Jacob Muller, Germany, did not return when regiment was on veteran furlough, he being partly deranged, and subject to delirium tremens; no inquiries were made.

John Schon, Germany, deserted at Newport News, Va., Nov. 13, 1863; arrested, sentenced to six months' hard labor, and to forfeit all pay and allowances for that time; left from Fort Monroe, joined his regiment, and deserted again at Bogue Sound, October 24, '64.

Ludwig Ludwig, Germany.   M. Schields, Ireland.

Recruits received 1864.

F. G. Peach, Germany, wounded in left side, at Swift Creek, May 10, '64; died at Point of Rocks, June 7, '64.

H. W. Nutt, Trenton, killed, Minnie-ball entering forehead, Cold Harbor, June 12, '64.

Philipp Spoonheimer, Elizabeth, wounded, in left leg, at Drury's Bluff, May 15, '64; discharged at Newark hospital, for wounds received.

William Fry, Germany, missing, Drury's Bluff, May 16, '64; died in rebel prison, Andersonville, Ga.

J. L. Deemer, Germany, missing, at Drury's Bluff, May 16, '64; died in rebel prison, at Andersonville, Ga.. June 27, '64.

J. J. Corine, Newark, deserted at Yorktown, Va., May 1, '64; returned to Co. January 22, '65; he being an imbecile, and not able to take care of himself, no charges were made against him.

P. Hegel, Germany, wounded, in third toe of left foot, at Drury's Bluff, May 15, '64.

M. Hill, Millford, missing, Drury's Bluff, May 16, '64; returned to regiment May, 1865.

C. Wilson, Easton, Pa., wounded in right thigh, at Drury's Bluff, May 14, '64.

E. S. Stewart, Sussex, wounded in left arm, at Drury's Bluff, May 16, '64.

E. Dyer, Bucks, Pa., wounded in left shoulder-blade, by shell, at Wise's Fork, N. C., March 10, '65; mustered out June 14, '65.

J. King, Ireland, deserted at Bogue Sound, October 17, '64.

J. McCarty, "   "   "   "

M. Dingler, Germany.   J. Dalton, Frankfort, Pa.
J. H. Williams, New Jersey.   Jacob Kline, Germany.
Lewis Conrad, Germany.   G. Koch,   "

Mustered out June 14, 1865.

Wm. Frederick, Bucks, Pa.
Jacob Conover, Somerset.
T. F. Terrell, Newark.
A. H. Gardener, New Jersey.
R. Wurgeler, Swiss.
L. Violet, France.
H. Fahrer, New York.
W. H. Johnson, Canada.
Archilla Chizzola, Italy.
H. Fanau, Germany.
P. Graff,   "
J. Glasser,   "
J. Kratz,   "
J. Long,   "

A. Michou, Belgium.
H. Morgan, Ireland.
Daniel Kennedy, Ireland.
J. Riley,   "
J. Wentz, Germany.
J. Muller,   "
A. Weissler,   "
L. Berry.   "
A. Biermann,   "
G. Neushafer,   "
L. Roin,   "
F. Schieler,   "
C. Cutler,   "
G. Hamlin,   "

Valentin Ritchie, Germany.

Recruits received 1865.

Louis Covert, Morrisson.
John Hearing, Germany.
John Murray, Ireland.
John McDonald.

C. F. Stalford.
David Reed.
Francis Schick.
J. M. Holstein.

The following five men were taken up, and dropped again, on Company rolls, by General Order, No. 305, of War Department, A. G. O., dated December 27, '64.

Wm. H. Donelly, Philadelphia. Adam Frederic, Germany.
L. H. Gause, Chester.   B. Gleissner, Atlantic.

Isaac P. Yane, Pennsylvania.

Company H.

J. J. HENRY, Captain.

JAS. STEWART, JR., 1st Lieut.   J. B. LAWRENCE, 2d Lieut.

Enlisted Men.

A. E. Armstrong, Johnsonberry, killed at Roanoke, Feb. 8, '62.

Wm. Aumick, Frankford, Pa., wounded at Roanoke, Feb. 8, '62 ; discharged at Newark, September 8, '62.

Jacob R. Aumick, Frankford, Pa., wounded at Newbern, March 14, '62 ; discharged at Newark, September 8, '62.

Ch. Alston, Burlington, a coward ! he run at the battle of Roanoke Island, Feb. 8, '62, and deserted on the morning of the Newbern fight, March 14, '62.

Thomas Burns, Warren, wounded at Roanoke, February 8, '62 ; wounded at Kinston, Dec. 14, '62 ; discharged at expiration of time of service, December 7, '64.

S. C. Brown, Warren, died, Roanoke, April 10, '62; typhoid fever.

James Barrigan, Ireland, mustered out at Beaufort, Nov. 10, '62 ; general debility.

August Boyd, Warren, discharged at Newbern, May 19, '62; chronic rheumatism.

John Brown, Ireland, killed at Drury's Bluff, May 16, '64.

Fredr. Brehm, Swiss, transferred from Co. L ; discharged at Carolina City, May 28, '63 ; disability.

Jacob Bettinger, Germany, transferred from Co. L ; discharged May 28, '63 ; disability.

John E. Cook, Hunterdon, died January 23, '62 ; inflammation of the lungs.

Thomas Cooper, Sussex, mustered out at Trenton, Nov. 1, '61 ; neglect of duty.

Wm. Comer, Oxford Furnace, discharged at Newbern, May 28, '63 ; disability.

E. S. Carroll, Warren, discharged for promotion, March 9, '62.

Nelson R. Cramer, Monroe, Pa., died at Beaufort, October 3, '64 ; yellow fever.

H. H. Cook, discharged at Trenton, Nov. 1, '61 ; unsound mind.

Timothy Callahan, Ireland, killed at Walthall, May 6, '64.

A. Deforest, East Madison, died at Roanoke, February 25, '62 ; typhoid fever.

W. D. Forgus, Alexandria, died at Roanoke, March 4, '62 ; typhoid fever.

Joseph Durant, France, discharged at Newbern, Nov. 23, '62; disability.

John Dickey, Warren, discharged, Newbern, July 19, '62; chronic rheumatism.

D. L. Duncan, Orange, discharged at Newbern, July 22, '62; disability.

F. Donnelly, Hunterdon, wounded, thigh, Kinston, Dec. 14, '62; discharged at expiration of time of service, Dec. 7, '64.

F. Gilles, Scotland, discharged at Newbern, Nov. 23, '62; disability.

B. Hartsell, Warren, wounded at Whitehall, Dec. 16, '62; discharged at Newbern, July 18, '63.

S. A. Hagermann, Bloomsberry, died at Newbern, April 17, '62; typhoid fever.

G. Hubbs, Baptistown, mustered out Nov. 10, '62; disability.

M. Higgins, Ireland, discharged at Newbern, Nov. 23, '62; disability.

J. L. Hawk, Warren, wounded at Whitehall, Dec. 16, '62; discharged for promotion, Dec. 23, '62.

Jacob Hadley, Hope, transferred to Invalid Corps, Dec. 28, '63.

J. W. Haggerty, Screpton, wounded in 4th left toe, at Drury's Bluff, May 15, '64; discharged at expiration of time of service, Dec. 7, '64.

James Hoffmann, Sussex, transferred to Co. C, U. S. Artillery, November 19, '62.

Wm. A. Johnson, Hunterdon, discharged and drummed out of Camp Olden, November 1, '61; neglect of duty.

C. P. Levers, Easton, discharged at Newbern, Aug. 15, '63; disability.

John Miller, Broadway, died at Roanoke, March 5, '62; typhoid fever.

John E. Matthew, Doylestown, mustered out at Beaufort, Nov. 10, '62; disability.

Francis M. McCue, Quincy, Mass.; discharged June 23, '62; varicose veins of leg.

James S. Van Campen, Warren, discharged March 14, '63, on surgeon's certificate.

R. Nast, Germany, transferred from Co. L; transferred to Invalid Corps, November 28, '63, by order of War Department.

E. S. Pullen, Mercer, discharged for promotion, Dec. 23, '62.

M. B. Philipps, New York, died at Newbern, Oct. 16, '64; yellow fever.

A. P. Keysar, Holland, transferred to Invalid Corps, Dec. 28, '62.

Geo. F. Ribbon, Warren, went home on furlough; did not return; reported as a deserter.

John Rink, Germany, transferred from Co. L; discharged at Newbern, Oct. 14, '63; disability.

A. D. Staples, Warren, died at Newbern, April 20, '62; typhoid fever.

F. R. Sylvester, Fairfield, discharged at Newbern, June 9, '62; disability.

Edward Scofield, Westchester, transferred to Co. C, 1st U. S. Artillery, November 19, '62.

Joseph Warner, Trenton, died at Roanoke, April 5, '62; typhoid fever.

Jeffrey W. Wethrel, Salem, Pa., discharged at Beaufort, October 22, '62; disability.

E. W. Welsted, Northampton, Pa., discharged for promotion, Aug. 12, 1863.

Discharged at expiration of time of service, December 7, 1864, at Trenton, N. J.

C. Dieber, Germany, transferred from Co. L; wounded in shoulder, at Kinston, December 14, '62.

Lycidius Hamilton, Belvidere.   G. W. Parker, Hunterdon.

Richard Harrisson, Hunterdon.   J. P. Smith, France.

—— Harrisson, Mt. Bethel, Pa.   John T. Van Normann, Easton.

Edward Levers, Easton.   C. A. Wolverton, Hunterdon.

John Moore, Holland.   J. McGrow, Ireland.

J. M. Miers, Warren, wounded by shell, in left foot, on Goldsboro' Expedition, 1862.

D. W. Shoemaker, Warren, wounded by grape-shot, in bowels, on Goldsboro' Expedition, 1862.

M. Scanton, South Lee, Mass., wounded in leg, at Whitehall, December 14, '62.

William A. Ward, Rahway, wounded in heel, at Kinston, N. C., December 14, '62.

Re-Enlisted November 25, 1863.

J. L. Aumick, Frankfort, Pa., wounded, leg, Whitehall, Dec. 16, '62.

John Bittinger, Germany, transferred from Co. L.

Daniel Eyer, Germany, transferred from Co. L; wounded in right chest, at Walthall, May 6, '64.

Marshall Howell, Warren, wounded in arm, at Goldsboro', December 17, '62.

H. C. Powers, New York city, wounded, at Kinston, Dec. 14, '62.

G. W. Taylor, Hunterdon, wounded in right arm, at Cold Harbor; arm amputated; discharged at U. S. General Army hospital, Alexandria, Va., August 23, '64.

Joseph Willgus, Sussex, wounded in right hand, at Cold Harbor, June 11, '64.

S. Worthington, Bucks, Pa., severely kicked in the face by a horse, at Petersburg, June 13, '64.

Patrick Cahill, Ireland.   T. M. Devoe, New York.

M. M. Fiske, Connecticut.   A. G. Hauk, Easton.

G. W. Miller, Warren.   E. Worthington, Bucks, Pa.

John Edmonds, Hunterdon, wounded in chest, at Walthall, Va., May 6, '64.

Re-Enlisted January 18, 1864.

P. Beam, Warren, wounded left shoulder, Drury's Bluff, May 16, '64.

Henry Bittinger, Oxford Furnace, wounded, rupture. at Roanoke,
Feb. 8, '62 ; wounded in both thighs, at Walthall, May 6, '64.

J. Deischler, Germany, transferred from Co. L ; wounded in hand,
at Drury's Bluff, May 16, '64.

A. L. Duncan, Orange, wounded, thigh, Cold Harbor, June 7, '64.

John Donnelly, Milford, injured in feet, while destroying houses
standing in range of artillery at Wise's Fork, March 8, '65.

Daniel Hallowell, England, wounded in right arm, at Cold Harbor,
June 11, '64 ; died at Campbell U. S. A. hospital, July 13, '64.

John Hirt, Germany, wounded at Kinston, Dec. 14, '62 ; killed
at Drury's Bluff, May 16, '64.

Augustus Lott, Bloomsburg, taken prisoner at Butler's Bridge,
Dec. 12, '64 ; returned May 17, '65 ; mustered out June 14, '65.

C. P. Little, Newark, wounded at Newbern, March 14, '62 ;
wounded in leg, at Kinston, December 14, '62.

Jacob Meyers, Swiss, wounded in foot, at Greensboro, Dec. 17, '62.

John Meiers, Germany, killed at Swift Creek, May 9, '64.

C. R. Nycomer, Sweden, taken prisoner at Southwest Creek,
December 13, '62 ; returned December 20, '63.

R. B. Philipps, Sussex, missing, Drury's Bluff, May 16, '64 ; died
in rebel prison, at Charleston, S. C.

G. A. Stout. Hunterdon, wounded, shoulder, Kinston. Dec. 14, '62.

John F. Schafer, Lehigh Co., Pa., wounded in right chest, Walthall, May 6, '64.

Jacob Schick, Germany, transferred from Co. L ; wounded, head,
at Petersburg, August 24, '64.

John Schwarz, Germany, transferred from Co. L ; wounded at
Goldsboro', December 17, '62.

John P. Taylor, Oxford, shot accidentally, thumb off, Jan. 19, '63.

Abram Vangarden, Warren, went home on furlough ; did not return ;
arrested as a deserter, court-martialed, and sentenced to forfeit
all pay and allowances from March 26, '62 till Jan. 14, '64 ;
returned to regiment ; wounded in thumb, at Drury's Bluff,
May 16, '64.

A. Bertrand, Germany, transferred from Co. L.

G. Hoffmann,   "   "   "   "

S. R. Buckley, Philadelphia.   Wm. J. Decker, Newton.

J. F. Butler. Little York.   D. S. Johnson, Readington.

J. W. Creveling, Warren.   W. G. Kitchen, Warren.

E. Cooley, Hunterdon.   John Loftus, Montono.

E. Clayton, Warren.   John Levers, Easton.

W. W. Clark, Hunterdon.   J. F. Sutphen, Germantown, Pa.

William Vangarden, Warren.

Re-Enlisted March 24, 1864.

Jacob Yeomans, Bleyerstown, wounded in cheek, at Drury's Bluff,
May 16, '64.

Recruits received 1862.

C. Dieber, Germany, transferred from Co. L: mustered out June 14, 1865.

John H. King, Philadelphia, wounded at Whitehall, Dec. 16, '62; re-enlisted March 7, '64; discharged September 30, '64, to be promoted 2d Lieutenant Co. A, 35th Reg't N. J. V.; did not report at headquarters, as ordered; reported on Co. rolls as deserter; order for promotion revoked by order of War Department; returned to regiment, and was taken up again on Co. rolls.

William Koenig, Germany, transferred from Co. L; discharged at expiration of time of service, March 16, '65.

A. W. Little, Clinton, mustered out June 14, '65.

J. Rosenbury, Cherryville, deserted at Trenton, March 16, '64, when the regiment was on veteran furlough.

F. Streining, Germany, transferred from Co. L; mustered out June 14, '65.

L. Schriff, Germany, transferred from Co. L; wounded at Whitehall, December 16, '62; mustered out June 14, '65.

B. Schafer, Germany, transferred from Co. L; wounded at Whitehall, December 16, '62; discharged November 20, '63.

A. H. Valentine, Paterson, wounded slightly in shoulder, on the Goldsboro' Expedition, 1862; mustered out June 14, '65.

Recruits received 1863.

John Daws, Hunterdon, deserted at Carolina City, Feb. 18, '65.

James Graham, Halifax.

M. Hussey, Ireland, wounded in head, at Swift Creek, May 9, '64; discharged at Fort Monroe, June 8, '65

William Idesson, Boston, wounded in left arm, at Swift Creek, May 10, '64; deserted at Goldsboro', March 30, '65.

John A. McClausland, Canada.

H. Keenan, Rochester, N. Y., wounded, Drury's Bluff, May 16, '64.

Recruits received 1864.

Z. Snover, Warren, discharged at Willett's Point, N. J., August 16, '64, by order of Major General Dix.

Henry Losey, Sussex, died at regimental hospital, Nov. 18, '64; remittent fever and epilepsy.

John W. Osborn, Penn'a, missing, Drury's Bluff, May 16, '64.

A. G. Spangenberg, Warren, wounded, Drury's Bluff, May 16, '64.

A. M. Vangarden, Warren, wounded in hand, at Cold Harbor, June 3, '64.

J. S. Vangarden, Warren, wounded, right hand, at Cold Harbor, June 3, '64.

J. A. Vangarden, Warren, wounded in thumb, at Drury's Bluff, May 16, '64.

Henry Beck, Germany.   J. Ozenbough, Warren.
Caspar Losey, Sussex.   D. H. Terrill,   "

T. G. Courtright, Monroe.
W. H. Crossman, Bucks Co., Pa.
S. A. Cole, Pennsylvania.
W. H. H. Harman, Penn'a.
S. J. Schipman, Warren.
James Smith, Pennsylvania.
E. Smaley, Warren.
R. Weaver, Pennsylvania.

Mustered Out June 4, 1865.

J. J. Berry, New Jersey.
E. Butler, Hunterdon.
James Coughle, Warren.
John Frank, Germany.
J. F. Hart, Germany.
Wm. Hummer, Hunterdon.
R. McCush, Ireland.
W. G. Smith, Hunterdon.

Recruits received 1865.

E. Bennett, Middlesex.
John Bechtel, Germany.
James Cannon, Indiana.
James Colfer, Ireland.
Thomas Coyle, Dublin.
James Casey, "
S. Courtright, Trenton.
Ch. Dyer, Germany.
John Gerbeck, "
Thomas Grady, Ireland.
James A. Houthon, Newark.
Ch. Kerby, New Hampshire.
John Metzler, "
William Moore, Warren.
William Mullnia, Trenton.
John Oldham, England.
G. F. Whaller, Warren.
Paul Wax, New Hampshire.

M. Gumpert, Germany.

G. King, Monroe, deserted at Goldsboro', April 4, '65.
James Woodruff, Clinton, deserted at Kinston, March 20, '65.

Company I.

Henry F. Chew, Captain.

Samuel Hufty, Jr., 1st Lieut.   E. M. Pinkard, 2d Lieut.

Enlisted Men.

Robert Aldron, Ireland, discharged at Newbern, Aug. 25, '62; disability.

J. C. Bowker, Burlington, discharged for promotion, Dec. 29, '62.

H. Bramble, Salem, discharged at Beaufort, Nov. 18, '62, by General Order 154, War Department.

C. Brown, New Brunswick, died at Beaufort, August 16, '62; pneumonia.

W. B. Birch, Atlantic, wounded, rupture, Newbern, March 14, '62; discharged at St. Helena Island, March 17, '63.

R. P. Craigg, Cumberland, discharged at Beaufort, Nov. 18, '62; by General Order 154, War Department.

Wm. P. Corliss, Philadelphia, discharged at St. Helena Island, March 24, '63; disability.

G. W. Cowmann, Gloucester, wounded in hip, at Roanoke, Feb. 8, '62; discharged at expiration of time of service, Dec. 7, '64.

E. H. Davies, Salem, wounded at Newbern, March 14, '62; deserted when home on furlough, August 18, '62.

Philipp Ebert, Germany, transferred from Co. L; discharged Feb. 25, '65, at Newark hospital.

L. Eckert, Germany, transferred from Co. L; discharged at Beaufort, September 13, '63; diarrhœa.

F. Felmy, Philadelphia, discharged at Beaufort, November 18,' 62, by General Order 154, War Department.

H. A. Hartranft, Philadelphia, discharged at Beaufort, Nov. 18. '62, by General Order 154, War Department.

J. H. Harvey, New York, wounded at Roanoke, Feb. 8, '62; discharged by General Order 154, War Department.

J. W. Harbison, Salem, discharged at St. Helena Island, March 24, '63; disability.

W. G. Hartline, Salem, wounded at Roanoke, Feb. 8, '62; died at Beaufort. February 3, '63; icterus.

R. Islan, Salem, wounded, Roanoke, Feb. 8, '62; disch. Beaufort, Nov. 18, '62, by General Order 154, War Department.

J. N. Johnson, Salem, appointed Drum-Major at Camp Olden, '61.

W. B. Loper, Salem, discharged at Beaufort, Nov. 18, 1862, by General Order 154, War Department.

C. G. Lorch, Philadelphia, discharged by General Order 126, War
Department.

S. M. Laymann, Salem, discharged at Beaufort, January 18, '63;
hypertrophy of heart and old age.

Samuel Lester, Atlantic, discharged at Beaufort, March 30, '63;
hypertrophy of heart and old age.

E. L. Metlack, Salem, discharged at Washington, Nov. 17, '62;
by General Order 154, of War Department.

C. B. Mesvic, Philadelphia, discharged at Beaufort, Nov. 17, '62;
by General Order 154, War Department.

Edward D. Mattson, Gloucester, lamed in action, Goldsboro', Dec.
17, '62; discharged expiration of time of service, Dec. 7, '64.

J. P. Mattson, Gloucester, wounded at Newbern, March 14, '62;
index finger of right hand, at Drury's Bluff, May 15, '64;
discharged at expiration of time of service, Dec. 7, '64.

John E. Johnson, Flensburg, wounded at Kinston, Dec. 14, '62;
died December 15, '62.

C. Oatanger, Germany, wounded at White Oak, July 26, '62;
discharged at St. Helena Island, March 24, '63; disability.

John Powell, Salem, deserted from Christopher Street hospital, at
Philadelphia, August 18. '62.

Jacob Rose, New York, wounded at Newbern, March 14, '62; discharged at Beaufort, Nov. 18, '62, by General Order 154, War
Department.

G. Rottenhofer, Germany, transferred from Co. L; discharged at
St. Helena Island, March, 30, '63; disability.

J. Reeves, Cumberland, wounded at Newbern, March 14, '62;
discharged at St. Helena Island, March 24, '63; disability.

R. Segraves, Burlington, died at Beaufort, October 2, '62.

C. P. Springer, Salem, discharged for promotion, March 9, '62.

C. J. Staincup, Salem, wounded at Roanoke, Feb. 8, '62; killed
at Whitehall, December 16, '62.

R. Swain, Philadelphia, discharged for promotion, Aug. 15, '62.

C. Schephard, Burlington, appointed commissary-sergeant, December 20, '63.

Philipp Schmidt, Germany, transferred from Co. L; discharged at
Hilton Head, S. C., May 9, '63; disability.

H. Streibert, Germany, transferred from Co. L; discharged at Newbern, September 11, '63; hypertrophy of heart.

C. Taylor, Salem, wounded at Newbern, March 14, '62; discharged
at Philadelphia, June 23, '63.

James W. Tasch, Queen Ann, Md., discharged at St. Helena
Island, March 24, '63; disability.

Aaron Vanculen, Salem, died at Beaufort, Aug. 22, '63; diarrhœa.

John Warfle, Cumberland, discharged by General Order 126, War
Department.

G. G. White, Salem, died at Newbern, April 18, '62; typhoid fever.

Wm. Williams, Salem, discharged at Washington, May 17, '62;
disability.

David Wensell, Salem, discharged at Newbern, April 7, '63; disability.

Joseph West, Salem, wounded at Roanoke, February 8, '62; discharged at Beaufort, June, 1863.

C. Wellendorf, Holstein, transferred from Co. L; wounded, left thigh, on Goldsboro' Expedition, Dec. 15, '62; discharged at expiration of time of service, February 7, '64.

J. Walker, Germany, transferred from Co. L; deserted at Newark, November 9, '63, while home on furlough.

Isaac Zanes, Gloucester, died at Newport Barracks, May 3, '62; typhoid fever.

B. Gill, Gloucester, wounded at Newbern, March 14, '62; discharged November 18, '62.

Discharged at expiration of time of service, December 7, 1864, at Trenton, N. J.

Enoch Cordory, Cumberland.   Thomas H. Kiger, Salem.
C. D. Mulford,   "   G. L. Turnbull, Philadelphia.
W. H. Toukey, Burlington.

Henry Loper, Salem, wounded at Newbern, March 14, '62.

I. H. Vining, Salem, discharged at Portsmouth, March 31, '64.

Re-Enlisted November 25, 1863.

Joshua Anderson, Cumberland, wounded, Newbern, March 14, '62.

J. Dubois, Salem, wounded in right leg, at Drury's Bluff, May 16, '64; transferred to Veteran Reserve Corps, by order of War Department.

J. L. Elkenton, Gloucester.

J. Sparks, Salem, missing, at Drury's Bluff, May 16, '64; never heard of; dropped as dead, on Co. rolls.

G. W. Townsend, Salem.

Re-Enlisted December 20, 1863.

C. F. Beyer, Germany, transferred from Co. L.

James V. Clark, Salem, wounded in right hand, at Drury's Bluff, May 16, '64.

Henry Eifert, Germany, wounded at Newbern, March 14, '62; wounded in left hip, on Goldsboro' Expedition, Dec. 15, '62.

Louis Murphy, Salem, wounded, hand, Drury's Bluff, May 16, '64.

John E. Taylor, Swiss.

Re-Enlisted January 18, 1864.

John Bennett, Salem, wounded in both hands, at Drury's Bluff, May 16, '64.

John Brady, New York, wounded at Whitehall, Dec. 16, '62; wounded at Swift Creek, May 9, '64; wounded at Drury's Bluff, May 16, '64.

A. Cowmann, Gloucester, wounded at Kinston, December 14, '62; missing, Drury's Bluff, May 16, '64; never heard of, and dropped from Co. rolls.

Wm. B. Davies, Gloucester, deserted; enlisted in the 85th N. Y. Vols.; was seen and recognized on the Goldsboro' Expedition, by Capt. Samuel Hufty, Jr.; claimed, and returned to the "Ninth N. J. Vols.;" killed at Drury's Bluff, May 15, '64.

C. P. Goodwin, Salem, wounded at Newbern, March 14, '62.

E. H. Green, Salem, discharged for promotion, Feb. 5, '65.

A. J. Hanley, Philadelphia, taken prisoner at Butler's Bridge, Dec. 12, '64; died in rebel prison, at Salisbury, Feb. 22, '65.

S. B. Harbison, Salem, wounded in thigh, Drury's Bluff; transferred to Co. I, 21st Veteran Reserve Corps, March 31, '65.

M. Hepburn, New York, died at Newbern, Oct. 10, '64; yellow fever.

C. Hoffmann, Salem, wounded, White Oak, July 26, '63; wounded at Cold Harbor, June 3, '64; wounded mortally, at Cold Harbor, June 4, '64; died at Cold Harbor, June 4, '64.

A. Kauffmann, Germany, wounded in left thigh, at Drury's Bluff, May 16, '64.

C. Keen, Salem, wounded at Roanoke, Feb. 8, '62; wounded in right cheek, at Drury's Bluff, May 16, '64.

David Kille, Camden, discharged for promotion, July 24, '64.

S. M. Laymann, Salem, wounded at Cold Harbor, June 10, '64; taken prisoner at Butler's Bridge, December 12, '64.

G. H. Lott, Philadelphia, wounded, leg, Drury's Bluff, May 16, '64.

T. W. Lummis, Salem, wounded, hip, Drury's Bluff, May 16, '64.

C. H. Miller, Salem, died at Fort Monroe, Aug. 23, '61; sun-stroke.

A. C. Mifflin, Philadelphia, deserted from U. S. General hospital, Newark, March 31, '65; returned to regiment June 3, '65; no charges made against him.

S. M. Mosure, Schuylkill, wounded at Kinston, December 14, '62; killed, shot in the stomach, at Cold Harbor, June 3, '64.

John Newkirk, Salem, wounded, contusion of right arm, Drury's Bluff, May 16, '64.

Wm. H. Nonnemaker, Montgomery, Pa., wounded, Cold Harbor, June 5, '64.

J. A. Patten, New York, wounded in head, at Drury's Bluff, May 16, '64.

A. Remming, New York, killed at Drury's Bluff, May 16, '64.

John Shull, Salem, wounded in left shoulder, at Drury's Bluff, May 16, '64.

William C. Sparks, Salem, wounded at Newbern, March 14, '62; wounded in shoulder, at Whitehall, December 16, '62.

Jacob Schmitt, Germany, transferred from Co. L; wounded at Kinston, December 14, '62.

John Schwebel, Germany, transferred from Co. L; wounded in finger, at Walthall, May 7, '64; transferred to Co. F, 22d Reg't U. R. C., March 31, '65.

Joshua Wensell, Salem, wounded at Roanoke, Feb. 8, '62; killed at Drury's Bluff, May 16, '64

Daniel Whitney, New York, discharged for promotion, Mar. 24, '65.

M. L. Carney, Salem.
J. W. Daniels, New York.
J. D. Haines, Salem.
A. K. Harbart, Salem,
J. S. Hampton, "

L. S. Mickle, Salem.
Th. Parsons, England.
R. R. Pittmann, Salem.
J. C. Smith, Gloucester.
S. B. Taylor, Salem.

J. W. Hilliard, Gloucester.
Fred. Weber, Germany, transferred from Co. L.

Recruits received 1862.

John Ostertag, Germany, discharged at expiration of time of service, June 4, '65.

Albert Reiss, Germany, mustered out June 14, '65.

H. Scholz, Germany, wounded at Whitehall, Dec. 16, '62; discharged at Hilton Head, S. C., May 19, '63.

L. Stoll, Germany, discharged at Newbern, July 17, '63; rheumatism.

Recruits received 1863.

D. J. Miller, Reading, Pa.   Robert Green, New York.

Recruits received 1864.

Wm. E. Creed, Boundbrook, wounded, scalp-wound, Drury's Bluff, May 16, '64.

S. A. Ewing, Nashville, Tenn , wounded in hip, at Cold Harbor, June 4, '64; died at Washington, July 8, '64.

P. J. Garrisson, Warren, discharged at Greensboro', May 11, '65; mental imbecility.

August Noll, Germany, transferred at his own request to Co. A.

J. McCormick, Newark, wounded in left hip, at Drury's Bluff, May 16, '64.

Thompson Mosher, Essex, deserted from U. S. General hospital, Newark, April 13, '65; returned to regiment June 3, '65.

Irwin Odenbough, Northampton. Pa , wounded in leg, at Drury's Bluff, May 16, '64.

Tyler Reynolds, Ocean, wounded in both thighs, Cherry Grove, April 14, '64; taken prisoner; exchanged.

Daniel Parr, Warren, wounded in stomach, at Drury's Bluff, May 16, '64; died at Drury's Bluff, May 29, '64.

A. J. Schuler, Warren, discharged from Newark hospital.

S. J. Tinsmann, Warren, wounded in hand, at Drury's Bluff, May 16, '64; discharged February 17, '65.

S. H. Vining, Salem, Vet. Vol., wounded in arm, at Drury's Bluff, May 16, '64.

James Vangarden, Warren, wounded in finger, at Swift Creek, May 10, '64.

Mahlon Vangarden, Warren, wounded, hand, Drury's Bluff, May 16, '64; died at Fort Monroe, July 30, '64; chronic diarrhœa.

A. J. Vangarden, Warren, wounded in left foot, at Drury's Bluff, May 14, '64; transferred to Co. F, 22d V. R. C., by order of War Department.

Joseph Wolff, Philadelphia, wounded in nose, at Cold Harbor,
   June 4, '64.

L. E. Alvord, Bradford.   John Muller, Germany.
George Courtright, Warren.   James McGhie, Scotland.
A. M. Dickerson, Mannington. E. Sullivan, Ireland.
C. Klapproth, Germany.   Wm. Speakmann, Chester, Pa.
E. Madara, Cumberland.   C. Vanaman, Cumberland.
J. B. Mitchell, Gloucester. William Warford, Bucks, Pa.
          E. S. Woolbert, Atlantic.

Mustered out June 14, 1865.

Joshua Ballinger, Salem.   S. C. Park, Camden.
John M. Davies, Camden.   A. Strickland, Atlantic.
William Floyd, Salem.   Wm. B. Stretch, Salem.
W. 11. Harper, New York.   F. C. Straun,   "
W. H. Harris, Salem.   J. W. Somers,   "
David Morgan, Union.   C. Weitzel,   "
Daniel Meyers, Salem.   F. A. Woodside,   "
G. N. Newkirk, Camden.   G. L. Webster, Pennsylvania.

Recruits received 1865.

Charles Schnable, Germany.   William Thompson, England.
Wm. Measey, Harmony, N. J.   James McDonald,   "
Jas. Mandeville, "   "   John Welsh, Ireland.
Enoch Julen, Atlantic.   S. Perkins, Burlington.
Wm. G. Youmann, Ohio.   B. C. Estlow,   "
John L. Christ, Cumberland. Nathan Kell,   "
John L. Cliff, Camden.   Jos. Madara,   "
J. C. Butcher, Philadelphia. J. J. Harris, Salem.
Wm. H. Loughlin, Cumberland. A. F. Schoemaker, Salem.
          Francis Fagan, Ireland.
Thomas Fanning, unassigned recruit, deserted June 10, '65.

Company K.

Elias J. Drake, Captain.

W. D. S. Boudinot, 1st Lieut. Jonathan Townley, 2d Lieut.

Enlisted Men.

Wm. Aschley, Bath, discharged at Newbern, July 10, '63 ; disability.

M. Atkinson, Pemberton, discharged at Newbern, May 11, '62 ; disability.

P. Allgeier, Germany, transferred from Co. L ; discharged at Beaufort, March 19, '63 ; varicose veins.

Ezra Ayres, Metuchin, transferred Nov. 18, '62, to Co. C, 1st Art. U. S. Army, by order of War Department.

J. Bural, Sussex, wounded at Roanoke Island, Feb. 8, '62 ; leg amputated ; discharged at New York city, Aug. 18, '62.

John Bell, Patterson, discharged June 14, '62 ; disability.

C. M. Billinger, discharged at Newbern, May 12, '62 ; disability.

W. O. Babcock, Sussex, discharged by General Order 126, of War Department.

Edwin Baldwin, Elizabeth, mustered out by General Order 126, of War Department.

R. Chester, Cape May, discharged at Beaufort, September 15, '63 ; disability.

J. M. Drake, Union, discharged for promotion, June 3, '63.

L. Davidson, Princeton, discharged at Carolina City, May 28, '63 ; disability.

Thos. Densmann, Elizabeth, died, Newbern, March 14, '62 ; fever.

Joseph H. Davies, Albany, mustered out Nov. 17, '62, by General Order 126, of War Department.

J. J. Derbrow, Holmesboro', Pa., escaped from guard-house at Carolina City, May 26, '63, while under charges for general court-martial.

Joseph Doran, Elizabeth, discharged May 7, '62 ; organic disease of heart.

L. Davies, Elizabeth, died on board " Durley Buck," while on his way home, at Hatteras Inlet, Aug. 20, '63 ; typhoid fever.

Isaac Fischer, Bedford, wounded when detailed on gunboat Southfield, engaged in battle of Blackwater river, Oct. 3, '62; died at Balfour hospital, Portsmouth, Va.

Thomas Freemann, Ireland, wounded at Newbern, March 14, '62 ; discharged at Fort Monroe, November 11, '62.

John H. Good, Elizabeth, discharged at Newbern, April 24, '63; chronic rheumatism.

E. C. Hale, Camden, discharged Nov. 23, '62; disability.

G. S. Hankins, Bristol, discharged at Newbern, June 24, '62; disability.

E. F. Hankins, Bucks, Pa., discharged June 1, '63; hæmorrhoids.

Adam Hicks, deserted at Trenton, November 10, '61.

J. E. Hillger, New York City, mustered out Nov. 17, '62, by Order 126, of War Department.

B. Hull, Seneca Lake, Pa., wounded in arm at Goldsboro', Dec. 17, '62; arm amputated; transferred to Veteran Reserve Corps, March 31, '64.

R. Hughes, Liverpool, discharged at Newbern, Feb. 28, '63; disability, and above age.

M. Koenig, Germany, transferred from Co. L; discharged at Carolina City, April 24, '63; chronic rheumatism.

J. Lawrence, wounded at Newbern, March 14, '62; both legs shot off; discharged at Trenton, September 30, '62.

D. Levi, Moscow, Pa., wounded at Newbern, March 14, '62; died at Newbern, March 17, '62.

E. S. Moffat, Oxford, discharged for promotion, April 27, '62.

Wm. D. Marshall, Philadelphia, discharged at Beaufort, June 1, '63; over-exertion in service.

J. S. Parkhurst, Elizabeth, wounded in head, at Newbern, March 14, '62; died at Newbern, Oct. 18, '64; yellow fever.

J. Romen, discharged at Trenton, March 3, '62; disability.

G. H. Smith, Springfield, killed at Whitehall, December 16, '64.

H. Spoce, Sussex, died, Newbern hospital, April 23, '62; fever.

Jervis Reeves, Bierton, discharged at Newbern, August 12, '62; disability.

William Southard, Flemington, transferred to Co. C, 1st U. S. Art., Nov. 18, '62, by General Order 154, War Department.

A. Schreeve, Burlington, died at 18th Army Corps hospital, Point of Rocks, September 19, '64; typhoid fever.

M. E. Townley, Union, died at Newbern, April 6, '62; fever.

R. Vincent, Blackwellstown, discharged Nov. 23, '62; general disability.

G. W. Watkins, New York City, discharged, Trenton, June 23, '64; disability.

A. Hamler, Sussex, wounded in leg, at Newbern, March 14, '62; discharged January 14, '64.

Discharged at expiration of time of service, at Trenton, N. J., December 7, 1864.

Thomas Delaney, Closh, wounded at Newbern, March 14, '62; wounded in leg, at Walthall, May 6, '64.

R. S. Williams, Union, wounded, arm, Drury's Bluff, May 16, '64.

R. Gerth, Germany, transferred from Co. A.

A. Lampe,   "   "   "   "

H. W. Bellis, Hunterdon.
E. P. Craig, Philadelphia.
John Conroy,   "
Wm. J. Doran, Elizabeth.
D. S. C. Higgins, Union.
J. R. Lemon, Monmouth.
Thos. McQuaid, New York City.
P. Randolph, Trenton.
G. W. Tonkin, Carpenter's L'g
E. C: Winans, Elizabeth.
J. Kuntz, Swiss, transferred from Co. L.

H. Cook, Montreal.
Edw. Condelly, Ireland.
S. W. Crane, Newark.
A. J. Gafney,   "
Henry Hoftellin, Ireland.
Wm. P. Levy, Pennsylvania.
J. C. Price, Branchville.
E. M. Swain, Whitfield.
Wm. H. Van Arsdale, Peapack.
J. W. Woolery, Carrollstown.

Re-Enlisted November 25, 1863.

Joseph Wright, Salem, wounded in shoulder, at Newbern, March 14, '62; discharged for promotion, April 16, '64.
G. W. Teates, Alamonchy, wounded, thigh, Walthall, May 7, '64.
S. J. Dilks, Carpenter's Landing, wounded in leg, at Gardener's Bridge, N. C., December 9, '64.
D. M. Rose, Hanover, wounded in hand, Petersburg, Aug. 26, '64.
L. N. Terrill, Newark, wounded in hand, Petersburg, Aug. 24, '64.
John Ward, Ireland, wounded in back, at Weir Bottom Church, May 9, '64.
J. Crowell, Cape May.   E. Moran, Ireland.

Re-Enlisted December 20, 1863.

A. Clark, Philadelphia.
J. E. Hamler, Canadatown, wounded in left leg, at Drury's Bluff, May 16, '64.
Wm. R. Knapp, New York.
J. O. Stearns, Stackstown, Vt., wounded in left arm, at Walthall, May 6, '64.

Re-Enlisted January 18, 1864.

G. L. Bryant, Elizabeth, discharged for promotion, August 1, '64.
J. H. Brown, Bridgeport, wounded in right ancle, on Goldsboro' Expedition, 1862.
A. S. Cadmus, Collwell, deserted while on furlough; arrested and sent back to regiment; court-martialed, sentenced to stoppage advance-pay, $13, arrest. $30, cost, $3.80; total fine, $46.80.
A. Hoever, Sussex, wounded in hand, at Newbern, March 14, '62; wounded in arm, at Walthall, May 16, '64; transferred to Veteran Reserve Corps, October 26, '64.
Wm. F. Ford, Hanover, wounded, left leg, Whitehall, Dec. 16, '62.
Thomas McCormick, Elizabeth, wounded, Kinston, Dec. 14, '62.
H. P Percel, New York, wounded at Drury's Bluff, May 16, '64; died at Newark hospital, June 15, '64; congestive fever.
Wm. H. Ross, Union, wounded, right hand, Walthall, May 6, '64.
John Skillmann, Trenton, wounded, arm, Whitehall, Dec. 16, '62.
Wm. J. Townley, New York, wounded in left leg, at Walthall, May 7, '64; discharged for promotion, Dec. 27, '64.

Adam Konder, Germany, transferred from Co. L.

John G. Klotz, Germany, transferred from Co. L; killed at Walthall, May 7, '64.

William Kurze, Germany, transferred from Co. L.

John Weder, Germany, killed at Walthall, May 6, '64.

John Anderson, Elizabeth.	J. W. Green, Princeton.
A. H. Berry, Green Township.	C. Hinton, Belvidere.
L. Campbell, Norfield.	J. Henry, Elizabeth.
James Cook, Cavendish.	J. Kerrigan, Vincentown.

J. F. Ewing, England.

Re-Enlisted March 12, 1864.

C. A. Williams, Elizabeth, wounded in arm, at Drury's Bluff, May 16, '64; discharged February 6, '65.

Recruits received 1862.

Tunis Peer, Newton, wounded in groin, Whitehall, Dec. 16, '62; missing, Drury's Bluff, May 16, '64; died in rebel prison, at Andersonville, August 16, '64.

J. Lynch, Ireland, deserted at Carolina City, March 8, '64; mustered out June 14, '65.

Joseph Niermann, Germany, transferred from Co. L.

H. Keyser, Poland, transferred from Co. L; wounded in foot, at Drury's Bluff, May 16, '64; wounded, contusion of right shoulder, at Petersburg, August 19, '64.

J. J. Kneller, Germany, wounded in left arm, Drury's Bluff, May 16, '64.

E. J. Cleveland, Elizabeth.	J. C. Decker, Union.
S. Ebert, Germany.	G. R. Townley, Union.

Recruits received 1863.

G. R. Keene, New York, discharged May 31, '65, by order of War Department.

W. H. Hemler, Sussex.

Recruits received 1864.

D. S. Giles, Metuchin, wounded in knee, at Walthall, May 6, '64; transferred to Veteran Reserve Corps, January 19, '65.

S. B. Gaston, New York, wounded, left thigh, Walthall, May 6, '64; transferred to Invalid Corps, October 22, '64.

F. Kneller, Germany, wounded, arm, Drury's Bluff, May 16, '64.

S. Lauer, Germany, accidentally wounded in knee, at Greensboro', May 4, '65.

Wm. J. Morris, New York, deserted at Carolina City, Jan. 23, '65.

Joseph Norton, Warren, fractured fibula of lower third right leg, May 2, '65.

G. A. Reinhard, Germany, wounded in head, behind left ear, at Drury's Bluff, May 16, '64; taken prisoner, returned to regiment Jan. 27, '65. (Read "Reinhard" in historical part.)

John Simmons, England, missing, at Drury's Bluff, May 16, '64;
died in rebel prison, at Andersonville, August 16, '64.

E. W. Thomas, Britain, wounded in right thumb, at Cold Harbor,
June 3, '64; transferred to Co. F, 18th Reg't Veteran Reserve
Corps, January 18, '65.

J. Trumbull, Ireland, died in regimental hospital, Carolina City,
October 19, '64; congestive fever and syphilis.

Daniel Webb, Ireland, wounded in finger, at Swift Creek, May
9, '64; deserted August 30, '64, before Petersburg, in front
of the enemy.

C. Wilson, Canada, deserted at Carolina City, January 23, '65.

B. Bankson, Sweden.	William Kneller, Germany.
J. Baker, Germany.	J. Kane, Ireland.
M. Cass, "	S. B. Moore, Brooklyn.
P. Condelly, Ireland.	R. Minnier, Ireland.
J. D. Dobbs, "	J. McGanvern, Ireland.
J. A. Davies, Albany.	Wm. McCarty, "
J. Farron, Ireland.	M. Sweeney, "
William Horton, England.	J. Shmidt, England.
J. Harrisson, "	P. Tracy, Ireland.
L. Heinlien, New York.	C. H. Wilson, Warren.
T. W. Hinton, Belvidere.	J. Vaughon, New Jersey.

Mustered out June 14, 1865.

J. Rame, France, missing, at Butler's Bridge, December 12, '64;
returned May 18, '64.

John Corcoran, Canada.	J. W. Ricketts, Washington.
A. Frank, Germany.	J. H. Rice, Canada.
J. Fairbrother, England.	F. Schneider, Germany.
C. Hoffmann, Germany.	J. Van Cloedt, "
J. Jackson, Canada.	William Williams, Ireland.
J. Lawrence, Ireland.	L. Wentzell, Germany.
Teacrell Loughtin, Canada.	A. Weiss, "
Tobique Loughtin, "	H. Wellbrook, "

Recruits received 1865.

G. W. Asch, Philadelphia.	J. J. Hartfield, Newark.
J. J. Bryant, Elizabeth.	J. C. Hubert, Warren.
M. Blackman, Hagerstown.	Thomas Matthew, Ireland.
M. Coyle, Trenton.	Thomas Murray, "
B. Castlow, Newark.	J. H. C. Nelson, New Jersey.
C. Cesar, New York.	John Peacock, Ireland.
Isaac Devine, "	H. Robertson, Salem.
B. Dillmore, Salem.	Lancing Seamann, Cape May.
G. Forsyth, Elizabeth.	J. H. Smith, Kent.

G. Forsyth, Union.

Company L.

CHARLES ERB, Captain.

HENRY M. HEYNOLD, 1st Lieut.   FRANCIS E. ADLER, 2d Lieut.

Enlisted Men.

John Muller, discharged for promotion, February 8, '62.

A. C. Moll,   "   "   "   "

Ch. Greene, deserted at Washington, D. C., January 4, '62.

M. A. Carl, died on board "Dragoon," on passage from Roanoke
to Newbern, April, 1862; typhoid fever.

H. Mathew, wounded at Newbern, May 14, '63; discharged.

H. Ensle, wounded at Newbern, March 14, '62; died at Newark
hospital, May, '62; discharged at Newport Barracks, Aug. '62.

A. Busch.   Anton Frank.

A. Hagel.   C. Kraft.

J. Muller.   H. Walters.

Edw. Zorn.

John Maertz, discharged at Beaufort, Sept. 18, '62; mustered out
November, 1862.

C. Graff.   Chr. Moll.

J. Buck.   —— Prin.

J. Wirth.   F. Weiser.

—— Hiller.

REMARKS.—Old companies A and L were consolidated into the ten companies, November,
1862. Names of men transferred will be found on the rolls of the Company to which they
were assigned. If the statements of the above are not entirely correct, it will be attributed
that the old Company records have been partly lost in action at Roanoke and Newbern.

Old Company M,—New A.

J. M. McCHESNEY, 1st Lieut.   THOMAS SMITH, 2d Lieut.

Enlisted Men.

Thos. B. Applegate, Middlesex, disch. for promotion, Mar. 8, '62.

Elias Bayles, Trenton, discharged at Camp Olden, '61 ; disability.

S. E. Brown, deserted at Newark, September 22, '61.

Dl. Burgard, Germany, transferred from Co. L ; discharged May 30, '63 ; disability.

C. W. Conover, Hightstown, discharged June 12, '63, to be promoted 2d Lieut. Co. D, 1st N. C. U V.

L. Conover, Mercer, discharged at Trenton, Aug. 23, '64, by order of Major General Dix ; disability.

A. B. Dunn, New Brunswick, discharged at St. Helena Island, March 28, '63 ; disability.

D. Dehart, Middlesex, discharged November 9, '61 ; disability.

Jos. P. Dobbs, Dublin,   "   "   "   "

John M. Davies, New Orleans, La., discharged for promotion, May 29, '62.

A. Dreher, Germany, transferred from Co. L ; died at Newbern, August 18, '63 ; jaundice.

A. E. Edwards, Prospect, discharged September 18, '63, to be promoted 2d Lieut. 1st N. C. U. V.

Thomas Eldridge, South Amboy, deserted at Trenton, Dec. 5, '61.

C. W. Grover, N. Brunsw'k, discharged for promotion, June 19, '63.

Joseph Grover, deserted November, 1861.

John H. Giles, Middlesex, discharged Jan. 20, '62 ; disability.

C. Graff, Germany, transferred from Co. L ; discharged Nov. 21, '62 ; disability.

James Hamilton, deserted December 2, '61.

M. Handell, deserted September 17, '61.

William A. Hunt, Middlesex, discharged May 28, '63 ; disability.

John Hiller, Germany, transferred from Co. L ; discharged at Newbern, November 23, '62 ; disability.

C. Hubner, Germany, transferred from Co. A ; transferred to Invalid Corps, September 1, '63.

William Harris, Middlesex, transferred to Invalid Corps, Newark, September 1, '63.

John Hopp, Germany, transferred from Co. L ; discharged at Newport News, November 19, '63 ; epilepsy.

R. S. Ingling, Burlington, killed, shot in head, Roanoke, Feb. 8, '62.

M. Jurgens, Germany, transferred from Co. L; discharged Nov. 23, '62; disability.

John Lee, deserted November 12, '61.

John E. McDougall, New York City, discharged for promotion, May 16, '62.

W. W. Messeroll, Middlesex, discharged, Beaufort, November, '62; disability.

M. Morris, deserted November 12, '61.

T. Muddell, Middlesex, discharged Nov. 21, '62; disability.

Dl. McElwill, Dougal, 	 "	 Oct. 22, '62; disability.

Thomas McLaron, Glasgow, killed at Kinston, Dec. 14, '62; shot through heart.

John Mulligan, Ireland, deserted June 18, '63.

M. McGintzy, Ireland, transferred to Invalid Corps, Sept. 1, '63.

J. G. Mount, Cranberry, wounded at Whitehall, Dec. 16, '62; discharged at expiration of time of service, Sept. 22, '64.

G. Marsch, Albany, killed at Drury's Bluff, May 16, '64.

H. Mathew, Glasgow, transferred from Co. A; wounded, leg, Whitehall, Dec. 16, '62; transferred to Invalid Corps, Sept. 1, '63.

J. Muller, Germany, transferred from Co. A; discharged August 19, '63; disability.

J. Nolan, Mercer, discharged June 1, '62; disability.

F. Obert, Middlesex, 	 "	 " 20, '62; 	 "

A. Perrine, Middlesex, died at Newbern, April 20, '62; typhoid fever.

S. Perrine, Middlesex, died at Newport Barracks, May 23, '62; typhoid fever.

D. A. Quigley, Albany, discharged Nov. 19, '63; disability.

Enoch Giles, Middlesex, 	 "	 May 12, '63; 	 "

A. Rudolph, Germany, transferred from Co. A; discharged May 28, '63; disability.

S. Slover, Middlesex, discharged June 19, '62; disability.

C. Schmalstich, Germany, transferred from Co. A; died at Fort Monroe, July 18, '64.

A. Schwinghammer, Germany, transferred from Co. A; discharged November 22, '63; disability.

H. Trilk, Germany, transferred from Co. L; missing at Drury's Bluff, May 16, '64; died in rebel prison, at Andersonville.

J. D. Voorhees, New York City, deserted December 5, '61.

B. Van Note, 	 "	 " November 12, '61.

James Vanderwater, Middlesex, disch. Dec. 4, '61; under age.

N. Van Northwick, Middlesex, dropped on Co. rolls, according to General Orders, November 21, '62.

Discharged at expiration of time of service, December 7, 1864, at Trenton, N. J.

R. Arlow, Ireland, wounded in leg, at Cold Harbor, June 3, '64.

P. Jones, New Brunswick, missing at Drury's Bluff, May 15, '64; paroled, exchanged.

J. Plondke, Germany, transferred from Co. A; wounded on Goldsboro' Expedition, 1862.

C. Voigt, Germany, transferred from Co. A.

J. Stussey, Swiss, " " "

N. Barricklo, Middlesex.	James Evers, Ireland.
D. C. Clayton, "	John F. Barrett, Newark.
C. Hoagland, "	S. F. Cox, Monmouth.
G. Perrine, "	M. J. Ives, "
Jos. Roxberry, "	C. G. Haines, Philadelphia.
A. Slover, "	Th. A. Jackson, Rahway.
C. C. Messeroll, "	S. Stultz, Prospect Plain.
G. W. Rolfe, "	J. S. Smith, Trenton.
S. H. Stillwell, Cranberry.	R. Silbey, New York City.

A. W. Smith, New York City.

E. Clevinger, Burlington, discharged at Fort Monroe, Sept. 17, '64, at expiration of time of service.

Re-Enlisted November 25, 1863.

John Applegate, Monmouth, wounded in right arm, Cold Harbor, June 4, '64.

Thomas C. Burke, New York City, wounded in left arm, at Walthall, May 6, '64; transferred to Invalid Corps, Sept. 3, '64, by order of War Department.

J. Barrett, Germany, transferred from Co. L; wounded in hand, on Goldsboro' Expedition, 1862; deserted February 16, '64; dropped from Co. rolls August 3, '64.

William Clayton, Mercer, missing, Drury's Bluff, May 16, '64; died in rebel prison.

C. Flower, Ireland, wounded, shoulder, Drury's Bluff, May 16, '64.

C. Hulfish, Princeton, wounded in right side and left under-arm, before Petersburg, July 11, '62; died at 18th Army Corps field-hospital, July 12, '64.

J. Reamer, Germany, wounded on Goldsboro' Expedition, 1862; wounded in right arm, right side, and right lung, before Petersburg, August 19, '64; died before Petersburg, Aug. 19, '64.

William Webb, West Indian, missing, Drury's Bluff, May 16, '64; died in rebel prison, at Richmond, May 22, '64.

W. H. Williams, Essex, missing at Drury's Bluff, May 16, '64; returned to regiment May, 1865.

F. Maker, Germany, transferred from Co. A; killed, ball entering head, at Cold Harbor, June 4, '64.

N. Buckley, Dublin.	H. Snedecer, Newark.
C. B. Hoagland, Somerset.	J. Wessell, Middlesex.
R. Snedecer, Middlesex.	M. Decamp, Princeton.

Re-Enlisted December 20, 1864.

William Hinton, Norfolk.

E. Schoertel, Ireland, died, Newbern, Oct. 27, '64; yellow fever.

A. Whitecraft, Middlesex.

A. Bauer, Germany, transferred from Co. L; missed at the Goldsboro' Expedition, 1862; exchanged, and returned to regiment July 17, '63; wounded in ear at Drury's Bluff, May 16, '64; taken prisoner at Free Bridge, June 16, '64; exchanged; admitted into U. S army hospital, at Annapolis, Md., for sickness contracted in rebel prison, Savannah; died at Annapolis.

William S. Wade, Union, appointed regimental hospital steward, October 3, '64.

Re-Enlisted January 18, 1864.

A. D. Applegate, Middlesex, discharged for promotion, Nov. 28, '64.

J. Albert, Germany, transferred from Co. L; missing, Free Bridge, June 16, '64.

L. C. Bonham, Cumberland, discharged for promotion, Sept. 29, '64.

Jas. Cook, Ireland, wounded, shoulder, Drury's Bluff, May 16, '64.

Thomas Dugan, Ireland, died at Newbern.

John Gary, Ireland, wounded in head, at Cold Harbor, June 5, '64.

R. Kuhn, Swiss, transferred from Co L; missing, Drury's Bluff, May 16, '64; died at Andersonville, Ga.

C. Muller, Germany, transferred from Co. A; wounded in left arm and chest, at Newbern, March 14, '62.

James Mathews, Monmouth, wounded in leg, December 16, '62.

J. V. Messeroll, New Brunswick, missing, at Drury's Bluff, May 16, '64; returned May, '65.

Hermann Noll, Germany, transferred from Co. A; wounded at Swift Creek, May 9, '64; missing, Drury's Bluff, May 16, '64; died in rebel prison, at Andersonville, Ga., Aug. 30, '64.

C. Petty, Middlesex, wounded, right thumb, May 16, '64; missing, June 18, '64.

Jos. Rieger, Germany, transf. from Co. A; wounded, head, Swift Creek, May 9, '64; died, Chesapeake hospital, May 15, '64.

J. Scully, New York City, wounded in right hand, on Goldsboro' Expedition, 1862; wounded in right shoulder-blade, cutting lungs, before Petersburg, July 7, '64; died, 18th A. C. field hospital, July 7, '64.

R. V. P. Wood, Middlesex, wounded in shoulder, at Swift Creek, May 9, '64; missing, Drury's Bluff, May 16, '64; returned May 24, '64.

W. H. Bendy, Middlesex.   Th. Perrine, Pittsburg.
James Cox, New York.   Wm. K. Stout, Middlesex.
James Dennemore, Middlesex.   M. A. Van Huise, Monmouth.
B. Nulty, Ireland.   J. Whitecraft, Middlesex.
F. Scholl, Germany, transferred from Co. A.

Recruits received 1862.

John Baader, Germany, transferred from Co. A; drowned at Newbern, July 10, '63.

J. G. Heilmann, Germany, died at Mowers' U. S. Army hospital, Philadelphia, December 7, '64; phthisis.

B. Yeager, New York, wounded in knee, Walthall, May 6, '64; discharged March 18, '65.

S. S. Stultz, Cranberry, missing at Drury's Bluff, May 16, '64; died at Andersonville, Ga.

Mustered Out June 14, 1865.

L. Probst, Germany, transferred from Co. A.

G. A. Schmitz, Trenton.

Recruits received 1863.

John Anderson, Scotland, discharged April 9, '64, to be promoted 1st Lieut. U. S. colored Battery.

Recruits received 1862.

John Conway, Ireland, transferred at his own request from Co. C; accidentally wounded by pistol-ball, in eye, at Greensboro', May 3, '65.

E. A. Bonmann, New York, wounded with shell, in right thigh, at Wise's Fork, March 8, '65.

John A. Kelly, Middlesex, wounded at Walthall, May 7, '64.

W. H. Silvers, Cranberry, died at field-hospital, before Petersburg, August 1, '64.

A. Noll, Germany, V. V., transferred at his own request from Co. 1; wounded at Swift Creek, May 9, '64.

R. Hendrickson, New York, missing at Drury's Bluff, May 16, '64; paroled; admitted into the U. S. A. hospital, Annapolis, Md.; died Jan. 3, '65, of sickness contracted in various rebel prisons.

C. W. Thompson, Albany. wounded in knee, Drury's Bluff, May 16, '64; deserted before Petersburg, Aug. 23, '64; dropped on Co. rolls, October 1, '64.

James Warren, Buffalo, missing at Drury's Bluff, May 16, '64; returned May 24, '65.

E. C. Neary, died at Division hospital, Greensboro', May 30, '64; typhoid fever.

G. F. Grinsley, Virginia, taken prisoner at Butler's Bridge, Dec. 11, '64; returned May 25, '65.

Mustered Out June 14, 1865.

G. Black, Ireland.	G. S. Hart, New Brunswick.
L. Eckardt, Germany.	S. F. Hopkins.
H. C. Fisher, New Brunswick.	A. W. Osborn, Ocean.

S. B. Foster, Hudson.

James Hanlon, New York, attempted to desert Oct. 19, '64; was arrested, and forwarded to the Provost-marshal at Newbern.

William Clark, deserted at Yanceyville, N. C., 1865.

John Baker, Ireland.	J. Fitzmeyer, Germany.
John Broughton, Ireland.	D. Finlason, Canada.
T. Barnburry, "	James Gold, Scotland.
David Brown, Scotland.	John Hoesel, Germany.
Jacob Bauer, Swiss.	J. J. Jennisson, Monmouth.

F. Bright, Germany.
George Brown, Canada.
John Beaver, Germany.
Henry Brown,   "
John Brockmann, Germany.
L. K. Carmann, Middlesex.
C. Conklin, Canada.
J. Demain, England.
C. Denninger, Germany.
E. Dieterich,   "
Hugo Els,   "

J. H. Johnson, Germany.
R. Inmeyer, Canada.
James Kenny, Ireland.
J. Nicholson, Virginia.
J. II. Martin, Ireland.
John Prochaska, Germany.
H. Schmith,   "
Jacob Suydam,   "
John Volz,   "
William White, Ireland.
G. Black,   "

R. Emery, Virginia.

Recruits received 1865.

H. D. Beckett, Gloucester.
W. Chew,   "
J. Crawford, Ireland.
B. F. Doughty, Atlantic.
J. E. Dawson, Baltimore.
G. V. Davies, Canada.
H. Essex, Camden.
H. B. English, Canada,
S. W. English, Williamston.
H. Frederic, Germany.

William Haggerty, New Jersey.
J. B. Lutz, Gloucester.
John A. Loring, Boston.
J. S. Parker, Salem.
R. Parker, Gloucester.
G. Schields, Philadelphia.
John Scanlin, Ireland.
Wm. Vanaman, Camden.
F. Wheeland, New York.
A. Zimmermann, Gloucester.

D. Frederic, Germany.

Musicians.

Mustered Out August 30, 1862.

PETER GAHN, Leader, Newark.

John Gahn, Newark.
Geo. Gahn, "
Godfried Kontenstetter, Newark.
Jacob Yost, "
Benjamin Lavere, Rahway.

John Mahler, Newark.
Albert Searing, "
John Jack, "
William Saxon, "
P. L. Starner, Rahway.

Gottlieb Hoyer, Co. B, and Thomas Pratsch, Co. C, detailed to the Band, were ordered back to their Companies at the mustering out of the other members.

Non-Commissioned Staff.

Armsteadt Gulick, sergeant-major, appointed Oct. 8, '61; discharged March 17, '62.

John W. Lewis, hospital-steward, appointed Oct. 8, '61; died at Hammond general hospital, Beaufort, Nov. 8, '62.

John Bamford, quartermaster-sergeant, appointed Oct. 8, '61; discharged, and commissioned 2d Lieut. 3d New Jersey Cavalry, December 4, '63.

Shmidt Bilderbeck, commissary-sergeant, appointed Oct. 8, '61; discharged Nov. 3, '63, by order of War Department.

C. F. Bonney, Paterson, appointed sergeant-major, April 2, '62; discharged for promotion, December 23, '62.

Mustered Out July 31, 1865.

Henry Van Schaick, Paterson, appointed sergeant-major December 29, '62; wounded, contusion of right foot, Aug. 24, '64.

William S. Wade, Newark, appointed regimental hospital-steward, September 1, '64, by order of Col. James Stewart, Jr.

Oscar Van Houten, Bergen, appointed quartermaster-sergeant, January 1, '64; received a commission as 2d Lieut. Co. E, May 5, '64, when the regiment was at Yorktown, preparing for active service; the commission was voluntarily returned July 27, '64, and former duty resumed.

Charles Shephard, appointed commissary-sergeant, Jan. 1, '64.

Officers.

PROMOTION AND RESIGNATION.

Joseph W. Allen, Bordentown, Colonel, commissioned Oct. 8, '61 drowned at Hatteras, January 15, '62.

C. A. Heckmann, Philippsburg, Major, comm. Sept. 20, '61; promoted Lieut. Col. Dec. 3, '61; promoted Colonel Feb 26, '62; appointed Brigadier General U. S. Vols., Dec. 22, '62.

F. W. Weller, Surgeon, comm. Oct. 8, '61; drowned at Hatteras, January 15, '62.

Lewis Braun, Elizabeth, Ass't Surgeon, comm. Oct. 8, '61; resigned March 20, '62.

Abram Zabriskie, Jersey City, Adjutant, comm. Oct. 8, '61; promoted Major April 10, '62; promoted Lieut. Col. Dec. 23, '62; promoted Colonel January 8, '63; wounded in the larynx, at Drury's Bluff, Va., May 16, '64; died at Chesapeake hospital, May 24, '64; buried at Greenwood Cemetery, Jersey City, May 28, '64.

Samuel Keys, Burlington, Quartermaster, comm. Oct. 8, '61; discharged at expiration of time of service, October 26, '64.

Thomas Drumm, appointed Chaplain October 8, '61; resigned October 15, '62.

James Wilson, Elizabeth, formerly Captain 2d New Jersey Vols.; appointed Major Dec. 5, '61; promoted Lieut. Col. February 26, '62; resigned December 1, '62.

A. W. Woodhull, Newark, formerly Ass't Surgeon 5th New Jersey Vols., comm. and mustered as Surgeon, Feb. 6, '62; wounded at Young's Cross-road, July 27, '62; also at Walthall, May 6, '64; discharged expiration of time of service, Feb. 8, '65.

F. B. Gillette, Salem county, comm. Ass't Surgeon, Aug. 20, '62; promoted Surgeon, Feb. 8, '65; mustered out July 31, '65.

J. J. Carrell, appointed Chaplain Dec. 27, '62; resigned Mar. 31, '64.

Hermann Rumpf, comm. Captain A, Sept. 20, '61; resigned December 3, '61.

Charles Hayes, comm. 1st Lieut. A, Sept. 20, '61; promoted Captain A, December 5, '61; mustered out November 18, '62.

Philipp Speer, comm. 2d Lieut. A, Sept. 20, '61; resigned October 11, '61.

Cornelius Castner, New Brunswick, comm. Captain B, September 18, '61; resigned October 8, '62, on surgeon's certificate, for disability.

L. Barthelmew, comm. 1st Lieut. B, September 18, '61; resigned May 1, '62.

C. H. Sofield, New Brunswick, comm. 2d Lieut. Sept. 18, '61; promoted 1st Lieut. May 16, '62; promoted Captain Oct. 11, '62; resigned April 14, '64, on surgeon's certificate for disability.

C. B. Hopkinson, comm. Captain C, Oct. 22, '61: resigned November 18, '62.

E. S. Harris, Hoboken, comm. 1st Lieut. C, Sept. 20, '61; promoted Captain Dec. 1, '63; killed in battle at Drury's Bluff, May 16, '64.

J. W. Cleft, comm. 2d Lieut. C, Oct. 22, '61; resigned Feb. 11, '62.

Thomas W. Middleton, comm. Captain D, Oct. 22, '61; contused wound of abdomen, at the battle of Newbern, March 14, '62; resigned Sept. 11, '62, on surgeon's certificate for disability.

G. G. Irons, comm. 1st Lieut. D, Sept. 23, '61; resigned Aug. 1, '62.

Edgar Kissam, comm. 2d Lieut. D, Nov. 1, '61; promoted 1st Lieut. D, Sept. 11, '62; promoted Captain D, Dec. 23, '62; taken prisoner at Drury's Bluff, May 16, '64; paroled, exchanged, and mustered out for disability, by order of War Department, Feb. 17, '65.

U. DeHart, comm. Captain E, Sept. 20, '61; resigned Mar. 11, '62.

Wm. H. Abel, comm. 1st Lieut. E, Sept. 20, '61; appointed regimental Adjutant, April 13, '62; promoted Captain E, Dec. 23, '62; appointed Ass't Adjutant General of Volunteers, and assigned to Gen. Heckmann, May 24, '63.

A. B. Beach, comm. 2d Lieut. E, Sept. 20, '61; promoted 1st Lieut. E, May 16, '62; dismissed December 29, '62.

Wm. B. Curlies, Camden, comm. Captain F, Sept. 18, '61; promoted Major, Jan. 8, '63; injured in leg, Point of Rocks, Va., May 12, '64; promoted Lieut. Colonel, June 15, '64; resigned at Carolina City, Feb. 17, '65, on surgeon's certificate for disability.

Augustus Thompson, Raritan, comm. 1st Lieut. F, Nov. 9, '61; promoted Captain F, Jan. 8, '63; resigned Feb. 8, '65.

J. W. Gibbon, comm. 2d Lieut. F, Nov. 9, '61; resigned April 27, '62.

J. P. Ritter, Elizabeth, comm. Captain G, Sept. 24, '61; wounded in leg, at Goldsboro', Dec. 17, '62; resigned April 6, '64, on surgeon's certificate for disability.

William Zimmermann, Elizabeth, comm. 1st Lieut. G, Oct. 7, '61; resigned December 28, '62.

W. H. Benton, comm. 2d Lieut. G, November 9, '61; resigned March 5, '62.

J. J. Henry, comm. Captain H, Oct. 30, '61; killed at Roanoke, February 8, '62.

James Stewart, Jr., Warren, comm. 1st Lieut. H, Oct. 30, '61; promoted Captain H, March 9, '62; promoted Major, Dec. 22, '62; promoted Lieut. Colonel, Jan. 8, '63; wounded at Drury's Bluff, May 16, '64; promoted Colonel, June 15, '64; mustered out July 31, '65.

J. B. Lawrence, Dover, comm. 2d Lieut. H, Oct. 30, '61; promoted 1st Lieut. H, March 9, '62; promoted Captain H, December 23, '62; wounded in leg, Drury's Bluff, May 16, '64; leg amputated; died at Chesapeake hospital, May 30, '64.

H. F. Chew, comm. Captain I, Oct. 8, '61; resigned March 8, '62.

Saml. Hufty, Jr., Camden, comm. 1st Lieut. I, October 8, '61; promoted Captain I, Mar. 9, '62; wounded, neck, Newbern, Mar. 14, '62; promoted Major, June 15, '64; wounded in left arm, at Petersburg, Aug. 16, '64; promoted Lieut. Colonel, May 24, '65; mustered out July 31, '65.

C. M. Pinkard, comm. 2d Lieut. I, Oct. 8, '61; promoted 1st Lieut. I, March 9, '62; resigned Dec. 28, '62.

E. J. Drake, comm. Captain K, Nov. 13, '61; resigned March 26, '62, on surgeon's certificate for disability.

W. D. Boudinot, comm. 1st Lieut. K, Nov. 13, '61; promoted Captain K, May 16, '62; discharged Feb. 17, '64, by order of War Department.

Jonathan Townley, Elizabeth, comm. 2d Lieut. K, Nov. 13, '61; wounded at Newbern, March 14, '62; promoted 1st Lieut. K, May 16, '62; promoted Captain K, May 11, '64; wounded at Drury's Bluff, May 14, '64; resigned Feb. 6, '65.

Charles Erb, Newark, comm. Captain L, Oct. 21, '61; mustered out November 18, '62.

Henry M. Heynolds, comm. 1st. Lieut. L, Oct. 21, '61; resigned February 8, '62.

Francis E. Adler, comm. 2d Lieut. L, Oct. 21, '61; resigned February 8, '62.

J. M. McChesney, comm. 1st Lieut. M, 1861; promoted Captain M, Nov. 12, '61; wounded at Newbern, March 14, '62; promoted and transferred Lieut. Colonel 1st Reg't N. C. Union Vols., March 29, '63.

Thomas Smith, comm. 2d Lieut. M, 1861; promoted 1st Lieut. M, November 12, '61; resigned March 8, '62.

Promoted from the Ranks.

Capital letters after the names, show the Company from which promotion was made.

Arunah D. Applegate, old M; promoted 2d Lieut. new A, Nov. 29, '64; discharged for personal reasons, May 16, '65.

A. Benson Brown, Bordentown, C; promoted 2d Lieut. C, March 9, '62; promoted 1st Lieut. C, April 30, '63; wounded, arm, Drury's Bluff, May 16, '64; promoted Captain C, Sept. 8, '64; resigned Feb. 21, '65, to be appointed Captain 11th Reg't Veteran Reserve Corps, by order of War Department.

C. F. Bonney, Paterson, E, appointed sergeant-major April 2, '62; promoted 2d Lieut. E, Dec. 23, '62; resigned July 3, '63.

F. G. Coyte, Coytesville, N. Y., promoted 2d Lieut. E, August 1, '63; promoted 1st Lieut. E, May 3, '64; appointed regimental Adjutant, May 16, '64; resigned Sept. 30, '64, on surgeon's certificate of disability.

R. E. Cogan, Newark, B, promoted 2d Lieut. B, October 9, '64; mustered out June 14, '65.

E. S. Carrell, H, appointed color-sergeant; promoted 2d Lieut. H, March 9, '62; promoted 1st Lieut. and appointed Adjutant, Dec. 23, '62; appointed but never mustered Captain Co. G, May 5, '64; killed at Drury's Bluff, May 16, '64.

Andrew Canse. M, promoted 2d Lieut. M, Nov. 12, '61; resigned March 8, '62.

John M. Davies, New Orleans, M, promoted and appointed Ass't Surgeon, May 23, '62; resigned June, 1865.

J. M. Drake, Elizabeth, K, promoted and transferred 2d Lieut. D, June 3, '63; taken prisoner at Drury's Bluff, May 16, '64; escaped and returned to regiment, Jan. 14, '65; promoted 1st Lieut. Feb. 9, '65; discharged on surgeon's certificate, April 7, '65.

A. J. Elberthson, D, promoted 2d Lieut. D, Dec. 23, '63; resigned May 30, '63.

Friedrich Felger, Newark, A, promoted 2d Lieut. A, Oct. 25, '61; promoted 1st Lieut. A, December 5, '61; mustered out November 18, '62.

Charles W. Grover, New Brunswick, M, promoted 2d Lieut. new A, July 1, '63; resigned October 31, '64.

Ethelbert Hubbs, New York, B, promoted 2d Lieut. B, December 29, '62; discharged December 8, '63; disability.

J. P. Heckmann, C, promoted and transferred 2d Lieut. G, March 5, '62; resigned June 24, '62.

Charles Hufty, Camden, D, promoted 2d Lieut. D, Sept. 5, '63; promoted 1st Lieut. D, Dec. 23, '62; promoted and transferred Captain I, July 25, '64; mortally wounded, left chest, Minnie-ball, at Wise's Fork, March 7, '65; died at Newbern hospital, March 14, '65; buried at Mount Vernon Cemetery, Philadelphia, April 10, '65.

Frederick Hobart, Elizabeth, G, promoted 2d Lieut. G, July 1, '62; promoted 1st Lieut. G, Dec. 29, '62; wounded at Walthall, May 7, '64; resigned August 19, '64.

John A. McDougall, M, promoted 2d Lieut. M, May 16, '62; promoted 1st Lieut. and detached A. A. Quartermaster June 19, '62; discharged February 18, '65.

George Mueller, old A, promoted 2d Lieut. June 24, '62; mustered out November 18, '62.

E. S. Moffat, K, promoted 2d Lieut. K, March 9, '62, and detached to the Signal Corps, at Newbern; discharged Jan. 26, '64.

John Mueller, L, promoted 2d Lieut. M, Feb. 8, '62; promoted 1st Lieut. M, August 15, '62; mustered out Nov. 18, '62.

Anton Moll, Newark, L, promoted 2d Lieut. August 15, '62; mustered out November 18, '62.

W. D. Rogers, C, promoted 2d Lieut. C, April 30, '63; promoted 1st Lieut. September 8, '64; discharged at Greensboro, June 5, '65; disability.

C. B. Springer, I, promoted 2d Lieut. March 9, '62 ; died at Hammond General hospital, Beaufort, July 31, '62 ; bilious remittent fever.

Joseph Schnetzer, Trenton, G, promoted 2d Lieut. G, December 29, '62 ; resigned April 6, '64 ; received his commission when home on recruiting-service, and was as officer never with the regiment.

Joseph Wright, K, promoted 2d Lieut. K, April 15, '64 ; promoted and transferred 1st Lieut. F, Dec. 25, '64 ; wounded, Minnieball, right foot, at Wise's Fork, March 10, '65 ; discharged May 15, '65.

Edward Willburn, old A, promoted 2d Lieut. A, Dec. 5, '61 ; promoted and transferred 1st Lieut. L, Feb. 8, '62 ; discharged August 15, '62 ; disability.

The following Officers returned with the Regiment to Trenton, and were mustered out July 31, 1865.

Thomas B. Applegate, M, promoted 2d Lieut. M, March 9, '62 ; promoted 1st Lieut. M, May 16, '62 ; promoted Captain new A, May 20, '63 ; promoted Major, April 23, '65.

L. C. Bonham, Cumberland Co., M, promoted 2d Lieut. new A, September 29, '64 ; promoted and transferred 1st Lieut. H, April 10, '65 ; promoted, transferred Captain A, June 30, '65.

Thomas Burnett, New Brunswick, B, promoted 2d Lieut B, June 11, '62 ; promoted 1st Lieut. B, Dec. 29, '62 ; promoted Captain B, May 11, '64 ; wounded at Drury's Bluff, May 16, '64.

John Bennett, New Brunswick, B, promoted 1st Lieut. B, April 26, '65.

R. J. Berdan, E, promoted and transferred 2d Lieut. C, September 9, '64 ; transferred back to E, Sept. 23, '64 ; promoted 1st Lieut. and appointed regimental quartermaster, March 5, '65.

J. C. Bowker, Salem, I, promoted 2d Lieut. I, Dec. 29, '62 ; promoted 1st Lieut. and transferred to D, July 25, '64.

G. L. Bryant, Elizabeth, K, promoted 2d Lieut. and transferred to E, Sept. 13, '64 ; transferred to C, Sept. 23, '64 ; promoted 1st Lieut. and transferred to G, March 21, '65.

Nicholaus Champion, Atlantic, D, promoted 2d Lieut. D, July 7, '65 ; not mustered.

J. W. Creveling, Warren, H, promoted 2d Lieut. H, July, 1865 ; not mustered.

A. H. Evans, Bordentown, F, promoted 2d Lieut. F, June 18, '64 ; promoted 1st Lieut. and transferred to E, Nov. 1, '64 ; taken prisoner at Wise's Fork, N. C., March 8, '65 ; escaped and returned to regiment at Goldsboro', April 1, '65 ; promoted Captain, and transferred to D, July 7, '65.

E. W. Green, Frederickstown, I, promoted 2d Lieut. and transferred to D, Feb. 28, '65 ; promoted 1st Lieut. and transferred to C, July 7, '65.

C. P. Goodwin, Salem, I, promoted 2d Lieut. I, July 7, '65; not mustered.

J. W. Green, Princeton, K, promoted 2d Lieut. K, July 7, '65; not mustered.

B. W. Hopper, Newark, E, promoted 2d Lieut. E, May 16, '62; promoted 1st Lieut. E, Dec. 23, '62; promoted Captain E, May 24, '63; wounded at Drury's Bluff, May 14, '64, and May 16, '64.

Henry Hopper, Newark, E, promoted 2d Lieut. E, March 5, '65; promoted 1st Lieut. E, July 7, '65.

J. L. Hawk, Carpentersville, H, promoted 2d Lieut. H, December 23, '62; wounded at the Half-way House, Drury's Bluff, May 14, '64; promoted 1st Lieut. H, May 16, '64.

David Kille, Auburn, I, promoted 2d Lieut. I, July 25, '64; promoted 1st Lieut. I, Mar. 24, '65; prom. Captain I, June 30, '65.

James Loughlin, B, promoted 2d Lieut. B, March 14, '64; promoted 1st Lieut. and transferred to G, Nov. 8, '64; promoted Captain, and transferred to C, March 5, '65.

H. B. Lenning, Pennington, F, promoted 2d Lieut. F, November 4, '64.

Samuel B. Moore, N. York, K, promoted 2d Lieut. B, July 25, '65; not mustered.

E. S. Pullen, Trenton, II, promoted 1st Lieut. H, Dec. 23, '62; wounded by a shell, in left shoulder, before Petersburg, June 29, '64; promoted Captain H, September 9, '64.

Geo. Peters, Elizabeth, G, promoted 2d Lieut.; comm. May 5, '64; taken prisoner, May 16, '64; returned April 10, '65, when at Goldsboro'; mustered in April 18, '65.

M. C. Runyon, Princeton, F, promoted 2d Lieut. F, May 16, '62; promoted 1st Lieut. F, January 8, '63; promoted and transferred Captain G, December 3, '64.

L. D. Shephard, Greenwich, F, promoted 2d Lieut. F, Jan. 8, '63; promoted and transferred 1st Lieut. B, May 11, '64; wounded at Drury's Bluff, May 16, '64; promoted Captain, and transferred to F, February 28, '65.

R. D. Swain, Salem, I, promoted 2d Lieut. I, Aug. 15, '62; promoted 1st Lieut. I, December 29, '62; promoted Captain, and transferred to K, Feb. 28, '65

W. E. Townley, Elizabeth, K, promoted 2d Lieut. K, Dec. 27, '64.

Wm Van Brunt, Mercer, C, promoted 2d Lieut. C, May 14, '65.

E. W. Welsted, Hunterdon, H, promoted 1st Lieut. E, May 24, '63; appointed regimental Adjutant, October 18, '64.

Daniel Whitney, Salem, I, promoted 2d Lieut. 1, March 28, '65; promoted 1st Lieut. and transferred to A, July 7, '65.

Collins B. Ware, Morris, E, promoted 2d Lieut. E, July 7, '65; not mustered.

R. V. P. Wood, Middlesex, A, promoted 2d Lieut. A, July 7, '65.

Additions to Company-Roll.

[The writing and printing of this History having been commenced while the regiment was stationed at Greensboro', N. C., and without the knowledge of the time of its final muster-out on July 31, 1865, the following additions are necessary, to perfect the record of those men not accounted for in the foregoing pages.]

John Applegate, new A, sick in hospital.
John Albert, new A, last heard from at Andersonville, Ga.
G. Black, new A, sick; left at Petersburg, when regiment went home.
C. Bough, B, never heard from since missing.
S. Barnes, B, left at Newbern hospital.
Henry Bittinger, H, sick in hospital.
John Baker, K, deserted at Greensboro', July 8, 65.
J. Crawford, A,   "   "   June 4, '65.
G. W. Church, B, sick at Newbern.
B. Clayton, B, deserted, arrested, and discharged at Newark.
T. G. Courtright, H, discharged June 19, '65.
William Devitt, B, deserted at Greensboro', July, 1865.
J. B. Dobbs, K,   "   Newark, January, 1865.
William Emery, E, transferred to Invalid Corps.
H. Frederic, A, died at Greensboro', June 20, '65.
J. Farron, K, deserted at Greensboro', July 20, '65.
A. Hundershot, E, sick at Carolina City.
P. Hegel, G, sick in hospital.
L. Heinlin, K, mustered out June, 1865.
J. Harrisson, K, detailed as carpenter, at 23d Army Corps headquarters; received a furlough; did not return; believed to be a deserter.
John Huff, B, sick at Newbern.
John A. Kelly, A, sick, left at Petersburg, when regiment went home.
E. King, E, discharged at New York.
J. Kent, E, sick at Newbern.
D. Kent, E, mustered out June, 1865.
Thomas Keenan, G, sick at Fort Monroe.
G. King, H, deserted at Goldsboro', April 4, '65.
William Kurze, K, deserted at Greensboro', July 8, '65.
J. Kane, K, deserted at Greensboro', June 20, '65.

Wm. H. Moore, B, wounded in leg, at Wise's Fork, May 10, '65 ; remained in hospital.

P. Meagher, B, sick in Hampton, Fort Monroe hospital.

E. Miller, B, deserted at Greenboro', July, 1865.

William Mullnia, H, deserted at Goldsboro', April 4, '65.

D. O'Comer, B, discharged at Wilmington, Va.

John W. Osborn, H, died in rebel prison.

C. Petty, A, sick in hospital.

William Randall, E, left at Greensboro'.

D. M. Rose, K, sick in Newark hospital.

Wm. H. Ross, K, sick in Morehead City hospital.

J. N. Rice, K, deserted at Greensboro', June 5, '65.

Wm. K. Stout, A, sick at Fort Monroe.

John Scanlin, A, deserted at Greensboro', June 20, '65.

P. Sherry, B, sick at Fort Monroe.

R. Schafer, B, deserted at Greensboro', July, 1865.

A. G. Spangenberg, H, sick in hospital.

George Sidel, G, sick in Newark hospital.

J. Shmidt, K, deserted at Greensboro', July 5, '65.

Hugo Schleicher, D, wounded, jaw-bone broke, at Wise's Fork, March 10, '65.

D. H. Terrell, H, sick in hospital.

G. W. Teates, K, when last heard from, at Andersonville, Ga.

J. Vaughn, K, deserted at Greensboro', June 30, '65.

Abram Vangarden, H, sick in hospital.

A. M. Vangarden, H,   "   "

J. A. Vangarden, H,   "   "

E. M. Ward, E, discharged at Newbern hospital.

C. D. Wallace, E, sick in Newbern hospital.

Joseph Willgus, H, sick in hospital.

C. Wilson, G,   "   "

John Ward, K, sick in Newark hospital.

C. H. Wilson, K, discharged at Newark hospital, July, 1865.

R. N. Gould, B, had the first finger of left hand shot off, while on picket, May 18, '62.

August Koenig, C, shot his finger off, May 24, '62.

H. McLarkin, F, shot finger off, May 24, '62.

All others were mustered out, as follows :—

Companies A, B, and C, Friday, July 28, '65.

"   D, E, F, G, H, and I, Saturday, July 29, '65.

Company K, and all the officers, on Monday, July 31, '65.

It is impossible to state in all cases at which hospital the sick or wounded remain, while some of the officers in charge of hospitals fail to make the required and very necessary information to regimental commanders.

Men discharged for promotion, only a few days previous to the disbanding of the regiment, were only commissioned, but not mustered in, as officers.

Daily Record.

From Oct. 8, '61, till Dec. 4, '61, the regiment remained at Camp Olden, near Trenton, N. J., engaged in organizing, drilling, &c.

December 4th. The regiment went per railroad to Washington, D. C., arriving on the 6th, and went into camp at Bladensburg toll-gate, one mile from the Capitol. James Wilson, from Elizabeth, N. J., formerly Captain of the 2d New Jersey Vols., who had been promoted and appointed Major of the "Ninth," joined the regiment.

December 14th. Review by Major General Casey, on Meridian Hill, near the Seminary, to which place the regiment also removed and encamped.

December 28th. The regiment drilled for the first time in Division, Major General Casey commanding.

December 31st. First regimental inspection and muster for pay.

1862.

January 3d. The regiment was paid by Major Allisson. The men were brigaded under Jesse L. Reno, 1st Brigade, Burnside's Expedition.

January 4th. Struck camp, and went per railroad to Annapolis, Md.

January 5th. Seven companies, A, C, D, E, H, I, and M embarked on ship Anna E. Thompson; five companies, B, F, G, K, L, on brigantine Dragoon.

January 9th. Sailed, both vessels in tow, for Fort Monroe.

January 10th. Came to anchor off Fort Monroe.

January 12th. The whole fleet set sail.

January 13th. Anchored off Hatteras Inlet, about 5 P. M.

January 15th. The commanding field and staff officers went ashore, to report to the General-in-chief; returning, the boat capsized and swamped. Col. Allen and Surgeon Weber were drowned; Lieut. Col. Heckmann, Adj. Zabriskie, and Quar. Master Keyes narrowly escaped; the 2d mate drowned also. Adj. Zabriskie made, with a self-sacrificing spirit, great and desperate exertions to rescue his Colonel, whom he saw struggling with the waves; but it was in vain! The decree of the Most High had gone forth. Human effort could not prevent His behest. Adjutant Zabriskie assumed command of the survivors. Their efforts for safety, without concert of action, were futile. His calm judgment so arranged the men that all could sustain themselves in the sea, and he, while hanging to the bow of the boat, by signals attracted the attention of the vessel that rescued them.

January 16th. Brigantine Dragoon entered Inlet.

January 21st. Ship A. E. Thompson, after much difficulty, entered Inlet.

January 30th. Brigantine crossed the Swash.

January 31st. Men on board the A. E. Thompson were carried by steamer Patuxent across the Swash, to steamer George Peabody.

February 1st. Two companies, D and I, were transferred from George Peabody to schooner Shmidt, and 60 men from different companies were detailed to serve on gunboats, for which they were promised extra pay, which they never received.

February 5th. Received signals to sail; Peabody, with Dragoon and Shmidt in tow, proceeded a short distance up the Pamlico Sound, and anchored.

February 6th. Weighed anchor at 9 A. M.; sailed and anchored about sundown off a point of shoals, about 12 miles from Roanoke Island. A. W. Woodhull, Newark, formerly Ass't Surgeon 5th N. J. Vols., promoted and commissioned Surgeon of the Ninth.

February 7th. Received signals to sail at 8 A. M.,—the gunboats in advance;—the firing upon the enemy's work began at 10½ A. M. Transports anchored out of range. At 3 P. M. the troops were ordered to land; the Ninth all landed by 9 P. M. Marched one-half mile through swamp and water, and bivouacked in a corn-field; it rained all night.

February 8th. The Ninth started about 6 A. M.; the 1st Brigade of Foster's in advance of ours, the 2d; at 6½ A. M. the advance, Foster's Brigade, engaged the enemy's pickets, and forced them into their works, "Centre Battery;" immediately the whole of the 1st Brigade was engaged; action began at 6½ A. M.; about 8½ received an order to pass the 51st New York, and report to Gen. Foster, for orders; received orders to enter the swamp on left of road, and engage the enemy; arrived in range of fort about 9 A. M. Entered swamp on left of road, in column by company, and formed line by Division after swamp was entered; advanced in this form to the edge of swamp, within about 100 yards of the fort; opened fire; the fire was returned from the fort by grape, canister, musketry, and solid shot. This continued for about two hours. Ascertaining that we were suffering mostly from their artillery, Col. Heckmann directed the attention of company commanders to the picking off of the gunners. This was successfully attained, and, in consequence, the enemy evacuated the fort. Lieut. Selden, of Wise's Legion, fired the last gun three times, and was shot in the act of firing the fourth. Col. Heckmann selected two men from Co. D, and ordered them to fire into the centre embrasure, on his giving a certain signal, agreed upon; the signal was given, and Selden fell, and with him the evacuation of the fort. About 10½ A. M. the enemy gave way. The 21st Massachusetts Vols. first entered the fort. The Ninth captured two guns. The total loss of the Ninth was nine killed and twenty-five wounded. During this day the Ninth subsequently marched about 10 miles, crossing a swamp at a side of the fort, which enabled them to attack the enemy in the rear, by which the victory of the day was gained: the enemy believing the crossing of the swamp impossible for human beings, were much puzzled and in consternation. The swamp was deep; some of the men sunk to their shoulders; cartridge-boxes were taken off, and carried in their mouths; for this undertaking the rebels for a long time called the Ninth the "Jersey musk-rats," the Ninth earning, for their coolness and steadiness under this, their first fire, for themselves and their gallant leader, the character of veterans. The Ninth quartered in rebel barracks at a northern point of the island; remaining here the regiment engaged in the usual company and battalion exercises. C. F. Burroughs, of Co. F, who had been color-bearer of the regiment, was ordered back to his company, for neglect of duty, and E. S. Carrell, of Co. H, was appointed to this post of honor.

March 3d. Early in the morning the regiment received orders to move. The right wing, seven companies, embarked on steamer Peabody; the left wing, five companies, on the brigantine Dragoon.

March 8th. Three companies, C, E, and H, were transferred to schooner H. T. Brown; four companies, A, D, I, and M, to steamer Albany; the other five remained on the Dragoon.

March 9th. Color-sergeant E. S. Carrell, having received commission for 2d Lieutenantcy, George Meyers, of Co. E, was entrusted with the important position, which he retained for over three years, a credit to himself and the regiment.

March 11th. At 8 A. M. signals for sailing; brigantine Dragoon and schooner Brown in tow of steamer Albany; anchored at sundown off Hatteras Inlet.

March 12th. Weighed anchor at 7 A. M.; sailed; arrived at the mouth of the Neuse river about 4 P. M., and anchored about 8 P. M. near the mouth of Slocum's Creek.

March 13th. Troops landed; all landed by 11 A. M. Marched 14 miles; bivouacked at 9 P. M., in wood; heavy rain all night.

March 14th. Column moved at 7½ A. M.; at 8 A. M. firing commenced in advance; the Ninth had the left of 2d Brigade, which was left of Division. After marching two miles on railroad, the Ninth filed to the left into the woods, took position, and deployed in line of battle; at 8½ A. M. engaged the enemy, who were behind earthworks. There were two batteries, one mounting three guns, the other two guns, bearing upon that portion of our lines held by the Ninth. The guns were silenced in half-an-hour, but the action continued for four hours, at which time the ammunition of the Ninth was reduced to five rounds a-piece. Colonel Heckmann sent a courier to Brigadier General Jesse L. Reno, commanding the 2d Brigade, informing him of the condition of affairs. General Reno sent back word that he might either retire, and give place to another regiment, or charge. The decision was instantly made, and "Charge! Ninth New Jersey!" echoed along the line, while over an almost impenetrable abattis, through pitfalls, ditches and mire, swept the gallant Jerseymen, and in a few minutes took the whole line of earthworks in front of them, capturing three guns. The flags of the regiment waved from three separate redans, from which the enemy had fled, and into one of which Colonel Heckmann was the first Federal soldier who planted his foot. This charge decided the day, and it was not long before the whole rebel front was flying in the greatest confusion. At 2 P. M. the regiment marched 4 miles, to the junction of the Neuse and Trent rivers, and bivouacked for the night. Adjutant Abram Zabriskie, being sick, went home on furlough. Lieut. W. C. Walker, comm. March 9, '62, and originally appointed to Co. A, but acting in this day's engagement with Co. H, was mortally wounded, and died on the battle-field.

March 16th. Received our tents, and encamped on Bivouac Ground; called it Camp "Reno." During stay here the regiment engaged in the usual company and battalion exercises, and many of the men being sick from fatigue and exposure, were allowed rest for recuperation. Surg. A. W. Woodhull joined reg't.

April 1. Received orders for a portion of the regiment to go to Carolina City, to relieve the 11th Connecticut Reg't, who had the small-pox amongst them. Eight companies went on board of the Union, steamed down the Neuse river, up Slocum's creek 5 miles, there landed; marched 10 miles to Newport Barracks, where the 5th Rhode Island Battalion was stationed; arrived about 9 P. M.; bivouacked for the night; four companies and the sick remained at Camp Reno.

April 2d. Received orders from General Parke to relieve 5th Rhode Island Battalion, and remain at the Barracks.

April 4th. The 5th Rhode Island Battalion left for Carolina City. The eight companies of the 9th N. J. Vols. at Newport Barracks, picketed the approaches to this place and to Fort Macon; one, Company F, at Havelock Station, 8 miles northwest; one, Company D, 3 miles down the railroad; one, Company K, 3 miles on Bogue Sound, and two or three other points west and southwest, at which the posts and number of men were frequently changed, generally taking one entire company.

April 7th. The rebel cavalry, about noon, charged upon a picket-post of ten men, posted about seven miles west from camp, and one mile from the company; nine men were taken prisoners, and one man badly wounded.

April 8th. Four companies from Camp Reno came to Newport Barracks; about 100 men sick and disabled remained in Camp Reno under command of Capt. Cornelius Castner, Co. B. Capt. Samuel Hufty, Jr., of Co. I, and two companies, burned bridge across Broad creek.

April 10th. A small detachment of mounted artillerymen, from Bellger's Battery, Lieut. Pope commanding, came into camp.

April 11th. The regiment was paid off.

April 12th. Lieut. Pope and command went on scout—of no importance.

April 15th. Col. Eglostein, of 103d New York, came into camp with his expedition, prisoners, and plunder; they have been three days absent from Newbern; came by Pollocksville, Pelticrs, &c. He lost one killed, and one wounded. They had Col. Robinson prisoner, and wounded, and another officer wounded through head, also eighteen other prisoners.

April 16th. Long-roll at night; false alarm.

April 18th. Long-roll at night; false alarm.

April 21st. Company H went on a scout.

April 25th. Heard in camp the bombardment of Fort Macon, which surrendered at 4 P. M.

April 29th. Quartermaster Keys left the regiment, having been detached as Acting Commissary 1st Brigade, 2d Division of Burnside's Expedition; 2d Lieut. E. S. Carrell appointed Acting Regimental Quartermaster.

May 3d. Long-roll at night; false alarm.

May 13th. Major Abram Zabriskie, formerly Adjutant, joined regiment again, having been absent, sick, since the battle of Roanoke, and promoted while home.

May 18th. Artillery returned to Newbern.

May 24th. Chaplain Thomas Drumm fell from his horse, and broke his leg.

May 26th. Very heavy rain; washed away the mill at Havelock; the regiment was paid off.

May 29th. Alarm and long roll at 10 A. M., caused by the officer of the day firing his pistol off. Long-roll at 11 P. M., false alarm. Wedding near the camp : a private of Co. E married to Miss Bell, from Newport.

June 3d. Adj. Abel went to Beaufort, and returned with Lieut. Leidig, aid to Gen. Parke. Row in camp; several officers were put under arrest, and one in guard-house, for resisting and abusing the officer of the day.

June 12th. Chaplain Thomas Drumm went North. On this day the first locomotive went over the Atlantic and North Carolina Railroad, afterwards named U. S. Military Railroad. News came into camp of the capture, by the rebels, of Rev. McMann, who lives 4 miles west of camp. Companies A and B went on a scout beyond his house; returned in the afternoon. Capt. James Stewart, Co. H, arrested two men at Jones' house; Co. C went out on distant picket.

June 13th. One company of 3d New York Cavalry came into camp from Newbern, at 6 P. M. Companies M and I started on a scout; cavalry followed at 11 P. M.

June 14th. Cavalry returned at 9 A. M; infantry returned at 3 P. M. They went to the rebel camp, about 16 miles; at White Oak road found the rebels had left; burned the barracks, and returned with three prisoners.

June 15th. Cavalry returned to Newbern.

June 18th. Monitor-cars went over railroad, mounting two guns.

June 21st. A splendid sword was presented to Col. Heckmann, by the company officers.

June 23d. Long-roll at 11 P. M.; false alarm. Col. Heckmann drilled the battalion while out, by the light of the moon.

June 24th. At 9 A. M. received news from Havelock that the enemy were lurking about, and that last night the pickets were driven in; the train was at the camp when the news was received; Col. Heckmann immediately left for Havelock, with Companies E, H, and I; Co. H went on to Newbern with the train, as guard. The two other companies went out 5 miles to Lewis & Brothers' plantation; found there that about 150 rebels had been across the swamp the night before, leaving their horses on the other side; they had gone back about four hours in advance of the arrival of our forces. Major Abram Zabriskie and Surgeon A. W. Woodhull followed the train in a hand-car, to Havelock. Co. I remained at Havelock, for the purpose of building a block-house. Companies E and H returned to camp in the afternoon, by cars.

June 25th. At 11 A. M. Major Lewis and 150 men of 3d New York Cavalry arrived in camp, and with Companies B, E, H and M, started on an expedition, to try to cut off some of the enemy. They marched six miles, and procured Mr. Roberts as guide; then marched six miles further, and bivouacked for the night, on the White Oak road; the guards were doubled around the camp.

June 26th. The expedition marched about twelve miles further, and finding the enemy had all escaped, they returned and bivouacked on the same place they did the night before.

June 29th. Started for camp at 4 P. M., and arrived at 10 A. M.; at 4 P. M. the cavalry returned to Newbern.

June 30th. Inspection and muster for pay. Co. E left for Evans' Mill.

July 1st. Lieut. E. S. Carrell, A. R. Quartermaster, returned to his company for duty, and Lieut. Thos. B. Applegate was appointed in his place.

July 3d. Companies A, Capt. Stearnes, and C, Capt. Jay, of 3d New York Cavalry, and two companies of Rockitt's Battery, with three rifled six-pounders, came into camp; Co. F, 3d N. J. Cavalry, Capt. McNamara, remained at Havelock.

July 4th. A salute was fired by the Battery.

July 7th. A man of Co. C, who was stationed about six miles west from camp, was shot in the knee, while on duty; supposed to have been done by some lurking bushwhacker.

July 8th. Alarm from the station of Co. C; Lieut. Col. Wilson sent out two companies of cavalry, and Companies B and C, under command of Major Zabriskie; upon their arrival, they found that the alarm was caused by the falling of burning trees and practice-firing in the vicinity;—they returned about sundown.

July 25th. During this interval, many expeditions of cavalry and infantry went out from the camp, generally being absent about 24 hours.

July 26th. At 4 A. M. six companies, B, C, D, H, I, and M, with three companies of cavalry and two pieces of artillery, started with the understanding that we should co-operate with another force, starting from Newbern, somewhere in the route between these two places, on the Pollocksville road. They marched on the White Oak road, at 12 M., twenty-one miles to Peltier's Mills, where they rested three hours, and took dinner; resumed march at 3 P. M.; marched five miles, and bivouacked for the night in a cornfield, near Davies' Mills; heavy thunder-showers during the night, which completely drenched the men.

July 27th. Regiment marched at 6 A. M.; built two bridges; marched ten miles, and arrived at Young's Cross-roads, at 11 A. M.; at 3 P. M. Col. Heckmann sent the three companies of cavalry to reconnoitre on three different roads; Col. Heckmann accompanied Co. F, Capt. McNamara, who proceeded on the Onslow road, which crosses the White Oak river, about one mile from where we halted; the bridge across the river was destroyed, and when the cavalry approached within range, they were fired upon by rebel bushwhackers, who lay concealed beyond the river. Such men of the cavalry who had rifles, dismounted, and deployed as skirmishers; the infantry-companies, B and D, were soon in the heat of action, and the fire of the enemy was materially slackened, when Lieut. Graham opened with grape and canister from one piece of artillery; after the first fire from the cannon, no response was made by the enemy; shells were fired as they retreated, gradually increasing the range; a bridge was constructed across the river, when many arms, sabres, &c., were found, showing that they had retreated in haste. Our wounded amounted to five men: two seriously, but none mortally; also Col. Heckmann and Surgeon Woodhull—the latter escaping a volley of musketry, with two balls wounding his body, one passing through his hat, and the fourth injuring his horse very badly. We had heard nothing from the forces of Newbern; strong pickets were posted on all the approaches, and we bivouacked at Young's Cross-roads. We had eighteen prisoners and many guns, taken in the neighboring houses, and a few horses belonging to rebel cavalry. The rebels who met us here were three companies: Ward's, Humphries', and Perkins', 150 men. From a negro was subsequently ascertained that four of them were killed and eleven wounded.

July 28th. Company H, with two companies of cavalry, marched ten miles to Pollocksville, and returned at 12 M.; found that the force from Newbern had marched to that place, met the enemy, and returned; at 3 P. M., the whole expedition, under Col. Heckmann, marched 10 miles, and at about 7 P. M. quartered in Seminary Building, situate 2 miles on Newbern side of Pollocksville.

July 29th. Marched at 5 A. M., 14 miles on the Newbern side of Pollocksville. Arrived at Newbern at 11 A. M.; infantry returned by cars to Newport Barracks.

July 30th. Cavalry and artillery returned to Newport Barracks.

August 4th. Company F was relieved from Havelock by Co. L, and went to Beaufort. Co. G went to Morehead City; Capt. Ritter, of Co. G, commanding post.

August 14th. One hundred men, taken from three companies of the Ninth, and two companies of cavalry, started for Cedar Point at 7 P. M., and marched by Peltier's Mill 30 miles before sun-rise.

August 15th. They arrived at sunrise at Hill's plantation, Cedar Point, opposite Swansboro'; they could procure no transportation to cross White Oak river, except one boat, that would hold fifteen men only. Capt. J. McChesney, of Co. M, with 15 men, started for the town, and was fired upon, and more than 200 cavalry appeared, when they returned; resumed march on return at 11 A. M.; marched 13 miles to Landers'; took dinner; marched at 4½ P. M., and arrived in camp at 9 P. M. During the last four hours of march it rained in torrents, and the night was pitch dark. On this expedition 53 miles were marched in 26 hours, with 8 hours rest; average, 2 17-18 miles per hour. Subsequent to the death of Surgeon Weller, Surgeon Minnies, of the 48th Penn'a Vols., acted in his place; after serving for a few days he died, when the regiment came under charge of Ass't Surgeon Braun, assisted by Lieut. Leonhard, assistant, until March, 1862; from this time the regiment was under the sole charge of Surgeon A. W. Woodhull, until August, 1862. Ass't Surgeon John M. Davies, promoted and commissioned from the ranks, May 1st, '62, was detailed in general hospital from the date of his appointment until August, 1862. When Dr. Davies joined the regiment at Newport Barracks, Surgeon A. W. Woodhull took charge of post at Beaufort, N. C.

August 21st. Company B relieved Co. A, at Havelock.

August 31st. Alarm at picket-station, two miles east of the camp, on the railroad; a corporal of Co. B was shot, and Companies B and E arrested two men and captured about 50 arms.

September 1st. The members of Co. H, whose commander, Captain James Stewart, Jr., had just returned from the North, marched in front of the Captain's quarters, when a committee of five non-commissioned officers waited upon the Captain, and announced the desire of the company to present to him a sword, sash and belt, as a token of good feeling, &c. On the part of the company, Corporal J. E. Matthews spoke about as follows:—

"CAPTAIN,—I am deputed by the members of Co. H to present you with this sword and sash; not so much as a token of the respect and love that we all feel for you as our commander—for we believe that feeling would be but feebly expressed indeed, were we to demonstrate it by so meagre an offering,—but we give you this emblem of your profession that in after years, when our present association is broken up, you may recall. through it, the brave deeds performed by yourself in this dark period of our country's struggle, as well to remind you of the gallant men who have followed you through every danger, and the confidence those men felt in their leader and Captain. May the reflection that you have our full respect and confidence, give you the same satisfaction as it does us in presenting to you a weapon which, while in your hands, we know will only be drawn in the cause of *justice* and *right*."

To which Captain Stewart responded, as follows :—

" Corporal and men of Company H,—But scarcely returned from an absence of over a month, I find myself taken completely by surprise—an agreeable one, I confess,—and one that any soldier, no matter how punctilious he may be regarding his duties, should be proud to have happen him. It has ever been a boast of mine, and one that our leader has frequently endorsed, that I had a company second to none in the service in point of discipline, drill, and efficiency ; and for me to know that in the difficult task of moulding a body of citizens into a company of soldiers I have not only succeeded, but at the same time have retained the respect and confidence of those men, is of itself a triumph one may be justly proud of. My interests and feelings have been identified with you from the organization of our regiment to the present time, and, God willing, that association shall continue until the mighty work which called us together has been successfully accomplished.

" You have already, during your brief connection with the service, been called upon, on more than one occasion, to test your patriotism and valor on the battle field, and many of our comrades, who started with us from our native State, full of life and hope, are now numbered among the dead, their bones left to bleach on Carolina's shore, far away from their kindred and friends. Nevertheless their brave deeds are remembered by all, and while we drop a tear to their memory, let us try and emulate their heroism, and prove to all our determination to defend to the last, and sacrifice life itself, if may be, to protect that Government which has nurtured and cherished us in the past.

" Having just returned from the North, and from the homes of many of you, I can give you the assurance that your conduct is closely watched by those who in '61 bade you God-speed on your mission, and that their prayers ascend daily for your safety and success. They are justly proud of your record thus far, and have no fears for the future. I, too, am well satisfied with the readiness with which you have obeyed all my orders, and the diligence you have displayed in acquiring a knowledge of your duties. Let the confidence which has heretofore existed been the officers of the company and the men continue, and I pledge you that the handsome gift handed me this day, while I shall ever cherish it as an expression of your good feeling toward myself, both as your

Captain and friend, I shall do all in my power to preserve, untarnished in any cause of injustice, but bright and glittering in the defence of *right*."

September 2d. Company M relieved Co. B, at Havelock; 2d Lieut. E. S. Moffat detached to the Signal Corps, at Newbern.

September 10th. Two false alarms in camp.

September 11th. Company E left camp for Morehead City. Ass't Surgeon F. B. Gillette, comm. August 20th, arrived, taking charge of the troops at Morehead City and Carolina City.

September 14th. Company B went to Morehead City, and Companies C and L to Beaufort.

September 15th. Company M was relieved at Havelock, by a company of the 27th Massachusetts, and went to Carolina City.

September 17th. Companies E and H, of the Ninth, and Companies A and C of the 3d New York Cavalry, started at 7 A. M., from Beaufort, and marched 20 miles towards Adams' creek; bivouacked in woods.

September 18th. Marched early 5 miles to Adams' creek, on a scout; started on return at 12 M.; marched 25 miles to Beaufort, arriving about 11 P. M.

September 19th. Company E returned to Morehead City.

October 2d. Surgeon A. W. Woodhull appointed in charge of Hammond General hospital, at Beaufort.

October 10th. Private Julius C. Salter, from Hague, New York, belonging to the 23d New York Battery, detailed as ward-master of the hospital of the Ninth New Jersey Vols.

October 15th. Captain W. D. S. Boudinot appointed Provost-marshal at Newark, N. J.

October 20th. Captain Samuel Hufty, Jr., ordered with a flag-of-truce to Swansboro', to deliver private Robinson, prisoner, on exchange.

October 29th. Companies B, C, E, G, H, I, M, and 25 men of Co. F ordered to depart on an expedition; started on cars for Newbern at midnight; arrived, and embarked immediately on steamer Patuxent.

October 30th. At 3 P. M. transferred on gunboat Huzzar.

October 31st. At 1 P. M. arrived and landed at Washington, N. C.; quartered near the city. About a half hour after our arrival, and the men not yet all at rest, a false alarm was heard of " rebels approaching!" The expedition was composed of the Ninth New Jersey, 3d, 5th, 17th, 23d, 24th, 25th, 27th, and 44th Mass., 10th Connecticut, 5th Rhode Island, 500 cavalry, and thirty-two pieces of artillery.

November 1st. Remained in quarters.

November 2d. Sunday; marched at 5 A. M. ; the troops were ordered to load arms, as soon as they came out of town; met enemy about one mile from the city; skirmished all day and all night; marched 19 miles to Rowles' Mills; about two miles this side the mill a deep swamp and morass had to be crossed, and the 44th Mass. was first ordered to cross; after they had marched a few feet into the mud, and being fired upon by the rebels from the other side, losing one killed and a few slightly wounded, they declared in a body to be unable to go any further: they were not used to wade mires, like the New Jersey musk-rats of Roanoke fame, and, though well-drilled, and particularly fitted for dress-parade and garrison duty, they did not, at that time, like the tune of rebel musketry. General Foster, commanding the expedition, remarked : "I know I have one regiment here which can and dares to cross this swamp," and at the same time sent his orders to Col. Heckmann, commanding the Ninth. In and through went the men of the Ninth, but on coming to the other side, it seemed as if the rebels had heard the remark made and order given, for no rebel was to be seen; arriving at Rowles' Mills, we found a few dead rebels; the mill was a corn-mill, and in operation; the covered bridge across the stream had been set on fire by the rebels, to obstruct our advance; Colonel Heckmann ordered 10 men of Co. G, of the Ninth,—which was posted at the right, in front of the bridge,—to extinguish the fire ; he, the Colonel himself, assisted in carrying water, and afterwards planks, to repair the damages; after the fire was extinguished, the Ninth was the first regiment that crossed the bridge; arriving at the other side, skirmishing began in all directions, but no enemy could be found ; pickets were posted, and the troops bivouacked, wet and weary after a long march and severe hardships.

November 3d. The Ninth, in advance, marched at daylight, 4 hours, nine miles to Williamston; halted 3 hours; at 1 P. M. marched 10 miles, and bivouacked at sundown in an open field.

November 4th. The Ninth, in advance, marched at daylight 15

miles; arrived at Hamilton at 2 P. M. A fire broke out in town, which laid one-half of the place in ashes; how the fire originated has never been ascertained. A part of the troops remained in and around Hamilton; the Ninth left Hamilton at 5 P. M.; marched about 3 miles further, halted, and bivouacked on a large plantation, in open field.

November 5th. The Ninth, in advance, marched at daylight 8 miles on road to Tarboro'; halted, and took dinner; marched again at 2 P. M.; turned south for one mile, then took the road for Halifax, about 7 miles; went across the Conecto swamp, and bivouacked 4 miles from Tarboro'.

November 6th. To quote the usual phrase: "the object accomplished," the return was commenced on this morning, the Ninth bringing up the rear; column marched in direct road 13 miles, to Hamilton; heavy rain all night; men quartered in barns, and other out-houses.

November 7th. Snow; on some places the snow was 3 inches deep; marched in early morning to Williamston; the whole regiment quartered in houses.

November 8th. Rest all day; *dress-parade in afternoon.*

November 9th. Left early; marched 11 miles to Jamestown; rested, resumed march at 1 P. M.; halted at 6 P. M., and bivouacked in open field, three miles from Plymouth. Total marched this day, twenty-two miles.

November 10th. Marched at 10 A. M. 3 miles to Plymouth; entered town at 12 M.; at 3 P. M. went on board gunboat Lancer; sailed; passed Edenton at 4 P. M., and anchored at 12½ A. M., near northern point of Roanoke Island.

November 11th. Sailed at daylight; entered Neuse river at 6 P. M., and anchored at 10 P. M. 7 miles from Newbern. A dispatch immediately arrived from Newbern, saying the city was threatened, and we were needed; we immediately steamed up, and landed in Newbern about midnight; marched to Fort Totten, and lay under arms all night.

November 12th. The cavalry left the city to find the enemy, but failed; here Co. K joined the rest of the regiment; the regiment remained near the fort all day; returned to the city at 9 P. M.; took the cars; arrived at Morehead City about 11 P. M., having been absent on this expedition exactly two weeks. The

Ninth lost only one man, of Co. B, who was accidentally killed at Williamston, and buried at Plymouth.

Some days after our return to Morehead City, from this expedition, the writer had an opportunity to peruse a copy of the Springfield (Mass.) *Republican*, of the 10th of November. The editor of that paper told his readers that Gen. Foster had driven the rebels out of Plymouth, taken the town, and a great many prisoners, capturing numbers of horses, mules, &c., &c. The good people of Massachusetts, many hundreds of miles from the place of action, did read, before breakfast, of deeds which many of her soldiers, commanded by one of her bravest and most gallant sons, only partly accomplished at noon on the same day. The fact is, the expedition entered Plymouth very peaceably : not a rebel soldier, not a rebel citizen, or other living human being was to be seen in the village, and no arms were taken at that place.

November 18th. By order from War Department, the regiment was consolidated into ten companies. Companies A and L were broken up ; Co. M took the place of Co. A, and with it its letter, A. Six officers, Capt. Charles Hayes, A, and Charles Erb, L, Lieut's Felger and G. Mueller, A, and John Muller and Anton Moll, L, also 37 men, were mustered out ; and 171 men of the two companies, A and L, were transferred to the other companies of the regiment. (See Company-Rolls.)

Up to this time the regiment, under command of Colonel Heckmann, was stationed at various points upon the Atlantic and North Carolina Railroad, and also upon Bogue Sound. Prior to the surrender of Fort Macon, the regiment had guarded the approaches from the enemy's lines. By the vigilance and untiring energy of Col. Heckmann, and the frequency of his expeditions, the Ninth alone kept in continual subjection the bands of guerillas that infested the borders.

December 1st. The Ninth was relieved by Massachusetts troops.

December 4th. The regiment went by cars to Newbern : encamped near the old site of Camp Reno. All present except Co. K, who were still in Bogue Sound.

December 11th. What is known as the Goldsboro' Expedition left Newbern. Colonel Heckmann had charge of an independent command, consisting of the Ninth New Jersey Vols., Belger's Battery, of six pieces, and a detachment of the 3d New York Cavalry.

Major Abram Zabriskie was in command of the regiment. At 7 A. M. marched 16 miles on the Trent road; when out 14 miles, the cavalry charged on abattis, and captured 2 prisoners; the Ninth had the advance on first day, and bivouacked beyond the abattis; this expedition starting to-day consisted of about 20 regiments of infantry—12,000, 40 pieces of artillery, and some 600 cavalry.

December 12th. The Ninth in advance; marched at 8 A. M.; skirmished all day, continually meeting the enemy in small parties; marched at 12 M., and bivouacked at dark about 10 miles from Kinston.

December 13th. The Ninth still in advance; marched at 8 A. M.; after proceeding 6 miles, came upon the enemy, entrenched beyond Southwest Creek, the bridge of which was destroyed; engaged the enemy; after three-quarters of an hour the Ninth crossed the creek, about 300 yards above enemy's guns, turned their right flank, and entered the earthworks, which we found evacuated; firing was then heard on the right; the Ninth yelled, and charged at a swift pace a force which, according to information received, consisted of General Evans' 2500 infantry and 4 pieces of artillery, stationed about 300 yards up the road; received a discharge of grape and canister, from a 12-pounder, which we charged and captured, with the men serving the piece; Col. Heckmann ordered a non-commissioned officer and 4 men to take charge of the gun, and with the regiment charged up the road, and captured the caisson of the piece, a guidon, horse, and several prisoners; the regiment rendezvoused at this point, and marched one mile towards Kinston, when they halted for dinner; resumed march about 3 P. M.; after marching two miles, again met enemy, consisting of three regiments, with two pieces of artillery, near the road, flanked on each side by two regiments; the Ninth deployed the whole right wing as skirmishers, and after a beautiful skirmish of three quarters of an hour this force alone succeeded in dislodging the enemy from his position, from which he retired with his guns; the loss of our forces was one wounded; the regiment bivouacked for the night on the field. At the time the Ninth advanced and came in hearing distance of the rebel guns, the officer commanding the rebel forces was heard to say to his men: "There comes the d——d Dutch Heckmann; you'd better save yourselves as well as you can;" and running, they did so.

December 14th. The Ninth, in advance, marched at 7½ A. M.; skirmishing commenced immediately; advanced skirmishers, until we received the fire from their artillery in our ranks; the Colonel sent a messenger to General Foster, informing him of the state of affairs, and received directions to ask for what he wanted, and act according to his own judgment; Morrison's Battery, the 3d New York, was called for, with a regiment of infantry, to support it, a whole brigade arrived with the battery; the Ninth skirmish-line were ordered to hold their position; Morrison engaged the enemy, and the Ninth were deployed to the right, in order to flank their position; the 17th Mass., Lieut. Col. Fellow's, joining them, moved briskly forward, and drove two North Carolina regiments before them, threatening their left-rear, and causing the main body to break pell-mell over the bridge that spans the Neuse river at that point. When the enemy was routed at all points, he fired the bridge, thus cutting off the retreat of about 300 rebels, who were taken prisoners on this side; the fire of the bridge was put out, and the Ninth were the first to cross and enter the earth-works, where they captured 100 prisoners, 5 guns, and one stand of Texan colors; the colors of the Ninth were pierced by two shots, fired by a South Carolina sharpshooter; our forces entered Kinston about 2 P. M.; remained there about one hour, during which our artillery from across the river shelled the enemy over the town; about 3 P. M. we left the town, and marched 3 miles on the road by Goldsboro', and bivouacked there.

December 15th. The Ninth, in advance, marched at 7½ A. M., to Kinston; re-crossed the river, burning the bridge behind; marched 14 miles on the road towards Whitehall, on the Neuse river; found the enemy in position on the opposite shore; the bridge across the river was burned the day before. The whole of the Ninth was deployed on the bank of the river, with thirty pieces of artillery firing over them across at the enemy; after an engagement of two hours, the ammunition of the Ninth gave out; they were relieved by the 17th, 23d, and 44th Mass.; after the action had continued for another hour, this attack being a feint to divert attention from the movement of the artillery and cavalry upon the railroad structure at Mount Olive; our forces resumed the march towards Goldsboro'; the Ninth waited for the rear to come up, in order to procure ammunition, and marched about 3½ P. M.

7 miles, and, after resuming its position in advance, went into bivouac at 12¼ A. M. The colors of the Ninth were pierced this day by many bullets.

December 17th. Marched at 8 A. M. 5 miles, to within 1½ miles of the Goldsboro' bridge ; the Ninth N. J. and 17th Mass. advanced towards the bridge ; when within quarter of a mile from the bridge the right wing of the Ninth were deployed to the right, along the bank of the river, when they were fired upon by pieces of artillery and about two regiments of infantry ; action continued about two hours ; the object being to destroy the bridge, volunteers were called upon, to set it on fire ; the call was responded to by many, and Lieut. Graham, aid to Col. Heckmann, privates William Lemons, of Co. E, and E. S. Winands, of Co. K, of the Ninth N. J. Vols., were selected ; they succeeded in accomplishing the act ; the Adjutant and one man of the 17th Mass., and three of the color-guard of the Ninth were wounded, while setting fire to the bridge ; the regiment was then, with other forces, withdrawn from the field. At 3 P. M. the return march was begun ; after proceeding 3 miles, heavy cannonading in the rear caused a halt ; the Ninth was ordered to return to the relief of the rear-guard ; it was ascertained that a heavy force had attacked the rear, when Belger's and Morrison's Batteries drove them back, with great slaughter ; the arrival of the Ninth found this state of affairs, and no further attack being apprehended, the rear of the column again moved on the return, and after marching 5 miles, bivouacked on the ground occupied the night before, at 9 P. M. Colonel Heckmann was, during this expedition, with his command, constantly in the advance, engaging and harassing the enemy : exercising so much prudence and skill in disposing his troops that the number of casualties was not only astonishingly small, but by his quickness and energy he made himself invaluable to the General commanding Expedition.

December 18th. Marched at 8 A. M. 17 miles, and bivouacked 9 miles from Kinston.

December 19th. Marched at 8 A. M. 15 miles, and bivouacked 7 miles from Kinston, on the Newbern side.

December 20th. Marched at 6 A. M. 32 miles, and arrived in Camp Reno at 5 P. M.

December 22d. The regiment was paid off. Col. C. A. Heckmann appointed Brigadier-General U. S. Vols.

December 23d. Surgeon A. W. Woodhull, of the Ninth, in charge of Heckmann's Brigade.

1863.

January 7th. The Brigade, consisting of the Ninth New Jersey, 3d, 8th, and 23d Mass., was reviewed by B. G. Naglee, Brigadier General commanding 2d Division, 18th Army Corps.

January 8th. Lieut. Col. Abram Zabriskie promoted Colonel.

January 13th. During the interval remained in Camp Reno, performing the usual company, battalion, and brigade exercises. In the morning the regiment left in cars, halted, and encamped at Carolina City.

January 20th. Marched to Morehead City; six companies. A, B, C, E, F, and I, embarked on board the Key West; four companies, D, H, G, and K, on board the Curlew.

January 29th. The fleet, consisting of nearly one hundred sail, all told, weighed anchor, and sailed at 3 P. M.

January 31st. Entered Port Royal harbor; the provisions were scarce, and the rations had been unusually small, and one day, when the quartermaster made his appearance, he was received with groans, and when a few hours later fresh meat was brought on board the boat, three times three cheers rent the air; so great was the appetite of the men, that an extra guard had to be detailed, to guard the meat, or else it never would have come over fire.

February 9th. The four companies on board the Curlew disembarked.

February 10th. The six companies on board the Key West disembarked, and the whole regiment encamped on St. Helena Island. Many other troops were encamped there already; soon after, from 12 to 15 negro shanties burned down; how the fire originated has never been found out, but the imputation was placed upon the Ninth by Major-General Hunter, and they had to suffer for it, for they received no fresh bread or fresh meat for a whole month, and other rations only in small quantities during that time. The roll had to be called every two hours, from reveille till taps. A small newspaper, issued at Beaufort, S. C., found great pleasure in publishing several articles concerning the accidents, to the injury of the

Ninth; but the gallant old regiment remained here long enough to completely live down all charges detrimental to their honor and their hard-earned reputation.

February 11th. Ass't Surgeon John M. Davies, of the Ninth, who had been in charge of Hammond General hospital, Beaufort, N. C., since December 6, '62, was ordered to take charge of General hospital, Portsmouth, N. C.

February 13th. The Division, under command of General C. A. Heckman, was reviewed by Gen. B. G. Naglee.

February 24th. All detachments of the 18th Army Corps now in the Department of the South, were reviewed on St. Helena Island, by Major-General D. Hunter. Many ladies were present.

March 5th. The following order was read to the men, at dress-parade :—

HEADQUARTERS NAGLEE'S DIVISION, }
St. Helena Island, N. C., March 5, '63. }

General Order No. 12.

Officers and Soldiers of my Division, and of my old Brigade:

I have been relieved of my command over you, and am ordered elsewhere. Let me entreat you to give implicit obedience to every order. Remember the sacred cause of our country, for which we have sacrificed our homes, and exposed our lives. Go on, and add to the gallant name your conduct has won, and, as before, again you will proclaim: "Truth is mighty, and will prevail."

With affectionate remembrance of the past, and a confidence in the future, I bid you farewell, and, with all my heart, "God bless you!"

By command of   B. G. NAGLEE,
Com'g 2d Division, 18th Army Corps.
G. A. JOHNSON, A. A. Adj. Gen.

March 5th. The regiment was inspected by the regular inspecting officer of the Department.

March 9th. The officers of the Ninth, and many others, bid farewell to General Naglee.

March 11th. Another fire; the guard-house of the regiment burned down; cause not known.

March 26th. The whole detachment, under command of General Stevenson, reviewed by General D. Hunter.

March 31st. Regimental inspection.

April 3d. Surgeon A. W. Woodhull rejoined the regiment.

April 4th. Seven companies, A, B, E, F, H, I, and K, embarked on the Key West; three companies, C, D, and G, embarked on the Tillie.

April 5th. Sunday; left Port Royal harbor, and came to anchor at North Edisto Inlet, at 7 P. M.

April 7th. Bombardment at Charleston harbor distinctly heard.

April 9th. Two companies, I and K, make a reconnoissance in North Edisto Inlet.

April 10th. Weighed anchor, and started for Port Royal at 1½ P. M.; towed barge Milton, and when we came up, cast her off, after being out one hour; took City of Bath in tow, she having injured herself in passing over the bar; towed her two hours; came to anchor off Hilton Head, and remained there all night.

April 11th. Entered Port Royal harbor, the right wing staying on board; the left wing landed.

April 13th. News had reached South Carolina of the investment of Washington, N. C., by the rebels, and that Gen. Foster was besieged with his brave garrison. Gen. Heckmann immediately applied to Major-General Hunter for leave to go with his Brigade to the rescue, and permission was given, and every possible despatch was made use of; the right wing, on board the Key West, started at 4 P. M., with ship Morton in tow; north-east storm.

April 14th. Cast ship off.

April 15th. Left wing embarked on steamer Belvidere, and sailed.

April 16th. The right wing entered Beaufort, N. C., harbor, at 9 A. M.; landed at Morehead City; took cars for Newbern; arrived about midnight; went into the vacated barracks of the 44th Mass.; men up all night, looking after and getting luggage into the barracks.

April 17th. At 8 A. M. ordered to march, the men having had no adequate food or rest. The left wing, Companies C, D, and G, arrived in Beaufort harbor; took cars for Newbern; left Newbern at 2 P. M.; crossed the Neuse, in steamer, and marched towards Washington 8 miles; marching very hard, water in some places very deep; bivouacked at dark, in open field.

April 18th. Marched at 6 A. M. 15 miles, and bivouacked one mile beyond Blunt's Mill, at 4 P. M.; here Major Curlies, who was in command of the three companies of the left wing, joined the regiment again.

April 19th. Sunday; marched at 5½ A. M. 10 miles, and arrived at 11 A. M. at Hill's Bluff, on Tar river, where we found our forces in possession of the evacuated rebel fort. The enemy had heard of our design, and of the approach of General Heckmann and his Star Brigade, and evacuated their stronghold but the day before, and Gen. Heckmann's veterans marched with no opposition over ground where, but the day before, had rested five times their number. Left at 2 P. M., in schooner, towed by a steamer, 7 miles to Washington; arrived 5 P. M, landed, and quartered in houses.

April 20th. Started on steamer Escort, at 10½ A. M.; anchored at night in Neuse river, 20 miles below Newbern; arrived in Newbern at 7½ A. M., and quartered in the barracks of the 44th Mass.

April 25th. Took cars, and arrived at Carolina City, at 1½ P. M., and encamped.

April 30th. Inspection and muster for pay.

May 2d. Quartermaster S. Keys relieved from Brigade, and detached as commissary of 2d Division, Burnside's Army.

May 18th. Colonel Abram Zabriskie in command of the District of Beaufort; Lieut. Colonel Stewart in command of the regiment. Lieut. Thomas B. Applegate, Co. A, Acting regimental Quartermaster, was ordered to return to his company for duty, and Lieut. Charles Hufty, Co. D, appointed in his place.

May 20th. Regiment inspected by Capt. Raulston, of the 81st New York, Brigade Inspector.

May 27th. Colonel Abram Zabriskie returned to the regiment, and took command.

June 1st. Company B went on picket on Bogue Bank.

June 7th.—   CAMP NINTH N. J. VOLS.,
                             Carolina City, June 7, '63.

Special Order No. 58.

Complaints having been made to the Col. Commanding, by the proper authority, that Lieut. Fredr. Hobart, Co. G, on June 6, '63, interfered with the sentinels in the execution of their duty, and by threatening language caused a sentinel on his post to violate the authorized instruction from the officer of the guard, the Col. commanding considers it necessary to express his censure of such behavior, and accordingly reprimands Lieut. Hobart for conduct so unbecoming an officer and so prejudicial to good discipline.

By order of   ABRAM ZABRISKIE,
                             Colonel Commanding.

                    E. S. CARRELL, Adjutant.

June 22d. Company B returned from Bogue Sound.

June 25th. Surgeon A. W. Woodhull ordered to superintend the erection of the hospital at Morehead City, afterwards named Mansfield General hospital. Regiment ordered to move to Newbern.

June 26th. Struck camp at 6 A. M.; started in cars at 8½ A. M.; went into barracks in outskirts of the city, near the Neuse river, and close by Fort Totten.

June 30th. Inspection and muster for pay. General Heckmann placed in command of the forces and defences at Newbern.

July 3d. The 3d New York Cavalry and 110 men of 1st Reg't N. Carolina Union Vols., mounted, started on a raid towards Keewansville. The Ninth New Jersey, 17th, 23d, and 27th Mass., 81st and 158th New York, Bellger's and Angel's Batteries were ordered to march.

July 4th. Marched at 4 A. M. to Pollocksville 12 miles, and rested; resumed march at 4 P. M. 8 miles, and bivouacked in open field, on McDonald's plantation.

July 5th. Marched at 3½ A. M., the Ninth in advance, and arrived at Trenton, 6 miles, at 7½ A. M.; after a short rest, marched 5 miles, to Scott's plantation; Companies B and F burned the bridge over the Trent; bivouacked on Scott's plantation.

July 6th. Four companies of the 23d Mass. and two pieces of artillery went about 3 miles to a school-house on the road towards the Free Bridge; about noon the rebels appeared on the other side of the river, and threw some shells; the Ninth New Jersey Vols. marched to their relief; deployed as skirmishers; shells were thrown, wounding two or three men of the Ninth, also fracturing the left clavicle of Lieut. Col. Chambers, of the 23d Mass. The rebels disappeared after a few rounds from one of our pieces; about 1 P. M. the cavalry made its appearance upon the Free Bridge road, and as the object of our presence was to sustain them, we returned to the place of bivouac at 8½ P. M. The cavalry raid was very successful, destroying several miles of railroads, a factory for making sabres and other arms,—government and commissary stores, &c., &c.; capturing also 300 horses, and bringing a large drove of negroes; made coffee, &c.; marched at 10 P. M.

July 7th. Arrived at daylight at the place of our former bivouac, 8 miles from Pollocksville; rested 3 hours; marched again at 7 A. M.; halted at the Seminary, and reached Newbern at 6 P. M.

July 12th. Sunday; in afternoon our pickets stationed at Deep Creek were driven in.

July 13th. The regiment went in cars to Newport Barracks; was joined there by the 23d Mass., two guns Co. I, 3d New York Artillery, and one company 3d New York Cavalry; marched at 10 A. M.; bivouacked at night.

July 14th. Marched at 4 A. M. 6 miles to Cedar Point; steamer Wilson, which was to co-operate with this force, got aground 10 miles below; bivouacked in Oak Grove; cavalry started for Young's Cross roads.

July 15th. Captain E. S. Harris, with 12 men, made soundings up White Oak river; the cavalry returned at 6 P. M.

July 16th. Marched at 5.10 A. M., and arrived at Newport Barracks at 11 A. M.: 18 miles in 5 hours and 50 minutes.

July 17th. Returned to Newbern in cars; Surg. A. W. Woodhull returned to the regiment. General Foster went to Fortress Monroe, to take command of Department of Virginia and North Carolina. Gen. Heckmann went to Newbern, to take command of Department of North Carolina.

July 22d. At 4 P. M. the regiment was ordered to march to Swift Creek, which was countermanded at 6 P. M.

July 23d. Five companies received orders to march; countermanded again.

July 24th. Received orders to march the following day.

July 25th. Expedition started for Winton; the force consisted of the Ninth New Jersey, 17th, 23d, and 4 companies of the 25th Mass., 81st New York, and Belger's Battery; the Ninth New Jersey embarked on steamer Convoy; sailed at 6 A. M.; arrived at the mouth of Chowan river, at 10 P. M.; anchored off Edenton.

July 26th. Steamed up Chowan river at 9.50 A. M., and arrived at Winton at 2½ P. M.; the Ninth took the advance, went one mile on wrong road; returned and followed 17th Mass. towards Hill's Bridge; 4 miles from Winton came up with the enemy behind breastworks; after a few volleys, they skedaddled, and reformed a mile beyond, behind fresh works, the other side of Pattocassey creek, tearing up Hill's Bridge; but they soon left again; the Ninth took the rebel camp at Mr. Tabor's church, about one mile beyond the creek; captured about 30 prisoners; bivouacked one wing on each side of the creek. The 17th Mass. had three or four wounded, the Ninth about the same : none seriously. When before Winton, and in bivouac, private Charles Muller, Co. A, from Newark, went into the woods for pleasure, carrying a small wooden stick in his hand, when he came up with three rebels standing under a tree, their loaded guns, with equipments, standing by their side at the tree ; to secure the arms and to tell the men that they were his prisoners, was the work of a moment, and carrying the arms himself, with the men walking before him, Charles returned to camp, still with the wooden stick in his hand. His march past the artillery and cavalry guards, and his arrival in the camp of the Ninth, caused much amusement among the men.

July 27th. Remained in bivouac ; the 1st New York Mounted Rifles, the 11th Pennsylvania Cavalry, and Stewart's Battery crossed Chowan river at Winton, having marched across from Suffolk ; they passed Pattocassey creek about 9 P. M. ; the object of this expedition seemed to be to destroy the railroad communication at Weldon ; this was to be done by the cavalry and artillery force that came from Virginia, while the forces from Newbern were to support them.

July 28th. Weather very rainy and very hot.

July 29th. In the afternoon one company of cavalry returned, with 40 to 50 prisoners, captured horses, carriages, and contrabands.

July 30th. All the cavalry and artillery returned ; they advanced about 2 miles beyond Jackson, where they met the enemy in force, and after an indecisive action returned ; the Ninth brought up the rear, marching for Winton at 12½ M. ; rained furiously ; marching very muddy ; in places the water was 3 feet deep ; the cavalry re-crossed the Chowan by 10 P. M. ; the Ninth guarded approaches to Winton ; all the troops were embarked by 12 M., and the last boat departed at 12½.

July 31st. Arrived in barracks at Newbern, at 8 P. M. ; private John Bauder, Co. A, drowned while bathing.

August 3d. Regiment paid off by Major Harbort.

August 5th. Three officers, with six men from the Ninth, went North, on recruiting service.

August 13th. Major-General Peck arrived, to take command of Department of North Carolina.

August 17th. Regimental inspection, by Captain Raulston, 81st New York Vols., Division Inspector.

August 26th. Regiment removed to Carolina City, as a sanitary measure, as there were many sick with remittent and intermittent fever; number of sick on daily report, from 200 to 250; remained at this place recuperating, and engaging in the usual company and battalion exercises.

August 31st. Regiment inspected and mustered for pay.

September 19th. Regiment inspected by Captain Raulston, 81st New York Vols., Division Inspector.

September 26th. Ass't Surgeon John M. Davies rejoined regiment at Carolina City.

October 10th. Regiment paid off.

October 12th. Ass't Surgeon F. B. Gillette ordered to report at Washington, N. C., to take charge of the 58th Penn'a Vols.

October 13th. Regiment reviewed by General Heckmann.

October 15th. Regiment received marching orders.

October 17th. Dr. J. C. Salter, Acting Hospital-steward of 9th New Jersey Vols., promoted Ass't Surgeon 1st North Carolina Union Vols. Dr. Salter was formerly a practitioner of medicine in Hague, Warren Co., N. Y., on the banks of Lake George. Upon the breaking out of the rebellion, the Doctor raised a company of artillery, with the expectation of being its commander, but owing to difficulties which subsequently existed, the company was consolidated, and he, not being willing to desert the men whom he had induced to leave their homes for a place in the army, himself enlisted among them, and was speedily appointed to the position of 1st sergeant of the 23d New York Independent Battery. In October, 1862, he was detailed to a position in the hospital department of the Ninth New Jersey Vols., and it was only the refusal of the permission of his Captain that prevented him from receiving a warrant as Hospital-steward of the Ninth. After the death of Surgeon Babbett, Dr. Salter was appointed Surgeon of the 1st North Carolina Union Vols. He earned, during the time he was with the Ninth regiment, the esteem and respect of every officer, and the love of every man,—the latter looking upon him with the fullest confidence. Dr. Salter may rest assured that he will always be remembered by the men of the Ninth for his untiring and friendly attention paid to the sick, and will find at all times the most hearty and cordial welcome by the men and families of the Ninth who were with him, or knew or heard of him.

13

October 18th. Took cars for Newbern: arrived at 7¾; embarked upon transports Albany and Jersey Blue; right wing upon former, left wing upon latter, but finding them to be too crowded, Companies A and K were left behind.

October 19th. Sailed half-hour after midnight; made Hatteras at 11 P. M., Cape Henry at 6 P. M., and arrived at Fort Monroe.

October 20th. At 9 A. M. sailed from there to Newport News, Va., and encamped near the Dock Ground; 23d, 25th, and 27th Mass., 81st and 98th New York Infantry, 3d New York Cavalry, Belger's, Riggs', and Howell's Battery subsequently arrived.

October 22d. Received marching orders at 3 P. M.; orders countermanded.

October 23d. Since our arrival Colonel J. J. Deforest had been in command of post, called Post of Mansfield, at Newport News; to-day General Heckmann took command of the post and garrison, consisting of six regiments of infantry, one of cavalry, and 3 batteries of artillery.

October 29th. Reviewed by General Heckmann.

November 2d. Reviewed by Major-General Foster; two officers returned from recruiting service; others left for that purpose.

November 10th. Ass't Surgeon F. B. Gillette ordered to take charge of post at Washington, N. C.

November 26th. Thanksgiving day; church attended by the whole Brigade; church was also held on Sunday mornings in the hospital and dispensary tents; many ladies being in camp, these assemblages were generally graced by their presence.

December 2d. Regiment paid off.

December 10th. Change of quarters and tents; the Ninth took the place and quarters of the 27th Mass., who were ordered to Norfolk.

1864.

January 1st. Sleighing in camp.

January 13th. Six officers and about 110 men, who had re-enlisted in November and December, 1863, went North, on veteran furlough. Col. A. H. Dutton, of the 21st Conn., in command of Brigade.

January 16th. Brigadier-General C. A. Heckmann left in the afternoon. The following farewell address was read to the Ninth, at dress-parade :—

HEADQUARTERS, NEWPORT NEWS, }
January 12, '64. }

General Order No. 2.

Having been relieved from the command of the Brigade, by Special Order No. 12, from Headquarters, Department of Virginia and North Carolina, I therefore bid farewell to the officers and men composing the command. The intercourse, both official and personal, between myself and those serving in the command, has been highly satisfactory, and will always be remembered with pleasure. To those troops which formed a part of my old command I bid an affectionate farewell. From my first association with them at Trenton, through the perils and affliction at Hatteras, the gallant charges at Roanoke and Newbern, the noble daring and brilliant deeds at White Oak, Southwest Creek, Kinston, Whitehall, and Goldsboro', my feeling towards them has been one of affection and pride.

Called to another command, I will continue to watch over you with unabated interest, feeling confident that your future history will be equally brilliant as the past.

By order of   C. A. HECKMANN.

W. H. ABEL, Capt. and A. A. G.

January 18th. Colonel Abram Zabriskie, of the Ninth, in charge of all the troops to attend the execution of H. C. Fuller, Co. O, 118th New York Vols., who was to be shot for desertion.

January 21st. Colonel Abram Zabriskie addressed the men of the Ninth, when on dress-parade, in regard to re-enlistment, assuring the men that he also would remain with the regiment for another three years, if God granted him life and health; in consequence of which the number required to give the whole regiment a veteran furlough, was filled the same evening.

January 22d. Major Curtis and several other officers left, with 231 men who had not re-enlisted, for Portsmouth.

January 26th. Five men of Co. F, and two of Co. I, returned from Portsmouth, to re-enlist. Ass't Surgeon F. B. Gillette re-joined regiment.

January 27th. Ass't Surgeon Gillette ordered to attend 16th New York Artillery.

January 28th. Recruits who had arrived on the 24th, went under charge of Lieut. Rogers to Portsmouth.

January 31st. Sunday; seven companies, 258 men, embarked on propeller Virginia, and three companies, 111 men, on Montauk; sailed; anchored near Fort Monroe, awaiting the paymaster.

February 1st. Paymaster arrived at 1 P. M., paying off in full all re-enlisted men who were two years in the service.

February 2d. About noon weighed anchor.

February 3d. Anchored near Jersey City.

February 4th. Weighed anchor about 11 A. M.; landed; the regiment marched through several streets of Jersey City, and partook of a collation at Taylor's Hotel. The regiment was formally received by the authorities and citizens of the city, and welcomed by the Mayor, to which Col. Abram Zabriskie responded; other speeches were made, one by Superintendent J. W. Woodruff, of the New Jersey Railroad, who remarked: "If I was the Colonel of that regiment," referring to the Ninth, "I would feel as proud as a President of the United States, and if I was the father of the Colonel of that regiment, I would feel as proud and happy as if I possessed the United States." Every effort had been made by the city to make our presence agreeable, and it was late in the afternoon when the regiment took the cars to Trenton, arriving at 8 P. M., marching to Camp Perrine.

February 5th. Governor Parker came into camp, addressed the Ninth, and taking regimental guard off, offered the men liberty and also the hospitality of the city. The men received their furloughs, dated February 6th, furlough ending March 7th. The first detachment, which had left Newport News, January 13, on board the City of Richmond, passed Fort Monroe on the 14th, arrived at New York on the 15th, and landed at Jersey City at 11 A. M. on the 16th; took cars to Trenton, at noon, where they received furloughs.

Men of the first detachment reported at Trenton on February 12th; left by cars to Philadelphia and Baltimore, arriving there at 3 A. M. of the 19th; quartered in Soldiers' Association Building; remained here on account of there being too much ice in the river; finally embarked on the 21st, on the mail-steamer Adelaide; sailed, arriving at 7 A. M., on February 22d, at Fort Monroe; went on board the Hudson; sailed to Portsmouth, arriving at 9 A. M.; took cars to Getty's Station, marching and arriving at Julian's Creek about noon; encamped. This detachment brought 41 recruits from Trenton. The first detachment received, on February 29th, an order from Colonel Steer, commanding 3d Brigade, Heckmann's Division, that 100 men should report to Col. Smith, of the 8th Connecticut, commanding post at Deep Creek, to support picket. The command started from camp at 2½ P. M., arriving at 4 P. M., at Deep Creek; met the enemy on March 1st, 7 miles beyond Deep Creek, on Dismal Swamp Canal road. Lieut. Thomas Burnett, Co. B, of the Ninth, in command of a small party of 25 men, engaged the enemy for about 15 minutes; the parties were only 9 yards apart, when the rebels opened fire from a dense thicket, at the left of our small force. The enemy was 150 infantry and 300 cavalry strong, the latter 800 yards in advance of us, masked by a bend of the road; our reserve, 70 men, was about a half-mile in rear of us, under command of Lieut. Col. Smith, 8th Connecticut, guarding a cross-road. We returned the enemy's fire immediately, and rushed into the thicket; perceiving the enemy, 150 men, moving at a double quick, with the evident intention of getting in our rear, to cut us off, we formed into the road again, retired by left flank, and, continuing to fire, at length compelled them to relinquish their design of cutting us off. We then retired slowly upon the reserve. Our loss was one killed and one wounded. A. S. Nutt, of Co. D, Veteran Vols., was killed during the engagement. He had six bullets through his body, and when it was received the day following, by our men, it had nothing on, except a shirt, drawers, and socks: the enemy had appropriated the rest of his clothing. Nutts' funeral started from camp-ground on March 1st, to Heckmann's Division Cemetery, at Getty's Station. Joel Huls, of Co. D, had six bullets through his clothing, and one through right arm and side, the ball lodging in the breast, causing death in three days; he died at the Balfour hospital, Portsmouth, where he was also buried. We took 3 prisoners; one of them remarked that their loss was one killed and two wounded. In the evening of the fight we were reinforced by 500 men, one company of cavalry, and two pieces of artillery; the following morning, March 2d, we advanced, General Heckmann in command, but the enemy would and did not stand; we followed them into North Carolina, 3 miles, when General Heckmann gave orders to countermarch. The enemy's force consisted of three regiments of infantry, one regiment of cavalry, and two full field-batteries, in command of General Ransom, and were greatly superior in numbers.

March 7th. The command reported to Col. Buchanan, at Trenton, and was ordered to Camp Perrine, near Trenton.

March 15th. The regiment, with a number of recruits, left Trenton by cars, at 8¼ A. M.; arrived at Philadelphia at 1 P. M., and at Baltimore at 11½ P. M.; quartered in Soldiers' Home.

March 16th. Embarked on steamer John Tucker; sailed at 2 P. M.; anchored at 8 P. M., at the mouth of the Rappahannock river; sailed again at 12.

March 17th. Came to Fort Monroe, at 11 A. M.; sailed again, at 11½ A. M., arriving at Portsmouth at 2 P. M. Took the cars to Getty's Station; marched to Julian's Creek; joined there with the first detachment, and the whole regiment combined again; encamped. The Ninth was again taken into Gen. Heckmann's command, which consisted of the 81st, 96th, 98th, and 139th New York, forming 1st Brigade; Ninth New Jersey Vols., 23d, 25th, and 27th Mass., forming 2d Brigade; 4th Rhode Island, 118th New York, 8th Conn., 10th and 13th N. Hampshire, forming 3d Brigade.

March 27th. First dress-parade again, after return; Col. Edgar Lee, 27th Mass., in command of 2d Brigade.

March 28th. Heavy snow-storm; snowed all night and on Wednesday forenoon; snow from 2 to 5 feet deep.

March 31st. Chaplain Carrell resigned, and since then the regiment has been without a Chaplain.

April 6th. Captain John Peter Ritter, Co. G, who was senior Captain of the regiment, and the only one who had left Camp Olden in 1861, as Captain, resigned on surgeon's certificate of disability. Captain Ritter carried with him the good-will of every brother officer and the respect of every soldier in the regiment.

April 13th. In the morning the regiment went out as parade-guard, at the execution of Charles Crampton, Co. F, 10th New Hampshire, who was sentenced to be shot for desertion; but the criminal being reprieved, the execution was postponed for seven days, and the regiment returned. Surgeon A. W. Woodhull detailed as Board to examine medical men who were candidates for position of Surgeons of regiments. Board convened at Portsmouth, Va. Colonel Abram Zabriskie ordered to preside on court-martial, at Norfolk, Va. Lieut. Col. James Stewart, Jr., in command of the regiment. Received orders for a move; regiment left at 4½ P. M.; arrived at Portsmouth at 6½ P. M.; embarked on John Tooker; sailed at 9, and arrived at Newport News, at 12, midnight.

April 14th. Weighed anchor at daylight; sailed up James river to Chucktuck river; followed Chucktuck for 3½ miles, and landed at Cherry Grove plantation; marched at 7½ A. M. a half mile in southwestern direction; halted on left of road, and rested till 9 A. M.; met 118th New York Vols. at 8 A. M.; marched at 9 towards Smithfield; met enemy; skirmished for 3½ to 4 miles; enemy retreating as we advanced; arrived at Smithfield at 4 P. M.; quartered over night in houses.

April 15th. At 7 A. M. went on board John Tooker; sailed at 9 A. M.; arrived at Portsmouth at 2 P. M., and marched into camp at Julian's Creek, where we arrived at 4 P. M.

April 20th. Company I, which had been on garrison-duty at Fort Walker, returned to the regiment.

April 26th. Left camp at Getty's Station, at 10½ P. M.; marched and arrived at Portsmouth at midnight; embarked on the steamer George Leary; weighed anchor.

April 27th. Arrived at 7 A. M., near Yorktown; troops transferred to ferry-boat Winnisimmit; landed at Yorktown at 6.20 P. M.; marched two miles above Yorktown, and encamped in open field.

April 29th. Regiment marched 6 miles towards Williamsburg; returned, and encamped near Yorktown.

April 30th. Inspection and muster for pay. Col. Abram Zabriskie returned to the regiment, and took command. Reviewed by Major-General Butler.

May 1st. Surgeon A. W. Woodhull returned to regiment.

May 3d. Order for a move; all regimental, medical and hospital stores which had not already been sent back to Norfolk and Portsmouth, were sent on board the barge Darnfield; even the indispensable stretchers. This showed, as time proved, very poor management on the part of the Surgeon and Medical Director at that time in charge of the Corps.

May 4th. Formed line at 6 A. M.; marched to and halted near the wharf; the Brigade consisted of the Ninth New Jersey, 23d, 25th, and 27th Mass.; the Ninth embarked on board the Nellie Bentz, at 10½ A. M.; sailed with barge Pilgrim in tow; steamer Wyoming, with Gen. Heckmann and staff on board, served as flagship. The whole fleet formed line about 2 P. M.; received signal to sail, about 4 P. M.; the whole fleet sailed, Wyoming ahead; went down York river, Chesapeake, and Hampton Roads, and anchored at 10 P. M., near Newport News.

May 5th. Weighed anchor at 6½ A. M.; at 10 A. M. the barge Pilgrim accidentally got loose, and ran aground; in consequence we had to stop; hailed Manhattan, but she refused assistance; hailed steamer J. Johnson, the Captain of which promised to free the barge, and either to bring or send her up, so we sailed again; about 3 P. M. men fell in by companies, and loaded arms; passed Harrison's Landing at 3½ and City Point at 4 P. M.; landed at 6 P. M., at Bermuda Hundred; marched about one mile, and bivouacked in open field. When leaving the Nellie Bentz, the Captain of the boat took an affectionate, friendly, and warm farewell of the men; he bid us God-speed, and hoped that he might see all on board again, but during the following 10 days too many embarked on their last, long voyage to a better life: their young and precious lives sacrificed on their country's altar.

May 6th. This day the summer campaign opened, which was followed by the siege of Petersburg. At 6 A. M. marched; advanced very cautiously, Heckmann's Brigade, and of this the Ninth, in advance; halted at 9 A. M., at Cobb's Hill plantation, north of Appomatox river, 3 miles from the Petersburg and Richmond Railroad. We passed a rebel camp, which they had left on the previous day; the barracks were burned down. All the troops concentrated and halted on an elevated portion of ground, on this plantation, surrounded with trees and bushes, most of which were burned down. General Heckmann, who had volunteered to attack the enemy, issued orders to the Colonels of the regiments of his Brigade to be ready for a move at 2½ P M. The Brigade, with two 3-inch Napoleon guns, marched at 3 P. M., Gen. Heckmann and staff ahead; met the enemy at Port Walthall Railroad Junction, at about 4½ P. M.; firing and engagement followed immediately. The enemy had two great advantages regarding position, the one being protected by earthworks thrown up on the other side of the railroad-track, while our men had no covering whatever; the other was, the enemy had the sun at his back, and thus shining full in the faces of our men, which permitted the enemy to aim sure, and at the same time preventing us from aiming with accuracy. The engagement lasted about two hours, and the regiment and the brigade returned about 9 P. M. to camp. The Ninth had about 4 killed and 30 wounded; the loss of the enemy could not be ascertained. When the engagement commenced, dispatch after dispatch arrived in bivouac-ground for ambulances, which gave much delay in the arrival of the wounded; stretchers were also needed: some regiments had one only, some had none; they were sent on board the barge Darnfield, when the troops were at Yorktown. Surgeon A. W. Woodhull, of the Ninth New Jersey, ordered to take charge of Brigade, and Ass't Surgeon F. B. Gillette was detailed to take charge of the 23d Mass., leaving the Ninth in charge of Ass't Surgeon Davies. The Brigade marched at 7 A. M., to the scene of yesterday's fight, the Ninth in advance, accompanied by two pieces of rifled artillery; engagement commenced early in forenoon, not with such ferocity as on the previous day, but lasting the whole day; the aim of the enemy with their artillery was very accurate: so much so, that by moving the regiment a short distance to the right it was out of range; one caisson of rebel artillery was blown up by a shell, and the enemy driven out of his position; our forces were entirely victorious at every point. The weather was very hot; a number of men returned to camp entirely exhausted; many were brought in sick with sunstroke. The regiment had one killed and ten wounded; all casualties were from spherical-case shot. About evening, the regiment and Brigade returned to camp; the house and other buildings on the Cobb's Hill plantation were torn down by our forces, to erect a fort.

May 8th. Sunday; the regiment remained in camp; heavy firing was heard in southern direction, coming from the gunboats; the enemy could be seen. About sundown 100 men of each regiment of the Brigade went on picket.

May 9th. Marched and removed camp at 4½ A. M, north of road on the same plantation, then the regiment went to the scene of action, meeting the enemy at Swift Creek, engagement commencing immediately (the fire from the enemy's battery was very heavy); the battery was soon silenced, and the enemy fell back. The regiment started for the rear of Petersburg; following the road to Petersburg for 3½ miles, the regiment crossed swamp, taking the Petersburg and Richmond Railroad track, destroying track and telegraph-line for about 3 miles; then taking turnpike again, marched 4 miles to near Petersburg, when skirmishing began, and when within 2 miles of Petersburg, we met the enemy in force, and a general engagement ensued. A notable circumstance at this time occurred,—the charge upon the 23d, 25th, and 27th Massachusetts regiments, by Hagood's Brigade, consisting of the 21st, 25th, 27th, and 7th Battalion South Carolina Vols : extremes opposed to extremes ; the one the greatest opponents to slavery, pitted against the other, the worst of traitors. A morning-report, dated May 1st, 1864, and found among other papers, at Greensboro', May, '65, after Lee's and Johnston's surrender, signed by R. F. Graham, Colonel commanding the said rebel Brigade, gives the effective strength thereof at 1,721. The engagement lasted from 12 M. till 7 P. M., when firing ceased till midnight, and the rebels made a charge on our pickets, but were driven back with heavy loss ; the regiment remained in arms the whole night ; over two hundred prisoners were taken on this day.

May 10th. After firing a few shots early in the morning, the enemy opened with artillery ; the men being exhausted from the fatigues of the previous day and night Heckmann's Brigade was relieved by Wistar's Brigade, at 10 A. M., and starting for camp, the regiment arrived at 4 P. M., having lost one killed and nine wounded.

May 11th. Remained in camp.

May 12th. Regiment and Brigade left at sunrise ; heavy rain commenced, which continued uninterruptedly till Monday evening, 16th. The first picket-firing began at 9½ A. M , and artillery-firing at 10½ A. M.; the rebel cavalry advanced by our left flank ; firing continued all day, till dark.

May 13th. Skirmishing began at 6 A. M., and the enemy was gradually driven from the whole line ; the Ninth, about two miles in advance, engaged the enemy about 2 P. M.; the engagement lasted till dark, but firing continued all night. On this evening two days' rations were cooked in camp, and sent out to the regiment, the regiment remaining in line of battle till next morning. On the morning of this day news came from the left wing of the army that the rebels were retreating towards Richmond ; the supposition was at once made, that Fort Darling was being evacuated, and General Heckmann was directed to send out a small party, to ascertain positively regarding the matter ; Capt. Samuel Hufty, Jr., with his Company I, was chosen for this undertaking, leaving the mode of procedure entirely with the Captain. Selecting a few brave men out of the Ninth, and procuring three men from the

1st U. S. Colored Cavalry, as couriers, the party started about 9½ P. M., passed without any guide beyond the picket-lines of the army, striking the James river at a distance of about one mile from the right flank of the army ; passing then under cover of the night and availing themselves of numerous deep and dark ravines up the James river, beyond the line of the enemy, until signals were observed at Fort Darling, in their front, another upon their left, apparently some 400 yards distant, another upon their left-rear, about a half-mile distant ; they also came upon one of the enemy's signal-stations, a log-hut, with a fire still burning in the fire-place ; having ascertained that the enemy still occupied the fort, with their lines the same as before dark, the party returned, without having fired a shot, or being discovered.

May 14th. The artillery opened at 6½ A. M.; our line gradually advancing; at 3 P. M. the enemy was driven from his first line of breastworks, which was near by the formidable intrenchments of a strong earth-work; the guns of this fort were silenced by our sharpshooters picking off the gunners. When the army had advanced so as to invest the fort at Drury's Bluff, Captain Hufty, with Co. I, was again sent to accompany Lieut. Forbes, of General Weitzel's staff, on a reconnoissance. They proceeded directly to the right, on the prolongation of the line of battle, driving the enemy's line of pickets, or videttes, until they reached the James river, which was about one mile from the right flank of the army ; here the country being open, our own cavalry-videttes were seen, half-a-mile to the rear. The party having accomplished their object, entered our lines again, and returned to their posts. The reconnoissance was as bold as dangerous, in regard to the country and position of the troops, and gave all credit and honor to those partaking in it. Two rebel officers, Capt. Campbell and Lieut. Gerard, of the 11th South Carolina Reg't, who were captured by the Ninth, stated that General D. A. Hill was in command of the rebel forces ; that Beauregard was hastening from Charleston, but that General Kautz had cut the line at Hixford, which left the main body of Beauregard's forces south of that point.

May 15th. Sunday ; continuous musketry and occasional artillery firing all day ; our lines held same position as on previous day ; at 12, midnight, the rebels began to flank our extreme right, held by Heckmann's Brigade, of which the Ninth held the extreme point, an open space being between it and the James river. General Heckmann, who had expected such a movement all day, had asked for reinforcements, first of Gen. Smith, and then of Gen. Butler; these two commanders either could not withdraw their troops from other points, or did not coincide with what Gen. Heckmann foresaw and foretold, and which proved afterwards too true and fatal to our cause, and our troops generally : particularly too fatal to Heckmann's Brigade.

May 16th. Night of 15th ordered entrenchments thrown up along our front. Early on the morning of 16th was attacked by five brigades of picked troops. The General, having expected the assault, was ready for it, and received them with a galling fire at short range, and forced them back. In three subsequent attacks they were repulsed with great slaughter. The enemy, being more than five times our number, and our right being open, the General ordered the Brigade to retire to a new position. In executing this movement, after having placed the Ninth in position, the General passed through a breach in the lines, and was captured. The morning was very foggy; it was impossible to see the length of a company. Before the General was captured, he said truly, and with bitterness : " I am outdone this time, when with only two sections of artillery and with one regiment and a half of infantry, as reinforcements, I would have been able to prevent the sad catastrophe." According to subsequent accounts, made by rebel prisoners and rebel official reports, " the loss of the rebels in front of this Heckmann's Brigade doubled in number the whole of that brigade!" The loss of the Ninth was ten killed, seventy-seven wounded, and seventy-five missing; the loss on Thursday, when regiment left camp, and on Friday, Saturday, and Sunday, was two killed and twenty-three wounded; making a total of twelve killed, 100 wounded, and 75 missing during this five days' engagement.

Color-sergeant George Meyers, who carried the emblem of a soldier's honor, took the same from the staff, and winding the treasure around his body, for better security, he fought like the others. Brave and heroic, as George always proved himself, the colors could not be carried by better and worthier hands.

Among the wounded in this engagement was Colonel Abram Zabriskie; he encouraged his men as much as circumstances admitted; calm and easy as ever were his orders given, noticing with quick conception the many dangers they all were in, and the extent of the great calamity. While thus engaged in encouraging the men, a ball struck him on the front part of the throat, and, passing through the windpipe, lodged in the vicinity of the spinal column, in the neck. Capt. Lawrence, who was near, was ordered to inform Lieut. Col. Stewart, who should assume command of the regiment, but Capt. Lawrence fell also, severely wounded in the leg, which had to be amputated, causing death May 30, '64, at Chesapeake hospital. Col. Z. now went himself for Lieut. Col. Stewart, and gave him the command, then leaning on Lieut. Burnett, he went to the rear; on his way, he saw some of his men in confusion, and attempted to rally them, but found that his voice failed him. Meeting General Heckmann advancing, and having, though wounded, a clear and cool comprehension of the way the fight was going, he stopped and told him the danger of our forces being surrounded—which event afterwards occurred. The Regimental Surgeon, A. W. Woodhull, in charge of Brigade hospital, dressed the wound, which he found and considered fatal at first. When under treatment of this skillful surgeon, the Colonel heeded not the surgeon's request to be quiet: his mind was with the men of his regiment, and all he said, was: " *Poor boys! poor boys! they are in a bad scrape!*" The tone in which this was spoken, proved how much he was attached to his men; how he loved them : and that his very heart was with them even in the hour of his death. Ambulances being in want, but soon expected to arrive, he was asked to wait; one, occupied by two officers of the Ninth, whose wounds made it necessary for them to lie, was ready to leave for the Army Corps hospital; there was one sitting-place at the side of the driver; this seat he took, as if to say, " I will be with you to the last." A trustworthy attendant was ordered by the Surgeon to accompany the Colonel, and to wait upon him with the greatest care. Though mortally wounded, and in great pain, and riding on a bad road, he did not ask for anything for himself; he had no wishes, no wants; his mind, his spirit, his soul, was with his regiment and the cause for which he soon should die. One question he made, inquiring what had become of the regimental colors, but no one present could answer. On Tuesday, the 17th, the Colonel was sent to Chesapeake hospital, where he arrived the next day. On the 20th his father and brother reached him; at first they were cheered by some appearance of improvement, but he soon began to sink, and, after great suffering, died on the evening of the 24th of May, eight days after receiving the fatal shot. He was not only highly-esteemed by all officers, but they looked upon him with a reverence dictated by a more noble, more sublime impulse than that of rank; it sprung from the superiority of principle, of knowledge, and of virtue, seldom found in one so young. The men respected and loved him; they looked upon him as children to their father; all called him the mother of the regiment; his orders were executed cheerfully and full of confidence, not because they knew that they were by oath bound to obey, and that punishment follows disobedience, but because they knew that no unnecessary orders would be given and nothing required except it was for the good of the cause for which they had left their homes, for the good of the regiment, or for their own benefit. The toast given by Superintendent Woodruff, on the occasion of a collation given to the veterans of the Ninth, on February 4th, may be said to have expressed, so far as regards Colonel Zabriskie, the opinion of every member of the Ninth, as there is no doubt but that all would have parted with that most dear to them to have saved his life.

With permission of Mr. A. O. Zabriskie, the following has been taken from a memorial issued at the time of the Colonel's death, by the members of the Bar of Hudson county.

"COLONEL ABRAM ZABRISKIE, the third son of Mr. A. O. Zabriskie—well-known to all Jerseymen, and a leader at the Bar of this State,—was born at Hackensack, N. J., February 18th, 1841. He was lineally descended from one of a family honored in Polish history, who found a refuge in this country, and settled in the county of Bergen, more than two centuries ago. The blood of the Huguenots and Hollanders also flowed in his veins. Contemplating the example, and imbibing the spirit of an ancestry devoted to civil liberty, may have stimulated this devotion to his country when in peril.

"Having lost his mother in boyhood, in 1849, he removed with his father to Jersey City, where, as well as at Edgehill School, he attended to his preparatory studies. He entered the College of New Jersey in 1856, and graduated 1859. From childhood he was distinguished by firmness of purpose, strong will, clear intellect, and capacity to master whatever he undertook. Upon leaving college, he entered his father's office, and prosecuted, until he joined the army, the study of the law as a profession.

"The elements of a strong character find occasions in which to manifest themselves, and the cool intrepidity of young Zabriskie was remarkably exhibited in a melancholy event that occurred at Long Branch in the summer of 1860. His elder brother, in company with his sisters and another young lady, had inadvertently got within the power of one of those resistless eddies that sometimes, after storms at sea, form along that beach, and are unseen on the surface. His sister became separated from her brother, and for a while was floating alone on the current. His brother, by determined effort, finally succeeded in reaching the shore with the other lady, his physical energies exhausted. Good swimmers having been attracted by the cry of distress and the sight of the danger, had swam towards them to render assistance. Two were forced back by the sea; two others, Dr. Dummer, of Jersey City, and Mr. Whitaker, of Trenton,—disinterested and determined men, and the best swimmers on the beach,—pushed to the rescue, but, powerless against the strong eddy, were overpowered, and lost their lives in the heroic effort. Abram Zabriskie, walking on the beach, heard the cry, and saw the peril;—an athletic swimmer, he plunged in, and taking a different course, swam to his sister; but, when he attempted to return with her, found himself seized by the current that had overwhelmed the others. It was a struggle for the lives of them both. For a short time the result was doubtful. His coolness and energy, by the aid of a kind Providence, enabled him to save his sister and himself from a watery grave. All this was the work of a few minutes, and when he stepped on shore, he saw that men in a boat were attempting the rescue of Dr. Dummer, and that Mr. Ardaugh, a young lawyer, from Trenton, who had gone to the assistance of Mr. Whitaker, and had reached him, was struggling with the sea, in peril. His quick perception instantly saw a means of help that had escaped the observation of others; he seized the bathing-rope, and moved towards the sea. His only response to the call of his father, who had witnessed the painful scene, was the holding up of the coil of rope, and rushing into the surf. The gentleman from Trenton, completely exhausted,

had given the body of Mr. Whitaker to a fisherman, and barely
reached the shore himself. By means of the rope, the fisherman,
the body of Mr. Whitaker, and Zabriskie were, by those on shore,
drawn to the beach. The unselfish bravery, the quick, cool dis-
cernment and energy which the youth of nineteen years evinced
in thus, under God's guidance, rescuing a loving sister and the fisherman from imminent danger, won the admiration of all, and was a
promise, afterwards fulfilled, of what his country might expect of
him when in equal peril.

"In the winter of 1860–'61, young Zabriskie had prepared himself to spend the ensuing year in the tour of Europe. He expected
to sail with the Hon. Wm. L. Dayton, deceased, our late Minister
at Paris. Then Sumter fell; his patriotism was roused. During
the absence of his father who, with others, had left home for Trenton, to aid in military arrangements, he gave up his state-room,
brought back the passage-money, and throwing down the gold,
said : ' *I am not going* to Europe ; I will stay, and do my part in
this war.' The inspiration that moved him to resist the fiendish
purpose which sought the destruction of our free institutions, was
paramount to the attractions which foreign travel presents to the
intelligent, educated youth of our country. Yes ; it was paramount
to his attachment to life, surrounded as it was with all the appli-
ances of happiness.

"His military career commenced, as the history of the Ninth
already shows, in September, 1861. His sickness, a combination
of typhoid fever and pneumonia, contracted by close confinement
on crowded transports, struggle on the sea, exposure at Roanoke,
was the first sickness of his life. It held him for weeks on the
verge of the grave.

"His noble deeds and achievements while with the Ninth, up to
the time of his fatal wound, have been told already. They were
acknowledged by the Governor and State of New Jersey, with
promotions : entering the service as Adjutant, in October, 1861 ;
receiving the Colonelcy in January, 1863, and yet not 22 years
of age. He commanded qualities, reputation. and position which
constitute the dignity of man. His tall, athletic figure indicated
his vigor. His ability, courage, patriotism, and disinterestedness
had been so proven that no one doubted. He commanded a regiment whose exploits had been more than once recognized by the

Legislature of New Jersey, and they were ready to meet death at the command of their Colonel. He was the pride of a large circle of influential friends, and his State was proud of him. But he had now done his part in this war, and his work was to be sprinkled with his blood. That keen eye was to become dim, that voice was to falter, and that manly energy to be paralyzed. He is gone."

The Common Council of Jersey City held a special meeting on Friday, May 27th, 1864, the members receiving a communication from His Honor the Mayor, in regard to the death of Colonel Zabriskie. Resolutions were passed, and the Board resolved to attend the funeral.

The *American Standard*, of May 28, 1864, published his funeral and obituary. Rev. Dr. Campbell, of Rutgers' College, N. J., pronounced an eloquent discourse on the deceased.

The *Newark Daily Advertiser*, of May 27, 1864, and the *American Standard*, of June 1st, 1864, also several other religious and other papers, referred in long articles to his life, death, and funeral; all lamenting, like the men of his regiment, his early loss.

Colonel Zabriskie was buried on Saturday afternoon, May 28th, 1864, in Greenwood Cemetery. The funeral ceremonies were conducted in the First Dutch Reformed Church, by Rev. Dr. Campbell, President of Rutgers' College.

While home with the regiment on veteran furlough, in February, 1864, a company of about thirty of the most respectable citizens assembled on Saturday, at 3 P. M., at the residence of A. O. Zabriskie, Esq., for the purpose of presenting to his son, Colonel Abram Zabriskie, a magnificent sword, belt, gloves, and aiguilette, as a token of their esteem. The presentation-speech was made by I. W. Scudder, Esq., as follows :—

"COLONEL ZABRISKIE : To be held in high appreciation by one's friends and neighbors is one of the greatest charms of life. Your friends and neighbors have come together, to testify their warm admiration for your patriotism and courage. Nurtured in ease and affluence ; surrounded by those incidents which make life pleasant and agreeable ; preparing for a profession which rewards those who labor in it with assiduity with high honors, you could not remain at ease when your country called. The roar of the cannon aimed at the Government erected by your fathers,—which has brought peace and prosperity to so many millions of people,—aroused you to energy and action, and you joined that illustrious band of patriots and heroes who were determined not to survive the destruction of the Union.

"With deep solicitude we have watched your course ; we observed the coolness and courage which marked your conduct when a noble-hearted Jerseyman, Col. Allen, was overwhelmed in the waves; Roanoke Island, Goldsboro', Kinston, and Whitehall attest your valor.

"We found you, at the commencement of your military career, a First Lieutenant and Adjutant, now we hail you as a leader of a gallant regiment, and on the honorable road to promotion.

"It has been boastfully said that the South gave to their cause the best blood of their sons. We, too, have sent, from the ranks of ease and elegance in social life, those who preferred freedom and constitutional government to arbitrary power. We feel that freedom and constitutional government ought to command as much of sacrifice and devotion as treason and tyranny.

"When we look to the great North : full of trade, business, and enterprise; engaged in great schemes of improvement; in commerce and manufactures; where the harvests are sown and reaped in security and plenteousness;—where the cataract, which leaps from the mountain-side, and coursing through the valleys, turns the wheels of successful business;—where there is an undoubted confidence in public security ; and ask ourselves from whence spring all these happy results in the midst of civil war ? the answer is, We owe these blessings to the valor of our armies and the skill of our officers; we owe these triumphs to such men as you.

"The North has, with undoubted confidence, trusted their fate to the Army, and the very peace and security in which we live is the most flattering eulogium that can be bestowed on those who carry the bayonet and wield the sword. Should our Army return with defeat and disaster, then discord, anarchy, and confusion would prevail here. Successful war in the South is peace in the North, and friendship in Europe. If we succeed, non-intervention will be the watch-word of European politics, and, above and beyond all, it will produce here a triumph of freedom, union, and constitutional government. You and your compatriots are battling for peace here, the restoration for the Union, and a proud position for our own nation among the people of the earth. We, therefore, hail you on this occasion as a representative of that grand army which has made its triumphant march along the banks of the Mississippi; which has stormed the heights of Vicksburg; which has raised the standard of the Union at New Orleans; which thunders at the gates of Charleston; which has penetrated North Carolina, rescued Kentucky and Tennessee, and which will not stay its victorious march until it shall reach the Gulf of Mexico.

"New Jersey is proud of her gallant sons, and your name will be recorded among the illustrious men who have taken up arms in defence of that which is most inestimable, the right of self-government.

"In presenting to you this emblem of professional pride, I have no special charge to make. It has been won by your skill and valor, and whenever you shall wield it, we know it will be in the thickest of the fight, and our prayer to God is that it may always flash with the beams of victory."

After which, Col. Abram Zabriskie made the following modest, manly, and dignified response :—

"MR. SCUDDER : I accept, with feelings of gratitude and pride, the beautiful present you have tendered me in the name of many citizen-friends of New Jersey. I thank you, gentlemen, for the gift of this sword ; I thank you, even more, for the feelings that prompted it ; and I thank you, sir, for the words of compliments and encouragement with which it was presented.

"The soldier, gentlemen, values a testimonial of this kind far more than you can think. Separated, as he necessarily is, from all the former associations of his life ; separated from all the amenities and comforts of his home ; undergoing many hardships, and encountering many dangers, it excites his patriotic zeal, enlarges his pride in his profession, and incites him to a more earnest performance of his duties as a soldier, to know that he is not forgotten by his friends, to know that his fellow citizens are watching his course with interest ; that they are ever willing to offer him their encouragement and assistance, and will do him justice according to his deserts. This smooths the roughness of his path of duty, and teaches him that his conduct is not unregarded, and will not be unrewarded.

"I accept this sword, gentlemen, as a New Jersey soldier, and I accept it with the proud boast that I am one of a band of volunteers that have never, on any occasion, dishonored themselves, their State, the uniform they wear, or the flag under whose folds they fight. The history of many a battle proves their efficiency, and the bodies of New Jersey's dead, now mouldering in numberless unknown graves, and the soil of almost every rebel State, testify to their unflinching execution of their dangerous and bloody duties ; almost every military Department has felt the benefit of their services, and every army has acknowledged its indebtedness to the soldiers of New Jersey, from the Mississippi to the Atlantic, from Roanoke Island, first, until Chattanooga, last, in many a battle. The soldiers of New Jersey have never fought but to fight well, and while doing their duty to the common country, have always reflected honor on their State and on themselves, and in every hard-fought field, bloodily won, or still more bloodily lost, the banner of New Jersey, floating in unison with the sacred emblem of the nation, has ever marked the spot where brave men were fighting, and where brave men were falling ; and as one of New Jersey's volunteer-soldiery, as *one* whom she has honored with an important trust, I accept from you, my fellow-citizens, and I accept with feelings of grateful pride, this testimonial of your confidence and regard."

Lieut. Col. James Stewart, Jr., was severely wounded in thigh ; Adjutant E. S. Carrell, son of the late Chaplain Carrell, and Captain Edwin Stevens Harris, were among the dead. The latter was shot through the breast. He was a son of the Rev. N. Sayre Harris, of Hoboken, N. J.; was born in Philadelphia; graduated at St. Timothy's Hall, Maryland, where he received the rudiments of a military education ; promoted to a Captaincy in '63, he resigned, with a view to the taking command of a battery of artillery ; anticipated in this, he was re-appointed to his Company ; he terminated his military service leading his men in a bloody slaughter. Captains Burnett, Hopper, and Townley, and Lieuts. Brown and Shephard were also wounded. Among the missing were Lieuts. Drake and Peters. Many privates were wounded, two, three, and more times. Private G. A. Reinhard received a fearful wound behind his left ear, the ball entering head; he fell; his intimate friends and comrades, who were nearest to him, believed him dead, and he was left on the battle-field. After two days, he was picked up by the enemy, and sent to a hospital in Richmond ; being a German, and not speaking English, he was most fortunate, coming under treatment of a German physician ; awaking from a sound sleep, on the third morning after his arrival in the hospital, the fifth day after he was wounded, he took out of his mouth the Minnie ball. After two months' stay in rebel hospital, he was removed to the Libby. He was in Andersonville, Savannah, and various other rebel prisons; finally being exchanged, he was sent to Newark hospital, and joined the regiment again January 27, '65 ; deaf from wound received, eyesight weakened from exposure and sufferings in rebel prisons, he remains a cripple for life.

May 17th. Captain Samuel Hufty, Jr., in command of the regiment ; Colonel J. Pickett in temporary command of the Brigade. Camp removed to place occupied upon our arrival, May 6th.

May 18th. General George J. Stannard in command of the Brigade. Continued artillery and musketry firing along the whole line ; more troops arrived, marching to the scene of action ; about noon, the regiment moved quarter of a mile south, close to the woods, and threw up breastworks.

May 19th. Again very foggy ; heavy cannonading west of camp.

May 20th. During the night the regiment was twice called out ; at 2 A. M. the enemy made a fierce assault on our centre, but was repulsed; at 5 A. M. the assault was repeated, and again repulsed; this time we captured Major-General Walker, several other rebel officers, and a number of soldiers.

May 21st. Major-General Butler sent, with a flag-of-truce, word to the enemy to exchange Major-General Walker for Brigadier-General Heckmann: this was refused; the rebels were not willing to exchange a Brigadier-General for a Major-General. This is, and ever will be, a great compliment to Brigadier-General Heckmann. It shows how much the enemy valued his capture, and how much averse they were to again have pitted against them a man of his fighting abilities. The cannonading continued during the day, and an attack was made on our right centre, but the enemy was repulsed.

May 22d. Regiment inspected by Captain Wilcox; regiment remained in camp; artillery and musketry firing all day; the firing from the gunboats was uninterrupted. Major-General Smith requested four men from the Ninth, to be sent by him as scouts into the rebel lines. Privates James Van Buskirk and Robert White, of Co. B, and privates Marshall Howell and Daniel Johnson, of Co. H, volunteered themselves, and were accepted for the dangerous and difficult undertaking. The first two were taken prisoners when only 200 yards from Petersburg; they were threatened to be hung. From the headquarters of General Beauregard they were sent to Andersonville and Savannah, prisoners; from here Van Buskirk was sent to Millen prison, remaining there 3 months; he was paroled, and returned to Annapolis, Md., where he was exchanged, and joined the regiment again on March 13, '65, suffering from scurvy, anasarca, and general debility, contracted during 10 or 11 months of life in the various rebel prisons. White was sent to Wiensburg (Florida) prison; exchanged after Lee and Johnston's surrender, and returned to the regiment in May, '65. Marshall Howell, who left camp at 4 P. M., noticed, when passing our outer cavalry-picket post, the rebel cavalry-picket guard only fifty yards in front of him; taking the woods to the right, he was not observed, but two other rebel pickets noticed and fired upon him, but without injuring him. Following and hiding himself in the woods, he finally came in the rear of the rebel pickets, in an open field, about one mile from Adams Mill, which had been burned; taking position in a ravine, on the very spot which Major-General

Smith had described to him, and instructed him where to take his post of observation. He saw the enemy engaged in reconstructing the railroad-track, which had been destroyed by our forces: also two battalions, with two stand of colors, and about 150 of our men, who had been captured, which passed close by him; remaining at his post from 7½ A. M. till 11 A. M.,—over three hours—he started back, not observing anything till he came to the mill at Walthall Junction; again turning to the right, and passing the same outer posts, he came in camp again, at 6 P. M.; reported to Major-General Smith, at 8 P. M., who, satisfied with his exploit, furnished him with the proper recommendation to Major-General Butler; upon reporting himself to Major-General Butler, the following morning, this officer paid Howell the promised reward of five hundred dollars in cash, for his daring and perilous enterprise. The fourth scout, Daniel Johnson, left camp in company with Howell, but leaving Howell also, he remained about two hours, somewhere on the Petersburg and Richmond railroad-track, on Butler's line, when he returned into camp.

May 25th. Heard in camp locomotive going over the road which had been destroyed by our forces on May 9th.

May 26th. At 10½ A. M. the bugle sounded for another move; the regiment marched about 11 A. M., and returned about 2 P. M.; the alarm was caused by picket-firing, south of camp. Late in the evening, such of the regiment which were not already on duty, marched north of camp, on picket.

May 27th. Ordered to move; marched about noon four miles; halted and encamped.

May 28th. Marched about dark; crossed Appomattox by pontoon-bridge, at Point of Rocks; marched then about 6 miles south of the river, and bivouacked in a wheat-field, within one mile of City Point.

May 29th. Marched early in the morning, to City Point, when nine companies embarked on steam transport Thames, and one company, I, on steamer Vidette; received orders to sail at 5 P. M., and to await General Martindale's orders at Fort Monroe; started at 5½ P. M. The Thames ran aground about 8 P. M., near Jamestown; the steamer Eastern State, which had the 23d Mass. and 89th New York Vols. on board, also ran aground, close by our side.

May 30th. Aground all day; several officers and men went ashore, over to Jamestown, which is one of the oldest settlements in the State of Virginia. The meeting-house is a very old structure, and in the neighboring burying-ground are monuments with inscriptions dated as far back as 1684.

May 31st. The ferry-boat Winnisimmit, which came to our relief, took also the 23d Mass. and about 600 men of the 89th New York on board; this crowded this old boat very much, even to such an extent that it seemed we would fare worse now on the Winni-simmet, than to remain on the Thames; although the difference between a cold drowning on the former, and being without provision or water on the latter is very slight. We sailed, and arrived near Fortress Monroe before sundown; here we not only ran aground again in front of the steamboat-landing, but another fatality was in store for us; the Winnisimmit had to call five times for a tug-boat, and then it was long before one came in sight. In want and need of water and provision, the Captain called first for water; it was an hour before the large steamer Massachusetts tried to run up to us; the Captain of this boat, not knowing the condition we were in, ran aground also, and found much difficulty in freeing himself. After the steamer Washington had come close enough to take the men of the 89th New York on board, the Ninth was enabled to go on board the Massachusetts, early on the following morning.

June 1st. We sailed at 3 A. M., with barge C. Gant in tow; the men received good, but not sufficient water, also two rations, or one loaf of bread, and a small piece of good bacon, already cooked. Sailing up the York river, we followed the Pamunkey river, with its windings, east, west, north and south, as there is perhaps not another on this continent nor in Europe with its picturesque scene-ries. Coming to White House landing, we passed, on both sides, a number of vessels of all descriptions, some of them with four, five, and six lights of different colors; it was a grand and beautiful spectacle, reminding one more of the entering of one of the greatest ports of the new or old world, instead of approaching of a nearly unknown place which, previous to the war, could hardly be found on any map.

June 2d. Landing, we met Ass't Surgeon F. B. Gillette, who had been with Co. I, on board the Vidette. Company I had already advanced to the front, Gen. Stannard leaving orders for the regi-ment to follow as soon as it arrived. Marching about 11 A. M., we crossed the Richmond and York Railroad, at Summit station ; we passed several wealthy plantations, among others, Dr. Webb's, which showed that their owners had been in good circumstances : but did not see any male people, not even a negro, and we bivouacked over night in the bushes, near Masson's Mill.

June 3d. Surgeon A. W. Woodhull and Ass't Surgeon John M. Davies were ordered to report at 18th Army Corps hospital ; Ass't Surgeon F. B. Gillette with the regiment. Marched to Cold Harbor ; met a great number of wounded, returning to the rear, mostly wounded in arm or hand ; arriving at Cold Harbor, the regiment went immediately into engagement, between Cold Harbor and Gaines' Mill : the Ninth, being in the front line, found itself greatly exposed to the certain aim of the rebel sharpshooters, as well as to the fire of the whole rebel line, there not being sufficient breastworks, and no shovels, no picks, or anything else on hand to work with, the men of the Ninth loosened the ground with their pocketknives and bayonets, threw it up with their tin-cups and bare hands ; the progress was slow, but finally accomplished, and our men were entrenched like moles, with clay. Late in the afternoon, engineers arrived to build a new fort ; to prevent this, the rebels charged, but we, expecting the assault, they were received with grape, canister, and small shot. The engagement lasted about one hour ; after half-an-hour's rest it was renewed, and lasted till dark, when it entirely ceased for the night. The fighting had been very bloody and murderous on this day ; the wounded and dead were carried in the whole night.

June 4th. The fighting was continued on the whole line.

June 5th. The Ninth was relieved from picket-duty, on which it had gone on previous day, and returned to breastworks at evening ; heavy firing on both sides.

June 6th. The picket-firing was during the night uninterrupted, and during the day the balls of the sharpshooters fell frequent and well-aimed. General Burnside sent, in the afternoon, a flag-of-truce to cease firing for three hours, so as to bury the dead and carry in the wounded, of whom great numbers lay between the two front lines of the contending armies ; this the rebels at first refused to accept, while our men continued to work on their earthworks, but it came finally to an understanding. Surgeon A. W. Woodhull, of the Ninth, was in charge of the flag-of-truce ; the sight which met the eye was sufficient to affect the hardest heart: as sad as it is impossible to describe. Graves were dug, and the dead buried by hundreds; wounded were carried in, who had lain on the battle-field over three days and nights, their wounds being filled with maggots. After the time had expired, firing commenced again, shells were thrown; the Army Corps hospital had to be moved, and the regimental hospital digged its quarters close in the rear of the regiment, as the Minnie-balls were not as frequent as the shells and solid shot. At that time we were, in direct line, only seven miles from Richmond. At evening, when our music-bands played rebel tunes, the rebels ceased firing, and cheered, but as soon as " Dixie," or others contrary to their feelings were played, they would groan like marmots, firing also in the direction where they believed the bands to be.

June 7th, 8th, and 9th, it was the same.

June 10th. The fire of the sharpshooters was uninterrupted and accurate. A sutler who was a sharper, accomplished even above his fellows, but who also possessed more courage than is usually found among this class, came up to the front with a cart full of goods, mostly chewing-tobacco, which he knew the men wanted much ; his prices were shameful, asking five dollars for a small piece of tobacco, formerly sold for 25 cents; this vampire of human blood and marrow wanted to become independent too fast; the ball of a rebel sharpshooter delivered the usurer of his ambition, and closed his book of abominable trade : the men in retaliation now appropriated his tobacco, and his body, with cart and horse, was sent to his friends at White House landing.

June 11th. The firing, particularly the artillery-firing, was very heavy ; mortar-shells were also thrown, and many rifle-pits were dug deeper; 18th Army Corps hospital moved further to rear.

June 12th. The Army Corps hospital moved to White House landing, and broke up ; all medical officers detached to it joined their regiments again. In afternoon, the Ninth received orders to prepare for a move ; left the rifle-pits at 8 P. M.; marched three miles, halted till troops who came by different roads arrived, when march was resumed, the Ninth bringing up the rear. If the rebels had known of our leaving, and followed us, they would have had a good chance of thinning our ranks, but they kept up shelling at random. The total loss of the Ninth at Cold Harbor, from the 3d until this day, was five killed and thirty wounded. During our stay, two buglers, belonging to the stretcher-corps, were picked up by the provost-guard, for tarrying and loafing in the rear, when their services were much needed in the front; as this was considered cowardice, they were tied for two hours to a tree in the front, by order of the General commanding.

June 13th. Regiment marched the whole night, eighteen miles; arrived at White House landing, 8 A. M.; rested; at 3 P. M., in nine companies embarked on board Albany, and Co. I on Claymont. Surgeon A. W. Woodhull and Ass't Surgeon J. M. Davies joined the regiment at White House landing.

June 14th. The Albany arrived at Bermuda Hundred at 9 P.M.; landed 10½ P. M.; marched four miles, and bivouacked in open field.

June 15th. Marched early in morning, to report to Brigadier-General Turner, by order of General Terry, commanding Division; halting near Point of Rocks, the order was countermanded, when we returned to camp-ground occupied on the 28th of May; receiving another marching order at 9 P. M., the regiment marched to near Weier Bottom Church; nine companies of the Ninth, and a part of the 23d Mass., all that were present from General Stannard's, formerly Heckmann's Brigade, were, with troops in similar condition, united under the name of Provisional Brigade, commanded by Col. W. B. Barton, of the 48th New York Vols.; this command was also temporarily transferred to the 16th Army Corps.

June 16th. Thursday; marched about 9 A. M. outside of our breastworks; entered rebel entrenchments, when skirmishing commenced, which lasted the whole day; the regiment destroyed two telegraph-lines running to and from the dwelling of a wealthy farmer. The owner had left, and the building had twice been used as the headquarters of Gen. Beauregard. Meeting the enemy twice, each time a short engagement ensued; once the rebels charged, but were repulsed; passing again by the aforesaid buildings, everything was set on fire; in an ice-house was found some ice, which came very acceptable, as the day was very hot; coming to the railroad, which had once been destroyed on the 9th of May, and since reconstructed by the rebels, the track was again torn up for about one mile; passing a very carefully, regularly built rebel fort, it was leveled down by our men. About sundown we entered our breastworks again; the enemy, who had been reinforced and followed us on our return, fired volley after volley when we entered our breastworks, but did us no harm. The regiment had marched on this day in different directions about thirty-five miles.

June 17th. Our pickets had been driven in on the previous night, at a place where Lieut. Pullen, of Co. H, of the Ninth, had charge of picket-post; the Colonel of the 8th Conn. arrived, inquiring whether the rebels held our lines or not, ordering Lieut. Pullen to send a trustworthy man to find out, and knowing Marshall Howell's particular shrewdness, Lieut. Pullen chose him. Howell, as usual, willingly consented, and again fulfilled the trust put in him, to the entire satisfaction of the General commanding, having been so close to the rebel lines as to drink water out of a well at which he saw the rebels filling their canteens just before he came up to it. Remained in camp.

June 18th. Ass't Surgeon John M. Davies, who had been with Company I, on board the Claymont, returned, informing us that Company I was with Gen. Stannard, doing Brigade Provost duty. Terrible artillery-firing was heard towards Petersburg.

June 19th. Sunday; the firing ceased, as if by mutual consent, to observe the day of rest. Surgeon A. W. Woodhull detached on hospital-transport Hero, of Jersey.

June 21st. Marched at 12½ A. M.; marched four miles; halted; resuming march at 8 A. M., we crossed the Appomattox by pontoon-bridge; took Broadway pike, which we followed for 5 miles; halted; rested two hours; marching again, we twice crossed the Petersburg and City Point Railroad; marched till 12 M., when we halted and rested; heavy cannonading was heard in front of us; here Ass't Surgeon F. B. Gillette received orders to take charge of the 55th Penn'a Vols. About 7 P. M. the regiment marched into the rifle-pits, taking position on the first line, in the centre, in front of the enemy; when marching to the front, Ass't Surgeon John M. Davies was ordered to the field-hospital, leaving the men without a medical officer, in the face of the enemy, and at the commencement of a bloody fight.

June 22d. Ass't Surgeon F. B. Gillette, of the Ninth, who was detached to the 55th Penn'a Vols., offers to attend to the Ninth New Jersey, also; the two regimental hospital departments joined and located together; at 11 P. M. the enemy charged, under heavy artillery-firing, but was repulsed; the Ninth had one killed.

June 23d. The firing continued all day; the Brigade consisted of Ninth New Jersey, 23d, 25th, and 27th Mass., 89th New York, 55th Penn'a, and 5th Maryland. At night the last six regiments were relieved, and moved one-and-a-half miles back of breastwork to encamp, or rather bivouac, in a ravine near a small creek; as enough troops had not arrived to relieve all, the Ninth volunteered to remain for two more days in the breastworks.

June 24th. Heavy cannonading on both sides; the rebels charged, but yelled too soon, as they were driven back, and our batteries advanced; the engagement lasted two hours; we took about thirty prisoners; picket and sharpshooter's firing was kept up all day; the regiment had two wounded this day.

June 25th. The rebels charged on our left at 8 A. M., but were driven back, after half-an-hour; in about one hour the attack was renewed on our right-centre, where mostly fresh colored troops were stationed, who became entirely demoralized, and, in the excitement, turned firing on our own men, wounding a large number; finally the rebels were repulsed. The intention of the rebels was to prevent the erection of a new line of breastworks in our front; the regiment had been relieved from the first, or front line of breastworks, and had already passed by the second and third line of breastworks, when the above charge was made; the regiment halted on the turnpike, in the rear of the third or last line of breastworks, to await the result. In this position the men were much exposed to the exploding of shells and dropping of solid-shot. The Ninth had one killed this day.

June 26th. Colonel A. Piper, of the 10th New York Artillery, in charge of the Brigade; at night, the rebels charged four times on our left, and were repulsed each time with heavy loss; the Ninth encamped about half-a-mile in rear of the breastworks, on a plantation belonging to Charles Frane, a resident of Petersburg; the dwelling stood on the top of a hill, offering a splendid view of Petersburg, only two miles distant, and served for Gen. Smith's headquarters.

June 27th. Many soldiers belonging to regiments in our brigade shot their fingers off; the regiment moved in afternoon to the front again, and held the first line of breastworks.

June 28th. Several mortar-shells exploded to the right, front, and left of regimental hospital position; one of these exploded above hospital-pit, and destroyed a rocking-chair, which had been taken from a neighboring building, and on which the acting hospital steward sat only half-a-minute previous; he had a narrow escape. Several pieces, of one, two, and three pounds weight, passed through the timber and bushes at the top of the rifle-pit, the dirt blinding one man for several days. The regimental hospital was moved further to the rear, and located near Gen. Turner's headquarters.

June 29th. Early in the morning, Lieut. Pullen, of Co. H, of the Ninth, was struck by a piece of shell on the right shoulder-blade, and five men of the 55th Penn'a Vols, under charge of Ass't Surgeon F. B. Gillette, were severely wounded by one shell. The regiment moved in the second line of breastworks; was relieved at night, and went into the skirmish line in front of the breastworks during the night.

June 30th. The regiment was relieved, and returned to the ravine, to rest. Received notice of Lieut. Col. Stewart's having been promoted Colonel, Major Curlies Lieut. Colonel, and Captain S. Hufty, Jr., Major: commissions dated June 15, '64. The regiments forming Brigade changed, Brigade consisting of the Ninth New Jersey, 23d, 25th, and 27th Mass., 55th Penn'a, and 10th New York. In the afternoon, the 89th and 98th New York, 5th Maryland and 112th Penn'a, one Division of engineers, two companies of pioneers, and one colored regiment marched to the front at the left; heavy cannonading and lively musketry was soon heard in that direction; the engagement lasted two hours, when the enemy was driven back, and the above regiments, who had marched out for support, returned. The regiment was inspected and mustered.

July 1st. The regiment moved in the first line of breastworks; during the night Petersburg was shelled from our forts, the rattling of stones, bricks, and lumber of destroyed buildings, could be plainly heard, also at intervals the fall of our heavy mortar-shells which were thrown over; soon a fire broke out in the city, the flames and smoke of which could be seen till noon the next day. The churches, foundries, machine-shops and fire-engine bells tolled forth the fate of the doomed city; a general engagement ensued also to our left, which lasted about three hours; the regimental loss was one killed and three wounded; the one killed, Robert J.

Sloan, of Co. G, had been wounded at Walthall, May 7th, again at Swift Creek, on the 12th, and was shot through forehead, ball entering the right and coming out of the left temple; he was shot while rising from the sink-pole. Isaac Myers, Colonel Stewart's servant, who had gone North with the Colonel when he (the Col.) was wounded, returned to the regiment with the news that the Colonel would soon follow; this pleased the men very much; contented faces could be seen and met with all over. The regiment moved in the evening from the first to the third, or rear-line of the breastworks.

July 2d. Unusual quiet during the day.

July 3d. Sunday; divine service in one of the farm-houses near General Smith's headquarters; in the afternoon, several shots were fired from our batteries over into Petersburg; about 4 P. M., three men of the 11th Connecticut, who had remained behind, without being excused by the medical officer, were drummed out of camp, to the front; their hair was closely cut and shaved; they had also a board hanging on their backs, with the word "Straggler" written on it. These three men, and several others who had been punished, deserted a few days after. At dark, the rebels threw solid shot and shell in quick succession over to our side, which was promptly answered by our forces; the duel lasted some time; several shells exploded around and near the regimental hospital location; one shell took a man's leg off, wounding two others in the arm; this man passing about 8 feet in front of our hospital.

July 4th. The reported and much spoken of attack on this day did not happen. The Anniversary day of Independence began and passed away very quietly.

July 5th. At night, regiment moved to front again: held second line of breastworks, the left connecting with Gen. Turner's right.

July 6th. Many shells exploded, and solid shot fell into the rifle-pits of our men; at evening followed the usual artillery-duel, which was followed by a peaceable night.

July 7th. In the evening the regiment was relieved from the breastworks; returned to camp; no casualties, but the number of sick was fast increasing.

July 8th. The rebels charged on our right; were received by musketry, and as soon as our small guns ceased firing, our batteries opened with such quickness and accuracy that the rebel bat-tories were soon silenced, and the rebels driven back; the pickets of our 2d and 5th Corps, and such of the rebels in front of them, agreed to stop all unnecessary firing, particularly the picket-firing, till a general engagement should ensue. The men on either side went out of their pits, took off their equipments, and laid down to rest and sleep. It so happened that one rebel, either carelessly or purposely, fired his gun, the ball lodging in the upper rail of one of our rifle-pits; in an instant, all were on their feet and to arms, when a rebel officer with a white flag appeared, inquiring if any one had been hurt; being told that the ball went into a rail, he asked for the rail, and punished the man who had fired his piece, by compelling him to carry the wooden pole in front of their first line of works for the whole day, remarking, loud enough for all the men on both sides to hear it : "The Yankees kept the bargain that was made, and my men shall do the same."

July 9th. The regiment went into the breastworks, holding the second line; all quiet during the day and night.

July 10th. Major Samuel Hufty, Jr., had formerly requested that Ass't Surgeon John M. Davies might be ordered back to the regiment, as Ass't Surgeon F. B. Gillette was with the 55th Penn'a, and the sick required more medical aid; Ass't Surgeon F. B. Gillette had also made a request for the same purpose, approved by the Surgeon in charge of Brigade. In consequence, however, of severe illness, Ass't Surgeon John M. Davies went to Fortress Monroe hospital; after making another request to be returned to his regiment, stating that the sickness of Dr. Davies was likely to continue; that the number of sick of the Ninth required all attention from its own physician; that Surgeon Merrick, of the 55th, was at the Corps hospital; and that it was necessary for the good of all the men that they should have the care of its own Surgeon, Ass't Surgeon F. B. Gillette was finally ordered back to the Ninth. In the afternoon was divine service in almost every regimental camp, and at evening prayer-meeting in one of the houses, at General Smith's headquarters; with the exception of the picket-firing, the night passed quietly. This picket-firing, so annoying, and so very unnecessary in most cases, was generally done by the negroes, as these troops need the sound of cannon-balls around their heads and ears to keep their eyes open. Regimental loss on this day : one mortally wounded.

July 11th. The regiment held the third or rear-line of breast-works during day; returned to camp in the evening; regimental loss, one killed and one wounded; at dark, it rained just enough to lay the dust.

July 12th. Regimental inspection.

July 13th. Quiet during day; late in afternoon the enemy fired from fifteen to twenty solid shots, which dropped all close by the regimental hospital; at night, the regiment went into the third line, to the right of the breastworks; regimental loss, one wounded.

July 14th. Quiet during day, but at evening, the usual artillery-duel.

July 15th. Early in the morning, heavy cannonading for about one hour and-a-half; regimental loss, one wounded.

July 16th. Heavy musketry to the left, and usual artillery-duel towards evening.

July 17th. Divine service in several regiments.

July 18th. All quiet.

July 19th. Heavy rain all day, and at evening heavy firing from rebel batteries, which was promptly answered by our forces, and the rebel batteries silenced; during the night picket-firing was very lively; the regiment held, during the day, the first, or front line, and came into camp during the night.

July 21st. The day passed quietly, but the usual artillery-duel at night occurred, which lasted four hours; this regular firing of solid shot and shell of evenings is done by the rebels from three pieces of flying-artillery, brought forward for each shot, changing place each time, which makes it difficult for our gunners to injure and silence them effectually. The regiment went into breastworks at night.

July 22d. The regiment held the third or rear-line of breast-works.

July 23d. Colonel James Stewart, Jr., returned to the regiment.

July 24th. Contrary to previous Sundays, this day the rebels fired solid shot and shells, and an artillery-duel followed, which lasted the whole afternoon; rain in the evening and during the night.

July 25th. Received intelligence of special order, dated Head-quarters of Virginia and North Carolina, July 15, 1864, that the different redoubts be called after the names of officers who had bravely fallen in battle, and the redoubt on Cobb's hill, near the signal-tower, was named "Zabriskie," in honor of Colonel Abram Zabriskie, deceased. Col. James Stewart, Jr., detached to command 1st Brigade, 2d Division, 18th Army Corps, relieving Col. Alexander Piper; Major Hufty in command of the regiment. In afternoon the usual artillery-duel; at night the regiment marched into the breastworks.

July 28th. Major Hufty, sick, went to field-hospital; Captain August Thompson, Co. F, in command of the regiment; the usual artillery-fire in afternoon; about 10 P. M. a fire broke out in Petersburg; the fire and flames could be seen; it lasted several hours.

July 29th. Regiment received marching orders: the men to take three days' rations in haversacks; about 8 o'clock the troops moved, 3d Division, 2d Corps, relieving 2d Division, 2d Corps; all the troops passed by the Ninth regimental hospital; it took five hours for all to march by; the Ninth marched at midnight about one mile, and halted.

July 30th. The regiment formed line of battle as reserve to the 9th Corps, and held this position till 2 P. M., when the regiment marched half-a mile to the left, and halted till night; then returning to camp in about an hour it marched into the breastworks, its right resting on Appomattox river. About 5 A. M., this day, the undermined fort, in front of Gen. Burnside's forces, was exploded; the explosion of itself was terrific, and was the signal for the commencement of the cannonading from all the batteries along our whole line, a distance of over forty miles; this was kept up for three hours; volley after volley of musketry was intermingled with it. The explosion buried a great number of rebels; our forces took three lines of rebel breastworks, when the rebels received reinforcements, who rallied and drove back such of their own forces as had previously broken and fled; they then charged Gen. Ferrero's colored troops, who were not able to stand the brunt; they broke and fled; many of these colored troops were killed. Through some mismanagement on the part of our Generals, the rebels retook their breastworks again, and the day closed with a loss of over six thousand on our side. The explosion, so long contemplated, and from which so great success was expected, was a failure.

July 31st. The regiment held the same position taken at midnight, and came into camp at night.

August 1st. Remained in camp.

August 2d. Quartermaster Samuel Keys returned to regiment, having been absent since April 29th, 1862.

August 3d. The regiment went into breastworks at night, taking former position, the right resting on Appomattox river.

August 5th. Same position; about 5 P. M. the rebels exploded their mine, made to reach one of our forts, but their engineers had miscalculated by sixty feet; the explosion made a great dust only; an engagement followed, which lasted till dark, but which resulted in the rebels falling back.

August 6th. Regiment in same position; regimental loss on this day, two wounded.

August 7th. Sunday; during the day the regiment held the same position; at night it returned to camp, having been out four days and three nights: on each of these nights one-half of the regiment went in front of the breastworks, on picket; Company I, which had been on Brigade-duty, joined regiment again.

August 9th. The regiment went into breastworks.

August 11th. The regiment returned into camp.

August 12th. Artillery-duel commenced at 7 A. M., and lasted till 11 A. M., caused by our forces erecting new breastworks.

August 13th. Regiment went into breastworks.

August 15th. The 10th Reg't New York Artillery left Brigade to go to Washington, D. C.; Brigade consisting of the Ninth New Jersey, 23d, 25th, and 27th Mass., and 55th Penn'a Vols.; in the afternoon a heavy storm, and rain in torrents; several dams at the upper end of the ravine broke through. The ravine, and the flat lands between the hills upon which we were located, and the opposite one, a distance of about 150 to 180 feet, was full of water, to the depth of about nine feet. A colored regiment was encamped between the two hills; they had bush-houses; the men fled on the opposite hill, leaving their guns, equipments, and everything else behind, so sudden and fast did the water rise. All were washed away: the tents and stores of sutlers and officers were lost, and such furniture as was made and used in camp; boxes with ammunition, and with arms, came down; among other things, a barrel of whiskey, about three quarters full, which was captured by the Ninth, and it served as an extra ration to all. It was amusing to see good swimmers swim after valuable or useful articles, particularly after the sutler's stores; and it was quite comical to see the colored troops skirmishing for their arms, equipments, and other property, when the water began to fall. But this freshet has also a sad record: about twelve lives were lost; the bodies of some were soon picked up, others not until after several days.

August 16th. Major S. Hufty, Jr., wounded in left arm. The staff of the regimental State colors was shot in two, receiving nine shots from a rebel sharpshooter At night the regiment came out of breastworks.

August 17th. The whole Brigade changed camp, to a position half-a-mile south.

August 18th. Artillery-duel commenced, and lasted about four hours.

August 20th. Rain all day.

August 21st. Received orders for a move; the regiment and the whole Brigade started at 4 P. M.; marched about five miles, and took position in right of centre of Burnside's Army, relieving a Brigade of New Jersey troops.

August 22d. Private C. W. Thompson, Co. A, a Southerner by birth, who joined the regiment in March, 1864, when on Veteran furlough, deserted. He was an intelligent man, of good manners, and he soon won the good-will and confidence of the officers, but the way he disappeared makes it more than certain that he entered the Federal service as a spy.

August 23d. The regiment moved two miles to the right, relieving a regiment of colored troops.

August 24th. Relieved about 3 P. M.; order for another move; the regiment marched near midnight up to General Ames' head-quarters, and halted; shortly before leaving the front of Petersburg, a piece of shell dropped on the right foot of Sergeant-major H. Van Schaick, cutting the upper-leather, and causing a contusion. Out of 64 days in which the regiment was present at the siege of Petersburg, it had been over 40 days and nights in the rifle-pits, where the men could not go for water or to other places of necessity without being a target for the rebel sharpshooters; besides this, they were often on picket and numberless other duties, full of dangers and hardships; in the breastworks troops could not be relieved by day or by moonlight: it had to be night, and a dark night, too; for this reason the men lost three nights of sleep two days in the works. When in camp, near the ravine, the washing of clothing was dangerous, as the shells and solid-shot dropped more around there than in the front.

August 25th. Regiment marched at 4 A. M.; crossed Appomattox river again, upon pontoon-bridge; arrived at Point of Rocks, and halted on Cobb's hill again; here the Brigade was formed in line, to receive Gen. Heckmann, who had been exchanged; the General was received with cheers, making a few appropriate remarks, of which the boys liked nothing better than the General's promise to use all his influence for the return of the regiment and the old Brigade to North Carolina. About 11 A. M. the regiment arrived near Battery Pruyn, or No. 6; halted, and bivouacked close by Redoubt Zabriskie, named after Colonel Zabriskie. The regiment received another order for a move, which was countermanded: a heavy rain and storm during the night.

General Heckmann was taken prisoner on May 16th; a few days after his arrival in Richmond, rebel newspapers, which had been exchanged for ours by the pickets, stated: "Amongst the distinguished Federal officers lately arrived was General Heckmann, who walked through the street, up and into Libby, as bold and as proud as if he had entered the city as a conqueror, at the head of his Star Brigade, with the Ninth New Jersey in advance."

C. A. Heckmann was born at Easton, Pa., on the 3d of December, 1822. He still retains all the elasticity and buoyancy of youth, and it would be only upon very close inspection that would be observed those lines on his face, which indicate a life of exposure and hardships. Gen. Heckmann is about 5 feet 8 inches in height; very erect in his carriage, and, without any superfluous flesh, possesses a general physique to which one would immediately adjudge great activity and powers of endurance. His hair is brown; his beard, which is by no means heavy, and is worn only on the chin and upper lip, has a decided dash of the sandy. His eyes are blue, generally mild and soft, but, under excitement, darken and gleam in a manner which it is utterly impossible to describe, but which, when once beheld, will never be forgotten. His voice, when issuing command, is loud, ringing, and sonorous. He is scrupulously neat in his personal appearance, and he seems, too, to have the faculty of preserving this characteristic under circumstances where but few would find it possible. His gait is light and graceful, but it is upon horseback that he appears to the best advantage. He is a bold and dashing rider, and seems a master of the whole art of horsemanship. He is an easy, ready, and intelligent talker, possesses a good fund of general information, and is a capital hand to make an extempore speech. He is passionately fond of music, and a brilliant performer on the flute, which ever accompanies him, and serves to solace many a weary hour, and lighten those burdens so many and so trying which ever follow in the track of desolating war. General Heckmann first entered upon a military career during the late war between the United States and Mexico. In February, 1848, he entered the U. S. service, as 1st Sergeant of Co. H, First U. S. Voltigeurs, Col. F. P. Andrew. While in this command, he participated in the battles of National Bridge, Contreras, Cherubusco, Molino del Rey, Chepultepec, and the City of Mexico. He served during the remainder of the Mexican war, and was mustered out when the Government deemed it no longer necessary to maintain those organizations, as previous exigency demanded. From the close of this war to the opening of the present rebellion, he was engaged in the employ of the Central Railroad of New Jersey. He had since removed to Philipsburg, and his interest and associations had become thoroughly identified with those of the State of his adoption.

In April, 1861, was issued the first call of the President of the United States for troops to aid in subduing the rebellious manipulation of the Southern faction. The subject of this sketch promptly responded to this call upon all loyal citizens to aid in restoring the integrity of our Union, and on April 20th, 1861, we find him commissioned as Captain of Co. D, 1st Penn'a Vols. He served in this capacity during the three months for which he was mustered in. This regiment had no active engagement with the enemy, but was employed in guarding points of great importance in the county and city of Baltimore, Md., where also they made very important arrests of persons plotting against the Government. At the expiration of the three months, he returned to his home in New Jersey, but his loyal heart and naturally active disposition would not suffer him to remain idle, while the great strife was still going on. Upon application to the Governor of New Jersey, Hon. C. S. Olden, he received a commission as Major, in the 9th New Jersey Vols.; what he accomplished while with this regiment, the celebrated Burnside's Expedition, up to his appointment as a Brigadier-General of U. S. Vols., is known to all. Upon one expedition, during the summer of 1862, he rode into an ambuscade, and at about fifty yards he became a target for a full volley, but only one ball hit him, and that was rendered harmless by passing through two thicknesses of his holster at his belt. At the Goldsboro' Expedition, in 1862, he was materially instrumental in bringing about the entire success. In January, 1863, General Heckmann, with his Brigade, constituted a part of the forces that removed from North to South Carolina, and amid all the intense and bitter feeling manifested, managed himself with so much judgment and dignity as to gain the respect and admiration of all with whom he came in contact. During the summer of 1863 he made several important expeditions, and perfect success never failed to attend him; among these were the expeditions to Trenton, Cedar Point, Winton, &c. At Newport News, Va., he had command of post and garrison; captured at Drury's Bluff, on May 16th, General Heckmann was in various rebel prisons; also under fire at Charleston, S. C.; finally exchanged on August 3d, he reported to Major-General Butler, and was ordered to take command of the Second Division, 18th Army Corps, relieving General Ames; was present at the attack and capture of Fort Harrison; the following day three attacks were made on the troops commanded by Gen. Heckmann, and not only repulsed each time, but two rebel regiments were captured.

Early in February, 1865, the 10th and 18th Army Corps were consolidated into the 23d and 24th Corps. Shortly after, another Corps, the 25th, was organized, consisting of all the colored troops attached to the "Army of the James." General Heckmann was put in command of the 1st Division of this Corps; after three days, he was put in command of the whole Corps. The work of moulding this mass of men was no easy task. But by diligent exertion, strict discipline, personal and constant supervision over their necessities: by unswerving justice, coupled with kindness, they soon became soldiers in the full sense of the word, and Gen. Heckmann was wont to regard them as men. He retained this command from this time until May 25th, 1865, when it seemed certain that the active campaign had ceased, and the war about ended. At this time Gen. Heckmann sent in his resignation, and it was accepted, and he embraced the opportunity to return to his home in New Jersey, and re-assume the more agreeable avocations of a peaceful life.

August 26th Colonel James Stewart, Jr., in command of the Brigade; Captain August Thompson commanding the Ninth; the regiment went on picket.

August 27th. The regiment returns to camp.

August 28th. Dress parade; an order was read off that by pay-day next no instalment of the U. S. bounty would be paid; this caused a general dissatisfaction.

August 29th. The regiment went on picket.

August 31st. The regiment returned in the morning; Surgeon A. W. Woodhull, who had been in charge of hospital-transport Hero, of Jersey, returned and took charge of Brigade. In afternoon the regiment was inspected and mustered for pay, and in the evening about 200 men went on picket.

September 1st. The men on picket returned to camp.

September 3d. The regiment went on picket, and returned on the 4th.

September 5th. The 23d and 25th Mass. left at 1 A. M., for Bermuda Hundred, to embark for North Carolina. Capt. Thompson, of the Ninth, with one man from each company, went to Norfolk for the knapsacks which were stored there when the regiment went on this expedition, in April last. The nights became cold and chilly, the men needed their blankets, overcoats, and change of clothing; after five months' hardships, it was difficult for the most cleanly men to appear properly after lying in mud and clay for such a length of time.

September 10th. Captain Thompson returned on previous day, and the men received their knapsacks, some of which were in good condition, many had been ransacked, and others were lost. Officers' luggage was also lost and stolen; Capt. Applegate had his stolen. Surgeon A. W. Woodhull had all his baggage stolen from a wagon, when at the White House.

September 11th. Divine service in camp; a member of the Christian Commission delivers the sermon.

September 13th. Brigade dress-parade; at evening, preaching again by the same gentleman; Surgeon A. W. Woodhull was serenaded; at other places bands of music were also playing; some men attended the divine service; others promenaded, or were engaged in other amusements, playing cards and all sorts of games. It was a splendid night: the moon was full, and the whole scene was one of the most interesting character.

September 15th. Divine service, held by the same gentleman.

September 16th. At dress-parade, an order was read, that the 9th Vermont should take place in the 1st Brigade, 2d Division, Colonel I. H. Ripley commanding Brigade; and another order for the Ninth New Jersey and 27th Mass. to be ready to move for North Carolina.

September 17th. The regiment formed line at 5 A. M.; marched and arrived at Bermuda Hundred at 9 A. M. Companies B, D, F, and I embarked on steamer Utica, and A, C, E, G, H, and K, on transport Convoy. The latter sailed at 10 A. M, arriving at Portsmouth at 6 P. M.; steamer Utica halted at Norfolk.

September 18th. All regimental and hospital-stores stored at Norfolk and Portsmouth were taken on board the boats. The Convoy left at 6 P. M., arrived at Fort Monroe at 9 P. M., and anchored; the boat was much crowded; rain all night.

September 19th. The Utica arrived at Fort Monroe; all the men and stores from the Utica and Convoy were transferred to the steamer United States; about 200 recruits, belonging to regiments stationed in North Carolina, also came on board; the steamer started immediately.

September 20th. Arrived, and stopped outside of the bar, at Fort Macon.

September 21st. Started at 10 A. M.; anchored, and landed at Morehead City, at 2 P. M.; seven companies marched immediately to Carolina City, halting near the old camp-ground; three companies remained, to bring stores from the vessel on the cars. All were in camp about 8 A. M. The 158th New York Vols., stationed at Carolina City, were ordered to the Peninsula; the Ninth waited for their departure, to take their camp. Heavy rain during the night, which continued for three days; the men being without tents, became very wet. Heard upon our arrival that Ass't Surgeon John M. Davies, who had become well again at the time when the regiment left the front of Petersburg, had already arrived at Newbern, and was ordered to report as the Surgeon in charge of one of the hospitals in that city.

September 23d. Colonel James Stewart, Jr., returned to regiment, and took command. Surgeon A. W. Woodhull joined regiment, taking charge; Ass't Surgeon John M. Davies married with Miss Eliza Allen, at Newbern.

September 24th. The 158th New York left, and the Ninth immediately took their camp and quarters, engaging in the usual company and battalion exercises.

September 25th. Inspection.

September 27th. Ass't Surgeon F. B. Gillette ordered to report to Surgeon in charge of Mansfield general hospital, at Morehead City; in the afternoon Company G left for Bogue Sound, to report to Lieut. W. McCherry, for garrison-duty.

September 28th. Lieut. Col. Curlies, who had been absent, sick, since May 12th, returned to the regiment, still using his crutches.

October 11th. The regiment was paid off, the men not having been paid in from 8 to 12 months.

Upon our return to North Carolina, it was found that at Newbern the fearful scourge of yellow-fever was raging. At the time it seemed impossible, satisfactorily, to account for its appearance here, but it was subsequently found out, as the whole world now knows, that we were indebted for this visitation to the infernal machinations of the rebel government, sanctioned by its leaders, and accomplished by the devilish ingenuity of Dr. Blackburn, who introduced trunks, filled with infected clothing, to be distributed in Newbern. The hellish plot too well succeeded, but it was upon the citizens that the plague chiefly worked. The soldiers were, of course, seriously affected by the epidemic, but at least nine-tenths of the deaths occurred among the citizens. Every precaution and preventative that sanitary science could suggest was adopted, to stay its increase, and with the best results. The medical department were unremitting in their exertions, as is evinced by the sad fact that thirteen surgeons succumbed to the disease. As many of the white troops as practicable were removed from the city. Badly-infected districts were burned, or removed, and every precaution was made use of to prevent the spread of the disease. Many patients were sent to Morehead City and Beaufort, and although it was a great benefit to those sent there, it had the effect of spreading the disease in those places. Many men of the Ninth, who were detailed to the Quartermaster's department in Newbern, died; but on account of the care observed in camp, only one case developed itself there. Great was the panic in the city; nearly all business was suspended; all who could, had left for more salubrious parts. Scarce enough nurses could be obtained to care for the sick, or bury them when dead. Gloom rested on every face, and the only gleam of hope or cheerfulness emanated from the faces of the hard-worked surgeons, of whom none worked with greater alacrity and self-devotion than the Surgeon and Assistant-Surgeons of the 9th New Jersey Vols.

About this time, as though misfortunes never come singly, the small-pox broke out in a negro regiment, encamped alongside of the Ninth; but by perfectly isolating every case, and cutting off all communication, the loathsome disease was kept from our ranks.

October 12th. Captain Jonathan Townley ordered to go with Companies I and K, to Newport Barracks, to guard against the threatened attack of the enemy.

October 14th. Captain Thomas Burnett ordered to go with Companies B and C, to relieve Captain Townley and his command.

October 21st. Four officers were ordered to accompany 108 men of the regiment, whose time of service had expired, to Trenton, N. J., the men to be mustered out and officers to return. Colonel James Stewart, Jr., sent Color-sergeant George Meyers to the North, to deliver to the Executive of New Jersey our worn-out colors. He carried with him the following letter to Governor Parker, of New Jersey :—

HEADQUARTERS 9TH N. J. VOLS., ?
CAROLINA CITY, N. C., Oct. 15, '64. ?

To His Excellency, Joel Parker, Governor of New Jersey :

SIR :—I herewith have the honor to forward to you for safe-keeping in the Archives of New Jersey, the National and State colors of the 9th Reg't New Jersey Vol. Infantry. Three years ago they were entrusted to our hands. How well we have performed our trust, our past record must show. In every engagement they have been with us, and battle-worn and bullet-riddled as they are, we can proudly look upon them with the consciousness that not upon a single thread is there the least speck of dishonor or shame.

At the expiration of original term of enlistment we now return them to the authorities of our State, well assured that they will sacredly cherish them as priceless relics of the brave men who have fallen, as well as the most precious deposit of those who remain.

Corporals Delany, Co. K; Hand, Co. C; Hubner, Co. A; Garthwaite, Co. G; Smith, Co. D, the bearers of the State colors, were severely wounded while bearing it at the battles of Newbern and Goldsboro', N. C., and Drury's Bluff, Cold Harbor, and Petersburg, Va.

Color-sergeant George Meyers has carried the National colors for the whole of the three years, and by singular good fortune his life has been spared, and doubtless he has known no prouder day than that in which he safely replaces it in the capitol of our State. Understanding it to be your intention to furnish the regiment with new National and State emblems, we can only say we shall be gratified to receive them, and it shall ever be our utmost endeavor to preserve them as unsullied as are those we now place in your hands.

I have the honor to remain,

Your Excellency's obd't servant,

JAMES STEWART, Jr.,

Colonel Com'g.

October 25th. Lieut. Colonel Curlies was detached to Newport Barracks, to take command of troops and post.

October 27th. Major Samuel Hufty, Jr., returned to the regiment, entirely recovered from his wounds.

October 28th. Quartermaster Keys leaves for the North, to be mustered out, because of expiration of time of service.

October 31st. Inspection and muster for pay.

November 14th. The regiment was inspected by Capt. Atwill, inspecting officer of the District.

November 17th. Ass't Surgeon John M. Davies relieved from duty at Newbern hospital, and ordered as Post Surgeon at Newbern, to take charge of the poor white and negro citizens.

November 27th. Color-sergeant George Meyers returned from the North, with new colors, bringing a very complimentary and satisfactory answer to the Colonel commanding, his letter, dated October 15th, accompanying the return of the old colors. Dress-parade in afternoon, when the colors were formally received. Private John Newkirk, Co. I, from Salem Co., N. J., married Miss Susanne Moyer, from Beaufort, N. C., by Squire Ward, of Carolina City; Mr. and Mrs. Pivor, of the latter place, appearing as witnesses.

December 7th. Received at 8 A. M. order to move, the men to be provided with three days' rations; the regiment marched to the railroad, awaiting return of cars from Morehead City; received about 10 A. M. order to wait for further orders.

December 5th. Took cars at 7 A. M.; arrived near Newbern at 9 A. M.; halted and bivouacked on camp-ground formerly occupied and called Camp Reno; at 8 P. M., five companies, A, C, D, E, and I, embarked on gunboat Reno, which carried six rifled guns; the other four companies, B, F, H, and K, on the steamer Massasoit: started, Reno in tow of Massasoit.

December 6th. Passed Roanoke Island at noon, when the seal of orders was broken, and the order of our destination read.

December 7th. Arrived at Plymouth at 4 A. M.; landed at 7 A. M.; the rebel ram Albemarle, sunk by Lieut. Cushing, attracted much attention; the regiment quartered partly in houses, partly in barracks: the latter were soon found to be full of vermin, left so by the rebels. The Episcopal and Baptist churches, the one of brick, the other of frame, were very much damaged by the late bombardment, during which the basement of the first had served as a bomb-proof for the few remaining citizens and colored people. Both edifices were bare of all furniture; the Baptist had owned a library worth some twelve hundred dollars, of which not a volume could be seen; the only moveable article remaining was the bell, made at West Troy, N. Y., 1854. The fences of both cemeteries were destroyed; tombstones scattered to pieces, and graves had been opened by the exploding of shells and dropping of solid shot. The family-vault of S. H. McRae was considerably damaged. McRae possessed formerly an independent fortune, raised a company, and held a Captaincy in the rebel service at the outbreak of the war, but two days previous to the battle of Newbern, March 14th, 1862, his courage failed him, he left his men and went home, serving the traitorous cause as a contractor and spy, by furnishing provision to his sham government whenever he had opportunity, and professing to be a Union man when necessary. He was several times arrested, and it was proved against him that he piloted the rebels into the place when they re-captured it. He always found a willing ear, and was left roaming around at large. Country produces were brought in on three days in the week, of which Provost-marshal Captain T. D. Kimball, of the 2d Heavy Mass., disposed at reasonable prices, but not "first come, first served," choosing his customers.

December 8th. When the regiment left the camp, the men had only been provided with three days' rations, and they called for hard-tack at the sound of the bugle for Surgeon's call. One citizen, formerly in comfortable circumstances, and also late Sheriff of Washington county, had several cattle, pigs, and a large number of poultry. A guard was posted on his property, to protect it by day and night, when our men were short of rations, and particularly when our unfortunate prisoners were suffering and starving in their filthy dungeons, of which numbers of deaths recorded on Company-rolls are mute witnesses, and of which Lieuts. Drake and Peters, and numbers of privates since returned, can add their sad testimony. This citizen, Charles Latham, though otherwise well spoken of by his few remaining slaves, had three sons in the rebel army : one a Major, the second a Lieutenant, and the third a private, all belonging to one regiment, stationed at Hamilton, in front of us. A diver arrived from Norfolk, to investigate the Albemarle, in regard to raising her (on this occasion, an officer appeared with a pair of pants made from a woolen blanket, and the initials of U. S. on his posterior) At night, four days' rations were given out, and the men ordered to be ready for a march.

December 9th. Regiment formed line at 5½ A. M.; marched, and halted outside the town, to await arrival of other troops : the expedition consisting partly of the Ninth New Jersey, 27th Mass., four Companies, A, D, E, and H, and a number of unassigned 2d Heavy Mass., Co. D, and a detachment of 85th New York; 48 men of 16th Conn., 48 men of 101st, and 55 of 103d Penn'a; 56 of Marine Artillery ; Company A, 3d New York, and 61 men of 12th New York Cavalry; also Capt. Graham's cavalry, and two pieces of artillery. Surgeon A. W. Woodhull Surgeon-in-chief of expedition ; Ass't Surgeon Meredith, of 103d Penn'a, in charge of the Ninth New Jersey ; Lieut. Kille, of Co. I, detailed to command Co. D, 2d Heavy Mass. After all the troops had loaded arms, the column moved ; marched about three miles, and halted ; passed Jamestown about 12 M.; met enemy about two miles above, at Gardner's Bridge ; the enemy consisted of about 200 cavalry, and intended to charge on Captain Graham, who had with his company of cavalry, the advance. The latter turned his howitzer, and fired a few shots, when the Ninth, with its gallant leader, Colonel James Stewart, ahead, charged in double-quick, dispersing the enemy immediately. The bridge was soon sufficiently reconstructed for our pieces to pass over, when all troops halted on the other side of the creek, taking dinner on Morris Gardiner's plantation, whose sole occupant was an old but as it seemed faithful negress. The rebels took away several wounded, leaving one behind, who died during our stay. We also took several prisoners; there was a fine snow-storm all day. About 3 P. M. the regiment marched again, halting and bivouacking for the night about one mile and-a-half from Foster's Mills. The foraging, so far, had been very poor; barns, granaries, and out-houses, which we found filled with a rich harvest at the Tarboro' Expedition, in 1862, were now entirely desolated; no men were to be seen. It rained the whole night; during the night heavy firing was heard, not far distant, which we subsequently ascertained to be from the naval portion of the expedition, ascending the Roanoke river, which was thickly planted with torpedoes: one of which this night blew up the Otsego, a large double-ender, and a steam-tug. The artillery-firing heard was caused by the Navy shelling the adjacent shores.

December 10th. Weather very foggy; column moved about 7 A. M.; met enemy at 9 A. M. at Foster's Bridge; a fierce engagement ensued, which lasted about one hour, when the enemy again took to his heels, after having destroyed the bridge, to hinder our advance; while the pioneers found more work here than on the other bridges on the previous day, we had the pleasure of seeing the rebels make a sham of a battle-line, before they made their final disappearance. The Ninth had two slightly wounded; the loss of the rebels is not known. We took several prisoners: one, Lieut. Trilo, of the 68th North Carolina Junior Reserves, who took the oath, and followed our expedition several days. After crossing the bridge, troops halted to take dinner; in Foster's Mill, near the bridge, was found a large quantity of flour; a number of pigs, sheep, and poultry furnished a good meal. Every man could be seen sitting near the fire, with a big piece of meat on a stick. Marched in the afternoon towards Williamston; after marching three miles, Capt. Graham observed the enemy on Asa Biggs' plantation, formerly U. S. Senator, now in rebel service. The Ninth New Jersey and 27th Mass., who were in advance, went on double-quick, with two pieces of artillery, but arriving at the crossing of the Hamilton and Williamston road, the enemy had again disappeared towards Hamilton and Rainbow Bluff. The woods were thoroughly shelled, but, receiving no answer, troops bivouac on this plantation.

December 11th. Some sixty hogs, a great number of poultry, etc., were seized at Biggs' plantation, for the use of the troops; about 3 P. M. column moved; skirmishers and flankers were out in double force, as guerillas were discovered in all directions; arrived at midnight at Spring Green Church; halted and rested one hour. Colonel James Stewart, Jr., was ordered to take the Ninth New Jersey, and Lieut. Col. Bartholomew's command consisting of the 27th Mass. and Co. A, 3d New Jersey Light Artillery, and to proceed down Butler's Creek to an old mill-dam, to cross if possible, and come in the rear of the enemy, at Butler's Bridge; the undertaking was very perilous, but it was in the hands of men who knew no failure, and shrunk from no risk. They passed silently down to the point indicating the site of an old mill; they noiselessly worked their way in single file along the mill-dam, and across the floating logs which bridged the stream. Nothing could be more picturesque:—the moon in her full brightness shed a flood of light upon the scene; the weather was intensely cold, but this could not chill the ardor of those brave hearts; still they pushed forward through the outer works of Fort Branche, and now the fort itself loomed prominently in the foreground, grimly but sleepily guarding the Roanoke, for, unchallenged, those braves pushed on *past* and *within one hundred yards* of the fort. Soon the advance, consisting of Co. A, Capt. Applegate, and Co. I, Captain Charles Hufty, commenced capturing couriers, cooks, pickets, and detached parties. Colonel Hinton, of the 68th North Carolina, commanding at Fort Branche, thinking that the troops were reinforcements which he was expecting, and which really were only 400 yards in the rear, rode directly into the line, and was captured by Colonel Bartholomew; the excitement at this time was intense, yet not a sound was heard but the occasional "halt!" or "Surrender!" as post after post of the unsuspicious enemy was captured; as the vicinity of the bridge was attained line of battle was formed, the Ninth New Jersey in the right and 27th Mass. in the left; Co. A was deployed as skirmishers, and Co. I in the road as support; the interior line of the enemy's works was carried without a shot as yet being fired, but soon a loud "Halt!" is heard, a shot, a rush, and the works are taken; Co. I charged after the flying rebels, and secured the bridge; the enemy had rushed, as Colonel Stewart thought, directly into the trap set for him, but, alas! Col. Frankle, of the 2d Heavy Mass., in command of expedition, had not secured the Tarboro' road, the only road they could fall back upon, and so the prey escaped. While still exultant over the victory, the cry is given the enemy is in the rear : they have occupied the interior line of works, over which our brave boys had just passed, and while Colonel Stewart, with the 27th Mass., proceeded to communicate with Col. Frankle, the Ninth, under Major Hufty, occupied the other line of works, and with bayonets for picks, and tin-cups for shovels, soon changed the slope of the works so as to cover them from the enemy, who proved to be the 68th North Carolina, and who, for more than a mile had been following our troops, unconscious of their presence. On the return of Colonel Stewart and Col. Frankle, with the rest of our forces, Co. K, Capt. Townley, which had been deployed to cover the Ninth while altering the works, was assembled, and the 27th Mass. charged the enemy in the second line, and scattered them through the works.

Besides Colonel Hinton, a Lieutenant, Ass't Surgeon Gregory, and a number of privates of some regiment were taken prisoners behind their breastworks and in the camp. If the command had been in the hands of Colonel Stewart, of the Ninth, Rainbow Bluff, with its guns and garrison, the whole rebel force in the breastworks, and in the adjoining camps, would have been taken, when, as it was, Col. Frankle, of the 2d Heavy Mass., failed to take advantage of the superiority we had gained.

December 12th. The Ninth New Jersey and the 27th Mass., who, as ever before, had been in advance, had again the pleasure of seeing the enemy in front of them, apparently consulting what to do ; it was thought a part of them wanted to surrender, and Major Samuel Hufty, Jr., and Captain Graham went out to them with a flag-of-truce ; these officers invited about fifty rebels to surrender, but they respectfully declined. The Ninth halted at this time on the same plantation they had bivouacked when at Hamilton during the Tarboro' expedition. About noon column began the return, not with the happy feeling and the assurance of "object accomplished," but feeling there had been exhibited on the part of our commander, Col. Frankle, a sad lacking of energy and promptness to turn to advantage our last night's success, which had been obtained with such hard fighting and so great suffering.

December 13th. Marched at daylight three miles, taking Liggit's Bridge, leaving Foster's Mill to our right; bridge, mill, and blacksmith-shop were burned down; the regiment arrived at Jameston about dark, and bivouacked in open field. The Col. commanding expressed a desire and determination to resume the expedition upon a different basis. The effective strength of the forces was taken, and it was found that hard marching, frost-bite, and blisters, had incapacitated many of the men from the ability to commence another long march; 600 men were pronounced unfit to march, many of whom were rendered so on account of their shoeless condition.

December 15th. The regiment went about noon on board John Faron, steaming for Plymouth; arrived at 2 P. M., taking the same quarters again, as before. Lieut. Kelly, Co. I, returned to his Company.

December 16th. Many females living along the road traveled by the late expedition, came in to demand the return of their horses and mules, declaring themselves to be loyal and professing Union sentiments; in most cases this was too readily complied with on the part of the Provost-marshal, as many of these noble animals would soon carry a bitter foe again. At night 40 men of the 27th Mass. and about 65 men of the 2d Heavy Mass. returned to Plymouth; they had sailed up Roanoke river on Wednesday evening, the 14th, landed at Cedar landing, where they expected to meet with another force, for the purpose of making another scout, according to the second plan lately proposed by the Colonel commanding expedition; but the latter's mind had changed soon after they had started, and the promised support was sent in another direction; they had not met the enemy. They brought in many horses, mules, a great lot of poultry, and other plunder. They reported the enemy, to the number of 2,000, engaged in rebuilding Foster's Bridge; expecting an attack on Plymouth, the order to be ready at a moment's notice was issued to all commands.

December 18th. Sunday; at night several houses burned down, which Col. Frankle did not fail to credit the Ninth New Jersey and 27th Mass. with.

December 19th. Rations were short; guards had to be posted on every corner and cross-road; provisions were so much needed, and the management of the commander of the expedition, Col.

Frankle, so poor, that regimental commanders threatened to let their men loose to help themselves, if they received nothing to eat. Coffee and crackers were borrowed from the gunboat Shamrock, and issued the same night, the quartermaster of the Shamrock saying it was a " d——d infernal shame to keep men waiting so long without provisions."

December 20th. The steamer Helen Getty came in with provisions, to the joy of all the men, and the great relief of Colonel Frankle and his Provost-marshal.

December 22d. Received order for another move; the weather *very cold ;* about 3 P. M. the Ninth New Jersey, 27th Mass., 2d Heavy Mass., a detachment of the 85th New York, 12th New York Cavalry, and Co. A, 13th New York Marine Artillery; two pieces and one section of artillery left; the first three embarked on the John Faron, the others on the Ceres; sailed up Roanoke river, the John Faron ahead, till dark, when the Ceres took the lead; the river being narrow, sharpshooters were called for, and posted on both sides of the boat. When between Jameston and Williamston, the boat ran into a network of brushes, the noise of which brought all the men to their feet, believing we had struck a torpedo, so numerous in this water. Coming up as far as two miles above Williamston, a gunboat came down, and recommended us to return, as a farther advance would be unsafe; sailing back, we halted, landed, and bivouacked at Jameston.

December 23d. The night had been very cold, and the men suffered much for want of blankets and tents; bridges were burned down to prevent a surprise.

December 24th. Another order for a move; went on board the Helen Getty, about 3 P. M.; sailed at 4, and landed at Plymouth about 7 P. M.; took old quarters.

December 25th. Christmas; Col. Frankle received a Christmas-gift, a song, in which the history of the late expedition was rendered in verse, in language more elegant than complimentary to its commander. A false alarm at night, caused by our outer pickets firing three shots. Lieut. Reid, of the 2d Heavy, who was officer of the day, and whose duty it would have been to inquire himself into the cause, sent out a sergeant and three men.

December 26th. Rain all day and night; officers who had been North with the discharged men, returned to the regiment.

December 27th. Weather clear, but rain all night.

December 29th. The remainder of the fleet up Roanoke river returned; one company of 2d Mass., one piece of heavy artillery, 12th New York Cavalry, and the pioneers of the Ninth went on a reconnoissance to Gardner's Bridge; met some 60 rebels of the North Carolina Junior Reserves; they were soon dispersed.

1865.

January 1st. New Year passed quietly.

January 5th. Lieut. Col. Strong, of the 1st North Carolina Union Vols., Chief of Gen. Palmer's staff, inspected all the troops; Surgeon A. W. Woodhull, in addition to his duties as Surgeon-in-chief, took charge of the regiment.

January 6th. The regiment was ordered to return to Carolina City.

January 7th. At 11½ A. M. went on board Helen Getty; sailed, and anchored at night near Roanoke.

January 8th. Took coal from a schooner; sailed at 11 A. M., arrived and landed at Newbern early next morning.

January 9th. Took cars for and arrived in camp at Carolina City, about noon. This closed the most tiresome and unprofitable expedition the Ninth ever took part in. Lieut. Col. Wm. B. Curlies, who had had command of troops and post at Newport Barracks, was relieved and ordered to take command of 2d North Carolina Union Vols., stationed at Carolina City.

January 14th. Lieut. J. Madison Drake, from Elizabeth, who had been captured on May 16, '64, returned to his regiment. The following is from his narrative :—

" After having been captured, we were hurriedly marched to the rear, to the James river. On our way to the wharf, several rebel officers told me that Major-General Heckmann was a prisoner in their hands, but this story I did not credit at the time. Reaching the river, we were sent down the wharf, where we found a rebel gunboat moored. Stepping on board, almost the first person I met was General Heckmann, and great was my surprise to find him there. Approaching, I said to him : ' General, it has long been the height of my ambition to be able to follow you into Richmond.' Extending his hand, he jocosely replied : ' Well, Drake, I think you are now in a very fair way of having your wish gratified.' In an hour or two we had left the wharf, and were slowly moving up the James.

"We landed at Rockett's, and marched up a number of filthy streets, halting in front of a dingy three-story brick building, from a corner of which projected a small, dirty sign, labelled as follows : 'Libby & Son, Ship Chandlers and Grocers.' Entering the bastile, we registered our names, and were then escorted by that noted villain, Dick Turner, into another room on the ground-floor, where we were relieved of our greenbacks, and rubber-blankets. Turner—commonly known as 'Thief Turner'—informed us that our money would be returned on leaving the prison, but General Heckmann told him plainly that it was unnecessary for him to add lying to his already long list of crimes—to which the villainous-looking keeper replied insolently, threatening to confine the General in the 'dark hole,' if he was farther insulted. As soon as we had 'forked over' our 'greenbacks,' we were stripped, and our clothing closely examined by the minions of Jeff. Davis, after which we were shown our quarters on the second floor, east room.

"May 17th. Rebel papers this morning acknowledge a loss of 5,040 in wounded alone, at the 'Bluff.' Several officers engaged in cutting dominoes, chessmen, &c. A small piece of corn-bread received for twenty-four hours.

"May 18th. Endeavor to procure a portion of our money, in order to buy some necessaries, but fail, of course. Hundreds of rebel wounded brought up from the 'Bluff' to-day.

"May 19th. Received some corn-bread, and then boiled it—answered very well as a substitute for coffee. Had some corn-mush for dinner—nothing for supper.

"May 20th. Mush and corn-bread for breakfast. Mush for dinner, and for supper we had mush. Nothing new to-day.

"May 21st. Mush and coffee for breakfast. Bread for dinner, and two or three spoonfuls of boiled rice for supper. Unusual commotion in the city ; bells rang all night ; citizens, &c., called out.

"May 22d. Mush (fried) for breakfast ; water, and a small piece of tobacco, for dinner, with the smallest quantity of rice for supper. Continue to hear favorable accounts from General Grant's army.

"May 23d. Mush for the morning meal. A few black, rotten beans for dinner, and a piece of toasted bread for supper. During the day a piece of bacon, weighing ten pounds, was issued to a party of sixty-two. It was received with three cheers. We lost no time in dividing it—for as it was ALIVE, we felt apprehensive of losing it.

"May 24th. Sour meal-cakes for breakfast; beans and maggots for dinner; a little rice for supper. Go to bed (?) hungry.

"May 25th. This A. M. we had mush for breakfast; the same quality of black beans for dinner, and mush for supper. We managed to procure a quart of sour molasses for sixteen dollars—this we considered quite a treat.

"May 26th. Nothing for breakfast; a very small piece of corn-bread for dinner, and rice for supper. Nearly starved to-day. Lieut. Peters paid one dollar for a small loaf of bread, two dollars for a common lead-pencil, and two dollars for having them brought up.

"May 27th. Mush for breakfast, bread for dinner, and rice for supper. Suffered a great deal to-day in consequence of extreme hunger. Could not sleep last night for the rats.

"May 28th. Fried mush for breakfast, fried bread for dinner, and for supper we had fried mush, which was quite a change.

"May 29th. Boiled rice for breakfast, bread for dinner, and rice, boiled, for supper. The 'rebs.' have been busily engaged in hauling locomotives, &c., from the York railroad, through the streets—twenty-four mules to each car.

"May 30th. Boiled rice for breakfast, corn-bread for dinner, and boiled rice for supper. Rebel gunboat passed through canal, with 'rag' at its stern. Feel that we cannot live much longer, unless we get more to eat. Heard Grant's guns very distinctly.

"May 31st. Aroused from our slumbers before daybreak, and ordered to roll our blankets—to go South. 'Thief Turner' did not make his appearance, but sent us word that our money would speedily follow us. In a few minutes, sixty-two officers and eleven hundred enlisted men (the latter from Belle Island and 'Castle Thunder,') were marching up Cary street, across the Mayo bridge to the Southside Railroad, in Manchester, where a cattle-train was awaiting us. Leaving Manchester at about 8 o'clock, we reached Danville at midnight. The country very hilly, and sparsely populated—hardly any signs of civilization being observed along this road. Danville—three or four small log-huts and a depot—is situated on the western bank of the river 'Dan.' Changed cars during the night; next morning started for Greensboro'—forty-eight miles distant—where we arrived at noon. About midnight we again started for Charlottesville—distant ninety-seven miles. We were packed like cattle: neither room to sit, stand, or lie down. Several of the enlisted men made their escape from this place. Capt. Carpenter was shamefully beaten with a musket, by a rebel guard. We passed through a number of small villages and towns, but nothing worthy of note occurred on the trip to Macon. At Augusta I met a Mr. Clark, formerly of Elizabeth, who was determined I should know him as a bitter rebel. He said he had two sons in Johnston's army, and if he had one hundred and two they should all strike for Southern independence. He owned a great many slaves, he said, and was considered wealthy. The North could never conquer nor subjugate them; and he repeated the same old story of last man, last ditch, &c. We arrived at Macon, and were marched into a four-acre lot, which was enclosed with a high stockade fence. Our entrance was greeted by the loud cries of ' Fresh fish !' ' Give them air !' ' Keep your hand on your pocket-book,' etc. At first I was somewhat surprised, but meeting some friends, the matter was soon explained. In this camp I found eleven hundred officers, who had been confined here about two weeks. We fared much better here, so far as rations were concerned, but had no quarters—no protection from the weather—the scorching sun by day, and heavy, sickening dews by night. On Sundays we generally had divine service, both in the morning and evening. One evening in June, Lieut. Gershou, while at the spring, was killed by a rebel sentinel. The guard received the customary furlough for killing a ' Yankee officer.' I may state here that inside the main stockade is a fence called the ' dead-line,' which no one is allowed to approach. To touch it would be certain death. The name is exceedingly appropriate.

" While at Macon, during June and July, a number of tunnels were completed, after an immense amount of labor, one being over eighty feet in length. Everything being in readiness, and several hundred prepared to leave the ' Corn-thievocracy,' we only awaited the shades of night, but were doomed to bitter disappointment; our plans had been betrayed, baselessly betrayed by one of our own officers, Lieut. Silvers, of an Illinois cavalry regiment. The rebels discovered the five tunnels, and destroyed them. Great was our indignation, and terrible the excitement. Silvers heard the tempest, and begged the rebels to give him protection, which was readily afforded. The rebels issued orders that if other tunnels were commenced, they would remove every board from the 'pen.'

"The time hung heavily, notwithstanding we played cricket, ball, &c. Classes for sword-exercises were formed, while many performed in gymnastics. During evenings the various glee-clubs would enliven the camp with soul-stirring melodies.

"Hotel-board was advertised at twenty-five dollars per day. Salt sold at sixty-four dollars per bushel; flour, one hundred and fifty dollars per hundred pounds; beans (poor quality), one dollar per quart; bacon, five dollars per pound; fresh beef, one hundred and fifty dollars per pound; baking-soda, twelve dollars; eggs, six dollars per dozen; blackberries, one hundred and twenty-five dollars per quart; butter, six and eight dollars per pound; molasses, eight dollars per quart; apples and onions one dollar per piece; newspapers, fifty cents each; watermelons, eight to twenty dollars per piece.

"After roll-call, Captain H. H. Todd, of the 8th New Jersey regiment, produced a small silk flag—presented to him last spring by a young lady of Jersey City. The appearance of the 'flag of the free' called forth the most vociferous cheers, from fifteen hundred officers. Cheer after cheer rent the air, while the 'Star-Spangled Banner' was sung by the entire assemblage, who adjourned to the large wooden building, where a patriotic prayer was offered by one of our Chaplains, after which eloquent speeches were delivered by a number of officers. I never witnessed such enthusiasm—never heard better orations. We did not adjourn our celebration till late in the afternoon, when the rebel 'officer of the day' entered the building with a large force, to stop the proceedings. Poor fellow! he had been trembling all day, and could not muster courage enough to inform us that our meeting was 'out of order.' The cannon placed around camp were manned, and double-shotted early on the morning of the 'Fourth.'

"On the 29th of July, six hundred of us were sent to Savannah, where we arrived the same day. All along the line of railroad we saw poor white people living in freight cars, huts, etc. These people had made their way from Atlanta, and were now thrown upon the cold charities of the world to freeze and starve.

Their condition was most wretched—their only food corn and meal. Reaching the city, the valorous 'Home Guards'—useful members of society—escorted us to the old United States marine hospital, where we lay on the ground all night; many of us being so weak that we could scarcely stand. Next day, however, tents and boards were issued to us—also plenty of rations. We were well treated at Savannah, receiving an abundance of corn meal, rice, and a pound of fresh beef each day. While confined here, we dug three tunnels, but they were discovered just in the 'nick of time.' We worked very hard on these tunnels, but had our labor in vain. Two of our party were sent to the city jail, and almost starved for several days for being connected with the enterprise. The First Georgia Regulars guarded us, and this accounts for our being well treated. Soldiers themselves, they knew how to use us.

"September 13th. We were sent to Charleston, S. C., and confined in the jail-yard, a most filthy place. Some few only had tents —the great majority being compelled to lie in the mud and water. We received half-rations here—just enough to sustain life. Our condition in the jail-yard was most wretched, and our treatment barbarous. A large number were taken sick. I believe that every rebel officer placed over us died of yellow fever, while no cases occurred among us. Some five hundred officers gave their parole in order to obtain healthy and pleasant quarters. General Foster sent his compliments (in the shape of one hundred pound shells) over the doomed city every fifteen minutes. Almost daily, shells would explode over and around our prison-home, the fragments often falling among us, but no one was ever injured by them. One morning the rebel commissary establishment was destroyed by a huge shell, and we were made the sufferers thereby—being compelled to go without rations three or four days. A day or two subsequently a monster-shell was thrown into the street, near the prison, labeled: 'Show me the way to the Arsenal.' The day after our arrival at Charleston several blocks of buildings were destroyed by our shells. Every day fires could be seen in different portions of the city. The fire-apparatus are run by the negroes, but they seldom go into service, owing to the severe shelling the city receives as soon as a fire breaks out. Our shells are thrown a distance of six and seven miles—often with good effect. It seemed to me that the best part of the city had already been destroyed. No business is done anywhere, the stores being all closed, and grass growing 'green and tall' in the principal streets. All the prosperous classes have long since vacated the place, leaving only negroes and those who are too poor to go away. There is much distress among those who remain. Hundreds sleep in the cars beyond the depot, so our barber told us, in order to get out of reach of our shells. Truly, the 'birth-place of secession' is reaping, tenfold, the reward her iniquities and folly so justly merit.

"On the 6th of October, six hundred of us were placed on a train of cars, and started for Columbia, S. C., about one hundred and thirty miles north of Charleston. Just before dusk I removed the caps from the guns of the guards, so we had no fear of being shot. After crossing the bridge over the Congaree river, four of us—Captain H. H. Todd, 8th New Jersey, Captain A. Grant, 19th Wisconsin, Lieut. J. E. Lewis, 11th Connecticut, and myself—leaped from the train (moving at the rate of fifteen miles an hour), although the night was black with darkness. Neither of us sustained any injury, and regaining our feet, we dashed into the woods. The train had gone a mile and more, perhaps, when the guards commenced discharging their fire-arms—thus giving the alarm. We lost no time in getting into a heavy, dense swamp, which we gained just as a pack of infernal bloodhounds came near. We continued to wade and beat our way through this swamp till daybreak, when we stopped to rest; but it was impossible to find a place large enough to sit or lie down, so bending some bushes, we propped ourselves against them till the next evening, when we sallied forth, the hounds having ceased their baying, and left our neighborhood during the afternoon. We marched altogether through woods and swamps during the first three weeks, and this at night : the moon and stars our only guide. For six days we lived on hard, dry corn, which we parched. We found persimmons, berries, apples, pomegranates, grapes, etc., on our route. When we had traveled some two hundred miles from the coast, we cultivated the acquaintance of the slaves, who, in every instance, divided their salt, corn-meal, etc., and in very many cases, cheerfully gave us the last morsel of meal in their cabins. While flanking the town of Dallas, N. C., one night, we accidentally met a Union man—the first white man that had seen us. Suspecting us, from our uniforms, he told us that if we were Union men he was a friend.

We eagerly embraced him, telling him who we were. Without any hesitation, he asked us to accompany him home, and he would see what he could do. Reaching his fine mansion, we found his lady still engaged in household duties, although the hour was very late. She at once commenced preparing a supper, which was steaming on a table in an hour. I never sat down to a more inviting repast—the nicest wheat-biscuit, roasted potatoes, pickles, preserves, milk, butter, and many other delicacies. The wants of the outer man having been amply supplied for once, the good lady filled our haversacks with everything that was nice. We passed some two hours with these good people, who were full of sympathy for us. Our 'host' was the owner of thirty slaves, and many broad acres, but he had ever remained true to the old flag—he was just as firm in his devotion to the old Government as ever, and he prayed daily for the overthrow of our common enemies, and the restoration of the American Union. He was an officer in a society called the 'True Heroes of America,' which had for its main object the dismemberment of the confederacy. Only last week, he said, he had kept six young men from being carried off to the rebel army, and he would never 'rest from his labors' until the 'last armed foe' expired. The members of the organization were determined to break up the power of the confederacy in the old North State. At times, in speaking of the old Government, which had ever blessed him, he became affected to tears. He gave us directions as to the best route to the mountains, etc., and conducted us beyond the reach of all danger, before he would part from us. I shall never forget the kindness of himself or wife.

"To cross Catawba river we found rather a difficult matter. We walked up and down the bank two days and a night in search of a 'canoe.' At length our labors were crowned with success—a boat was found, and the river safely crossed, although the stream is both deep and swift, with dangerous rapids. Gaining the opposite shore we almost felt ourselves safe. Just after crossing the river, it commenced raining very hard, so that we were unable to proceed through the woods. We halted for several hours, and being half famished, we visited a hut near by, and asked for food, but the woman said she could give us nothing; her husband was in the mountains, doing patrol-duty, and she and her children were in a starving condition, subsisting solely on corn and meal. Toasting our feet (my boots had long since 'played out,') we soon after left this scene of misery, and before dark reached a poor farmer's house, where we partook of a substantial supper, provided by two good Union women—one of whom had lost her husband at Gettysburg, and five brothers in various other battles. She had been robbed of her milch cows, hogs, and horses, for which the rebel government had never paid her. We gave her a twenty-dollar confederate note, which would purchase a quart of salt. She directed us to a number of old camp-meeting buildings, where we might pass the night in safety. As the storm did not abate, and the night was very dark, we concluded to rest in the buildings till next morning. About midnight we heard some little pigs running about the place. Lighting some pine-knots, and arming ourselves with sticks, we fearlessly charged, capturing in the sortie three fine little porkers, which were soon roasting on the cheerful and blazing fire. After breakfast, nothing but the 'har' remained as an evidence that 'piggy' had ever existed. In the morning we made for the mountains, some twenty miles distant. Several times during the day we saw, from our hiding-places, the lame, blind, and halt, boys of sixteen, and grey-haired men of sixty, dragged off by conscripting officers. Men who had been discharged from the army, for loss of limbs, were now compelled to leave their families, and hasten to the field again. An able-bodied man, except he be a deserter, cannot be found in Georgia, South or North Carolina—everything that can move has been conscripted.

"Reaching the base of the 'Blue Ridge' without a mouthful in our haversacks, we almost quailed at the prospect—as it would be impossible to obtain any food if we commenced the ascent of the bleak waste. As fortune would have it, we soon after saw two white women at work in a sugar-cane field. Representing ourselves as deserters from the rebel army, in a starving condition, they left their work, and returning to their cabin, they baked us several large 'pones,' also filling our canteens with sorghum molasses. Having spent our last dollar, we had no money to offer them, so Lieutenant Lewis presented one of the women with a valuable gold ring, which greatly pleased the recipient. These women informed us that the mountains were filled with 'deserters,' and that they would be pleased to see us. In less than two hours we were in a cave, among the mountaineers; they welcomed us with open arms, and promised to conduct us safely 'over the hills.' We slept soundly, awaking early in the morning, and accompanying one of the party to a spring, we found a splendid breakfast already awaiting us—brought there by a matron. At noon we enjoyed a chicken dinner. These deserters (together with those who have ever resisted the wholesale conscription act) are called 'Lyers-out.' They are all armed—though poorly—with old horse-pistols, squirrel-rifles, and old muskets. They are constantly 'bushwhacking' with the rebel forces sent to effect their capture, and who generally come off second-best. I saw men who, from their hiding-places on the mountains, had daily seen their families, but who had not for over two years crossed their thresholds. Their wives had brought them food—oftentimes at the imminent risk of their lives, while all the work on the farm had been performed by them and their little children. The rebels had repeatedly taken their last cow and chicken, and maltreated many of the women in a barbarous manner. One of these patriotic women piloted us seven miles through the laurel, one afternoon—then bidding us halt in a corn-field, she visited a farm-house near by—soon after returning with two young ladies, who, in turn, took us in charge, conducting us to a deep ravine, where they left us, while they returned to the house to prepare supper, which was shortly afterward brought us. They also furnished us a feather-bed, and several bed-quilts. At an early hour the next morning, these 'angels' served us with a warm breakfast, to which we did ample justice. Every day, for some two weeks, we continued to meet such friends. Never shall I forget these noble, brave, self-sacrificing Union women—who took so much pleasure in ministering unto our wants. The women, like the men, loathe the rebel government, which has caused them so much distress and suffering.

"While in Caldwell county, N. C., we organized a battalion of Union men. They detained us several days in preparing to leave their 'mountain-homes,' for Knoxville—distant about two hundred miles. Finally, everything being in readiness, we started across 'Grandfather mountain,' which was difficult to ascend, owing to its great height and steepness. One of our friends killed a large black bear, which we ate with the greatest relish. The meat tasted very much like fresh pork. Reaching 'Crab Orchard,' East Tennessee, we found two United States recruiting officers—Major

E. A. Davis, and Lieut. James Hantley, of Colonel Kirk's Third North Carolina mounted infantry. We were warmly welcomed by these officers, who at once took our party under their charge. Several fresh beeves were killed and roasted. After resting at the 'Orchard' a day or two, we again took up our line of march for Bull Gap—one hundred miles distant. Before starting, however, our North Carolina friends were sworn into Uncle Sam's service for three years. This seemed to relieve them of a great load : they were so happy, they said. All they wished was good arms and plenty of ammunition, to rid their neighborhood of rebel guerillas. Major Davis promised to arm them as soon as they reached Knoxville—then he would return at their head, and wage a war of extermination against the rebel bandits. Descending 'Big Butt' mountain, we heard the firing of cannon and musketry. Sending a woman, in advance, to reconnoitre, she returned with the information that Breckinridge, with four thousand ragged rebels, had driven our forces from Bull Gap, capturing six pieces of artillery, and that it would be impossible for us to enter our lines this side of Knoxville. This was, of course, a bitter disappointment to us, as we should not only have a long distance to march, but would necessarily be in more danger.

"Lieut. Lewis, myself, and thirty-five others, succeeded in reaching Knoxville on the evening of November 16th, having been just six weeks in marching six hundred and fifty miles, a portion of the distance in a barefooted condition. I was compelled to walk a long distance in four inches of snow, without a thing on my feet, which are badly frozen. We spent a pleasant evening at Knoxville, with a number of 'shoulder-straps,' who were much interested in the story of our miraculous escape.

"General Carter, Provost-Marshal General, furnished me with transportation to Washington, D. C. Arriving there, the General granted me leave of absence, and the Paymaster furnished me with a pile of greenbacks, which I have since found very useful.

"Let the loyal people of the North continue hopeful—this wicked rebellion cannot last longer than next Spring. The confederacy, as seen by me, is nothing but a 'shell.' While it has been my good fortune to be the bearer of glad tidings to many whose sons and brothers I left in exile, my heart has been sorely grieved when anxious kindred pressed me to assure them of the welfare of dear ones whom I knew were long since mouldering in unknown graves. Among those who will never return to the familiar scenes of youth is the brave Carroll, who was severely wounded in a desperate conflict, and when the tide of battle ebbed was missing. To the period of my return, fond hearts hoped that this officer survived among his captive associates. It was indeed a painful duty to undeceive them. The question is frequently asked me if my comrades in captivity ever attempted to escape. I answer that the love of liberty prompted many to peril life. Alas, that such acts of heroism proved unavailing! Of the scores of captives who eluded the vigilance of their jailors, none, so far as I am apprised, ever succeeded in getting out of the bounds of the accursed land where they pined for the air of freedom. Some who had almost reached the goal of their aspirations were doomed to bitter disappointment. Profiting by their experience, and directed by a Providence whose gracious interpositions often seemed as clearly revealed as the brilliant orbs of the firmament by which we determined our course, the writer and his associates escaped from the hands of the Philistines. A deliverance so remarkable as to excite the astonishment of hundreds familiar with the country through which we traveled, admonishes us to be profoundly grateful to the Preserver and Guide whose mercies are so deserving of thanksgiving. ''

At the return of Lieut. Drake to the regiment, he was offered a Captaincy, or the appointment as Quartermaster, if he wished to remain; neither of which he could accept, because of frozen feet and general debility, contracted and produced in rebel prisons, on long marches, and exposures of all kinds during his travels.

January 21st. Lieut. J. E. McDougall, of Co. A, Acting Ass't Quartermaster at Beaufort, married to Miss R. K. Johnston.

January 22d. In afternoon church was held in hospital-tent.

January 24th. Colonel James Stewart, Jr., in command of the District of Beaufort, N. C.

January 29th. Inspected by Major-General Palmer.

February 1st. Four companies, E, B, H, and I, under command of Major Samuel Hufty, Jr., took the cars for Newport Barracks.

February 2d. This command, joined by Captain Graham's cavalry, and one howitzer, commanded by Col. James Stewart, Jr., marched to Adams' Creek, thirty-one miles; bivouacked.

February 3d. Procured small boats, when three Companies crossed to Hard's Island; Co. I, under Lieut. J. C. Bowker, of Co. D, remained as guard. The troops were divided into sections, taking different paths, to hunt for guerillas and a number of deserters, who had assembled and were reported as being in that vicinity. After scouring the whole island in all directions, and not meeting with the enemy, they returned, re-crossed the creek, and bivouacked for the night.

February 4th. Troops started for Newport; arrived there at midnight; Companies C and I returned, by way of South Creek, to Turnican's Bay.

February 5th. Troops returned to camp; two corporals from the 2d North Carolina Union Vols., served as guides on this expedition; church in the afternoon.

February 8th. Surgeon A. W. Woodhull resigned, his time of service with this regiment (3 years) having expired; Ass't Surgeon F. B. Gillette appointed and promoted Surgeon.

DR. ADDISON W. WOODHULL.—The eminent services rendered by Dr. Addison W. Woodhull, as Surgeon of the Ninth, justly entitle him to something more than a "passing notice." This patriotic gentleman at the outbreak of the rebellion, feeling it to be his duty—notwithstanding a lucrative practice—offered his time and talents to Governor Olden, who immediately availed himself of them. During the first six or eight months he served in the Army of the Potomac and Lower Potomac. In the spring of 1862, he was appointed to the Army operating in North Carolina, under the heroic Burnside. Circumstances prevented him from reaching his new scene of labors until two days after the battle of Newbern. It was in the crowded hospitals of this place that his skill was required, day and night, for long weeks. Unremitting in his labors, assiduous in his attentions, gentlemanly in his deportment, exceedingly kind and anxious in the care of the sufferers, we may not wonder that hundreds to-day live but to bless and honor him.

At this trying period there were comparatively few surgeons at Newbern: a number remaining at Roanoke Island, and others being sick or disabled; consequently there was but little relaxation from labor. Never, perhaps, did men work with greater zeal or more cheerfulness; but none were more fully alive to the task of mercy than the subject of our brief sketch. The great skill with which Dr. Woodhull treated his cases, soon attracted the attention of the ubiquitous Burnside, who at once appointed him to a position of great responsibility. It was while filling the onerous duties of this position that the excellent administrative abilities of Dr. Woodhull were so clearly exhibited. The commodious hospitals, erected at that time, are not excelled for convenience, comfort, accommodation, or good order. The Doctor received many complimentary testimonials for the able manner in which he brought " order out of chaos."

During the summer of 1862, Dr. Woodhull, who always accompanied the intrepid Heckmann on his incursions, had his horse shot from under him, in the engagement at Young's Cross-roads ; the Doctor was wounded, and narrowly escaped. In the Fall, he was appointed Surgeon in charge of the Hammond general hospital, at Beaufort,—a position held by him until the departure of Generals Foster and Heckmann for South Carolina. On taking the field, Dr. Woodhull was made Surgeon of Heckmann's Star Brigade, in which capacity he faithfully served for a long time. In the summer of 1863, in addition to his other duties, he superintended the erection of Mansfield general hospital, at Morehead City, which has been pronounced in itself a model affair. Time would fail us closely to follow the Doctor through the several campaigns in the Carolinas and the bloody fields of Virginia, where the Star Brigade won never-dying laurels. When we say that Dr. Woodhull was *semper fidelis*, we only repeat that which every member of the Ninth so loudly boasts.

Upon returning to North Carolina, in the autumn of 1864, when the yellow fever was raging at Newbern, Surgeon A. W. Woodhull at once offered to assist in subduing the terrible enemy, and through the whole course of the deadly epidemic was found ever faithful, constant at his post.

But it is to the medical statistics of the regiment that he can refer with the greatest pride, and these are the best witnesses of his diligence and skill. These show that during each of the three years that he was connected with the regiment but three men died in camp or regimental hospital during each year, making nine in all, and this, too, when but few were sent to general hospital. This is doubtless due to the great care with which our Surgeon looked after the habits of the men, the condition of their quarters—the injunctions he always gave the soldiers to attend early to any indisposition they might feel—and the pertinacity with which he insisted upon daily inspecting the processes for preparing food. These, after all, seem to be the great duties of a regimental Surgeon.

When it became known that Surg. Woodhull intended to retire from the field, his time of service having expired, he was formally tendered the Lieut. Colonelcy of the Ninth, by the Col. com'dg, and was solicited to accept the position by all the officers of the regiment, who believed him possessed of qualifications which eminently fitted him for filling so important a position. But the smoke of the final conflict seemed rolling up; the end of the war appeared near, and he preferred to take advantage of the present circumstances, to resume the duties of private life.

New Jersey may well be proud of him. His indefatigable and patriotic labors, during four long years of war, exhibit a record which does him the greatest credit, and sheds lustre on the State which he so ably represented in the field.

February 11th. Surgeon F. B. Gillette relieved at Mansfield general hospital, at Morehead City, and joined regiment.

February 17th. Company G was relieved at Bogue Sound, by a company from the 17th Mass., and joined the regiment.

February 19th. Regimental inspection, by Lieut. L. K. Devendorf, A. A. Inspector-General.

February 22d. Washington's Birthday; firing of salutes at Fort Macon.

February 28th. Regiment inspected, and mustered for pay.

March 2d. Received orders to move: the men to have three days' rations in knapsacks.

March 3d. All regimental and hospital-stores, officers' luggage, and all the knapsacks, were sent to Beaufort and stored.

March 4th. Rain all day; waiting for transportation till afternoon, when, at $3\frac{1}{2}$ P. M., took cars for Newbern and Batchelor's Creek; arrived at midnight.

March 5th. Quartered over night in the barracks of the 132d Reg't New York Vols.; marched at daylight, following railroad-track; marched thirteen miles, to near Core Creek; halted; bivouacked; regiment brigaded. Brigade consisting of the Ninth New

Jersey, 23d Mass., four companies 2d Heavy Mass., 85th New York, and Battery C, 3d New York Artillery, under command of Brigadier-General E. Harland.

March 6th. Marched at 6½ A. M.; the Ninth New Jersey in advance, followed railroad-track, which was entirely broken up by the rebels.

March 7th. Marched at 9 A. M.; the Ninth, in advance, marched within five miles of Southwest Creek ; four companies skirmishing the whole day; advanced to rebel breastworks ; engagement ensued, in which the Ninth lost one officer, Captain Charles Hufty, who died on the 14th, at Newbern ; the engagement lasted till night ; Companies A, D, and G went on picket.

March 8th. The regiment returning three-quarters of a mile, then formed line of battle ; here the regiment was relieved by the 23d Mass., and took position near General Palmer's headquarters, on Tilghmann's farm, throwing up breastworks ; no shovels and picks being on hand, knives, bayonets, tin-cups, and bare hands were used ; the Ninth held position of extreme right of Brigade, in centre.

March 9th. In afternoon, the enemy made seven charges on our left, resting on Wise's Fork ; the Ninth was ordered, and went on double-quick to the scene of action ; the engagement lasted till night, when the enemy fell back, our troops returning to their former position ; picket-firing during night ; shells were also thrown. Lieut. A. H. Evans, and sixteen men, of Co. E, were missing ; that part of the 27th Mass. present were all taken prisoners, except Surgeon Fish ; rain the whole day.

March 10th. Early in morning the enemy renewed his charges ; they were made with great ferocity : four columns deep, and *eleven* times repeated ; they had received notice that other troops of ours were coming up in their rear, towards Smithfield and Goldsboro' ; they fought like devils, but it was all of no avail, they could not break our lines ; our men stood firm, repulsing every charge made, with a heavy loss to the rebels ; these bloody attacks were followed at evening by a remarkable stillness, indicating either that the enemy was preparing a ruse, or evacuating his strongholds. The Ninth had this day one officer and nine men wounded.

March 11th. Found in the early morning that the enemy had retreated ; the regiment held same position on Tilghmann's Farm, the owner of which was a guide in the rebel army, and his brother, a true, loyal man, acted in the same capacity for our Generals, and told our men to help themselves to whatever they could find, as his brother was one of the worst of traitors. This plantation lay two miles from Union Mills, in Jones' Co., near the line of Lenoir. Upon the battle-ground of the previous day we found about 800 dead rebels, and some 70 of our own men; lay in breastworks all day; four pieces of artillery were stationed to the left of our regiment, in the direction the enemy had taken their line of retreat. Towards Kinston heavy firing was heard; the fire from our gunboats, advancing up the Neuse river, could also be heard.

March 12th and 13th. Sunday and Monday; remained in same position.

March 14th. Marched at 9 A. M.; passed rebel breastworks on the other side of Southwest Creek; they were very formidable, and had had seventeen guns, all of which were taken away by the rebels; arrived at noon at Neuse river; found the bridge destroyed by fire, by the rebels; the woods, all bushes, even the large, dry grass and straw, on the field, had been set on fire by the enemy. Halted close by the place where the regiment had charged in 1862; found bones of human bodies and pieces of clothing laying all over the ground. After a short rest we marched again, leaving Neuse river and Kinston to our right; whole column bivouacked in open field, about half-a-mile southwest of Kinston.

March 15th. Marched at 2 P. M.; heavy rain, which drenched the men; crossed the Neuse river, by pontoon-bridge, at 7 P. M.; passed through rebel breastworks, and bivouacked southeast of Kinston; rain all night; near the camp-ground were several cemeteries, with a number of new graves of men who had fallen in the late charges at Wise's Forks; only a few had head-boards, among which were those of Colonel James H. Neal, and Adjutant S. G. Turner, of the 19th Georgia regiment. Kinston has three churches; the building of the Masonic Order was considerably damaged; the railroad-depot had no accommodations: one scale, a few freight-cars, and the caissons of two guns, comprised all that was there. Near the court-house was a whipping-post, for punishing negroes; the jail, or bull-pen, as it is called by Southerners, was a most dirty and filthy den; the hotel was used for a hospital.

March 16th. Remained: rain all day.

March 17th. Very cold during the night; clear at day; the men of the Ninth, and all troops along the line surrounding the city, built breastworks; in doing this, many torpedoes were found and dug out, which had been placed there by the rebels, to injure our men when entering the place. They were placed in such a way that anything weighing seven pounds stepping or dropping on to one would explode the infernal machine; one of these exploded, injuring the leg of a cavalryman, and killing his horse.

March 18th. Regiment inspected by Lieut. Col. Burnam, of the 16th Conn.; an order was issued for the Ninth to remain on garrison-duty, at which the men rejoiced.

March 19th. Received marching orders, contrary to all expectation, and contrary to all former arrangements; the Generals. well knowing the former deeds of the Ninth, did not intend to leave it on garrison duty; Colonel James Stewart commanded newly-organized Brigade, called 2d Brigade 1st Division of District of Beaufort, consisting of the Ninth New Jersey Vols., 25th Mass , and 85th New York Vols.; Major S. Hufty, Jr., in command of regiment; regiment formed line at 5 A. M., and moved immediately into breastworks east of Kinston, and halted there; passing through town, regiment halted near the Court-house, at post-commissary's headquarters, and received three days' rations. (The writer met with five women, living in one house, all widows of rebel soldiers, all of whom were pregnant.)

March 20th. Monday; weather very warm; troops moved at sunrise; marched, passing several large plantations, among which was one belonging to James Woods, whose negro-huts, about 40 in number, where formerly over 140 negroes had dwelt, were all vacant. Crossed railroad at Jones' road, about noon; halted, and bivouacked for the night. about three miles from Whitehall, and sixteen miles from Kinston.

March 21st. Tuesday; marched. the Ninth in advance; rain during night; weather clear in the afternoon; foraging plenty: bacon, ham, poultry, flour, meal, and quantities of other produce; Corporal R. Emory was wounded, kicked by Major Hufty's horse, which accidentally got loose, and became frightened. Halted several times, and rested for about one hour about four miles from Goldsboro'. Marched again about noon; came in sight of Wep-town: here, when skirmishing began, about 1500 rebel cavalry,

200 infantry, and some 25 belonging to the rebel Home-guard, all under command of Colonel S. D. Pool, of Beaufort, were met; the cavalry had dismounted, and entered Weptown, when the Ninth came up, charging into Weptown upon them, double-quick. Rebels retreated to Goldsboro'; our cavalry, which was relieved, by the Ninth, fell back; the Ninth skirmished from Weptown to Goldsboro', with huzzas and cheers. The rebel cavalry and infantry, in all 1700 strong, had disappeared in all directions; retreating, the enemy fired into their own town, wounding one citizen, at Weptown; the Ninth New Jersey was the first regiment to enter Goldsboro', where it was met by I. H. Privett, Mayor of the city, and Constable George Murray, the latter carrying a flag-of-truce, inquiring for General Cox, for the purpose of surrendering the town. The flag of the Ninth was the first Union flag raised over the city, on the top of the Court-house. The regiment marched through several streets, halting at the railroad-depot, sending different companies in all directions, to reconnoitre; soon other troops arrived; they entered the city with flags flying, bands playing, and drums beating; cheer followed cheer, and huzzah after huzzah, to the Union flag of the Ninth, waving from the Court-house. As soon as General Carter arrived, he turned the city over to the hands of Major S. Hufty, of the Ninth, detaching this officer for Provost-marshal; also ordering the Ninth to do the Provost-duty. The Ninth was partly quartered in the Court-house, partly in stores. In a large frame-building, standing on the Fair-ground, and which had lately been used for a hospital, we found 23 of our wounded men, four of whom belonged to the 27th Mass., wounded in the engagement at Wise's Fork. Lieut. Col. Bartholomew, of the 27th Mass., who had been severely wounded in the leg, was forced to march along, when the rebels left. The wounded and sick left behind were all serious cases; the men, the beds, yea, even the building itself, was completely alive with lice, and other vermin. Surgeon F. B. Gillette was ordered to take charge of the sick and the general hospital, by order of Surgeon D. W. Hand, Medical-director, from Newbern. Surgeon F. B. Gillette took the Female Seminary, a large brick-building, and well adapted for the purpose, to have it furnished for a hospital, but hardly had he commenced, when the advance of Sherman's army arrived, followed by some 3 to 4,000 of sick; Griswold's

and Grainger's hotels, and several large private houses, were turned into hospitals, and Surgeon F. B. Gillette who, with his other duties, still continued to attend to the men of the Ninth, and was also senior medical officer of the Brigade, requested to be relieved as Surgeon in charge of general hospital, which request was granted.

March 22d. The large freight and store-house of the upper depot was burned down by rebel citizens.

March 23d. The whole of Sherman's army having arrived by this time, quartered partly in town, but the most of them encamped around the city; General Sherman reviewed the whole, riding with his staff along the whole line of breastworks and all the camps. The men of the 14th Army Corps were very badly clothed; they had drawn no clothing or shoes since leaving Atlanta; had only received seven rations from the Government, living on what they found and captured; they entered Goldsboro' with wagon-loads of provisions, numbers of cattle and other live animals, carriages drawn by four and sometimes more horses;—in some cases it seemed as if they carried the whole farm. About 1,000 prisoners were brought in during the day. More than 1,000 white refugees, most of them females, or old, crippled males and infants, seeking the assistance of provisions and Government rations, to keep them from starving. Some 1200 negroes also came in : most of these were sent to Newbern.

March 25th. Seventeen cars, loaded with tools and materials for the Engineer and Construction-corps to rebuild the Railroad, arrived from Newbern, and from this time several trains arrived daily. The army rested, awaiting the arrival of clothing and shoes. As it was reported that the Ninth New Jersey should be relieved from Provost-duty, a petition signed by all citizens, was sent to the Gen. commanding, to allow the Ninth to remain, as the conduct of the men in doing their duty, etc., had given general satisfaction.

March 27th. Some men exchanged greenbacks for gold and silver; silver-plates and bars also came into market; one of Sherman's bummers found $1800 in half-dollar silver pieces; the money, packed in a tin-box, had been put in a well by the owner, who was betrayed by one of his slaves. Many men daily went out to forage, returning with boots, pigs, poultry, potatoes, and other produce; three of these were found dead, with labels fastened to their bodies, inscribed : "Death to foragers!"

March 28th. Many sutlers arrived, and other enterprising persons, to begin business; the storehouses were wanted; the regiment and all troops moved out of town, to encamp in open field; to-day a newspaper was issued, printed by Charles Hinton, of Co. K, called "The Loyal State Journal;"—the press and type were all found in good order, so hastily had Spellman, the former editor and proprietor, and many citizens, fled when we entered. A second petition was sent to the General commanding, to let the Ninth remain on Provost-duty, as it was understood that Gen. Carter wished to have this regiment tranferred to the 23d Army Corps.

March 29th. Rain in afternoon; about 200 prisoners were brought in, among whom were Col. Alfred Rhett, of the 1st South Carolina Artillery, who was one of the first to fire on Fort Sumter, in 1861. Private Bryant, of Co. K, 12th New York Vols., was shot for committing rape upon an old lady, having committed the same crime on a young girl, at Kinston; Captain Keenan, of the 17th Mass., was in charge of the guard and men detailed for the execution, which was ordered to be witnessed by all the troops.

March 30th. Rain during day and night.

March 31st. Clear in the morning; orders were issued from General headquarters to take up all horses, mules, etc., not allowed by regulations, or which could not be accounted for.

April 1st. Lieut. A. H. Evans, Co. E, taken prisoner at Wise's Fork, March 8th, returned to the regiment; when captured, they were brought to Manson, on the Raleigh and Geston Railroad; then marched, and arrived at Greesy Creek, near Clarksville, Va., on the evening of the 12th, the fourth of their capture; the Lieut. and a Captain of the 12th New York Cavalry escaped, returning on the same railroad-track, following then the first county pike: traveling through Halifax county, south of Roanoke, Northampton and Bertie county, west of Roanoke; marched to Plymouth, Washington county, where they embarked for Newbern. The rebels had only taken the sword of Lieut. Evans; he having hid his money, watch, etc. Negroes running around, and coming into town, were picked up, to work in the trenches; divine service every day, in the churches and meeting-houses; these were mostly attended by negroes and mulattoes.

April 2d. Sunday; nothing of importance.

April 3d. The regiment was transferred to the 2d Brigade, 3d

Division, 23d Army Corps, and consisted of the Ninth New Jersey, 65th Illinois, 65th Indiana, and 177th Ohio Vols., under command of Brevet Brigadier-General J. S. Ceasement, and in charge of Surgeon S. S. Burrows, of the 177th Ohio.

April 4th. Companies E and F, of the Ninth, arrested at Weptown some 50 men and women living in one house for disorderly conduct.

April 5th. Numbers of sick and wounded, from different commands, were sent to Newbern.

April 6th. A written Special Order, from General headquarters, was put up, and eagerly read by all, announcing the evacuation of Richmond and Petersburg, of the capture of 500 guns, three rams, and 2500 prisoners. Soon an extra edition of "The Loyal State Journal," printed by Charles Hinton, a private of the Ninth, circulated through town and in all camps, spreading the great news to all. Charles deserves credit for his labor.

April 7th. Private Robert Schafer, Co. B, who deserted in June, 1864, was arrested; he had re-enlisted in another regiment.

April 10th. Colonel James Stewart, Jr., returned to the regiment, and took command; Lieut. Col. Hufty, Jr., of the Ninth, Provost-marshal, was relieved by Col. Rumlet, of the 38th Mass., 19th Army Corps; this regiment also relieved the Ninth from Provost-duty; the Ninth, having received marching orders, marched at 2 P. M.; marched five miles, and bivouacked at 9 P. M., in open field. It had rained the whole day, and the roads were in bad condition. Lieut. George Peters, Co. G, of the Ninth, captured May 16, '64, returned to the regiment. This officer shared the same fate as Lieut. Drake, till the latter made his escape, October 16, '64. Lieut. Peters and others remained at Columbia two months; here many escaped, by passing the outer guards, on paying twenty-five dollars; others did not return when sent after wood. Lieut. Peters escaped in company with three other officers, from Columbia, S C., having been detailed upon the wood-relief parties; they took advantage of these opportunities, and struck out for the swamp. After dark, they traveled to the right of Lexington, in a northwesterly direction; at daylight they made six miles towards Saluta river, and remained on its banks; two white citizens passed by, but did not notice them; at sundown they looked for means to cross the river: not finding anything, they built a raft of rails, tied together with grape-vines ; when launching it, it was found not strong enough to carry all four, so three started first, intending that one should return, to bring the fourth, but the current of the river was very strong at this point, the rapids being only 2 or 300 yards above ; when the raft nearly reached the opposite shore, it parted, and all three were precipitated into the water, but succeeded in getting on dry land ; though it was their intention to return after the fourth, this was now impossible, and he was left behind with sorrow. Starting again, in a northwesterly direction, they mistook the right course ; they marched in a circle, and found themselves at the same place that they had started from in the morning ; in the evening, retracing their steps, they followed the road till morning ; hearing dogs barking, they hid themselves for some time ; being very hungry and cold, they tried to find the negroes, whom they had heard calling for their animals, but in vain ; remaining in the woods during the day, they came up to a negro-hut, towards evening ; the old man gave them plenty of corn-meal and milk, and filled their haversacks also, with biscuit. On the evening of the 29th of November, they came to a mill-dam, which they crossed with difficulty ; at the opposite side they found several houses, which were flanked ; they found a patch of radishes, which were first thought to be turnips : this was a God-send, as they were very hungry ; the houses all passed, another difficulty arose, from the joining of several roads ; they traveled several miles without interruption, halted, and rested about midnight ; while resting, they heard men approaching ; by the conversation, they knew that they were white men ; fortunately they did not notice us. Marching again in the morning, they came close to a house, which they were afraid to pass ; flanking it, they came, to their astonishment, but great joy and pleasure, up with Lieut. Alexander, who had been forced to remain on the other side of the river, a few days before. At this time, they believed themselves to be near Frog Level, which they did not like to enter by day ; so they rested, approaching the road at night ; they kept close to the fences, to watch the arrival of negroes, to receive something to eat ; meeting with one who promised them plenty if they followed him to his house, though very tired, they marched three miles back, in the expectation of a good supper ; arriving, they received a substantial supper, filling also their

22

haversacks; resuming march, and reaching the village, they flanked
the building; marched all night, hiding themselves by day. On
the night of the 2d of December, they again started: coming to
Newburry, they found themselves in a tight place, and kept close
to the woods. Here they met a negro with his team, on his way
home, who was startled to death by their appearance; convincing
him that no harm should befal him, he promised to furnish them
with provisions; waiting his return, the dogs made such an infernal noise, that they considered it best to move on until the morning of the 3d, when again they halted to rest; negroes and white
citizens were at work in the fields close by, so that they had to
keep very still. Traveling again at night, they tried to find something to eat, but instead of nourishment, they found that they were
at Hinton, when they expected to reach Lawrenceville, Lawrence
county; marched this night twenty miles: resting during the day,
and marching again at night, they had the great disadvantage of
there being a full moon; approaching a plantation, they were observed by a man on horseback: the man watched them coming
up, so that he bid them "Good evening;" it proved to be a physician, going out to visit a patient; directly after they met a negro,
riding a mule, who promised not to betray them; afterwards they
learned that the Doctor and negro met, when the latter was threatened to confess what he knew about them; fearing that they
would be retaken again, as a prevention, they put pine boughs
under their feet; not being able to find the road, on account of the
darkness, they came upon a turnip-patch, from which they ate
heartily, and laid down to sleep; they were aroused by four dogs,
it proved, followed by two negroes, who were out hunting, and they
showed them the Greenville road; when marching about five
miles the following night, dogs were again on their track, and not
liking to be torn to pieces, they climbed the trees: the men coming up, did not make any attack, for which they know no other
reason than that they were out-numbered; traveling again about
three miles, they came to a village; the dogs which were on their
track, again made a great noise; here they were also pursued by
three men, and they ran for three miles, resorting to pine-boughs
again; being tired and foot-sore, they laid down to rest till morning, when they concluded to travel by day, to be able to find out
their way, that part of the country where they were not-being

safe ; working on this plan, they met with great disadvantages in the beginning ; to come to another road, they had to pass over open fields, on hands and knees, to be unobserved from the houses, and from the people at work in the fields; at night they came to a negro, who was ploughing, a white boy being with him : the negro stated that the boy was the son of a Union man, but dared not bring them to him, the nearest neighbor being secesh ; he promised them something to eat, to show them to the right road, and to bring them to another Union man, who lived some distance off. Instead of all this he betrayed them : as they soon were halted by a party of citizens, with shot-guns and rifles, who demanded their surrender ; they surrendered, and moved on. (The following remainder of the account is given in the language of Lieut. Peters.) "After marching about four miles, we came to a house, where the lady invited us to supper ; supper had been already prepared, which convinced us that our arrival had been expected. The lady was very inquisitive : she had never seen any Yankees before in her life, and had undoubtedly prepared this supper to have a chance to gratify her curiosity ; she was very much astonished to find us men, like all others, and without horns ; she asked a number of questions ; supper over, we marched two miles farther, to Johnson's Store, where we were turned over to the commanding officer. This was on the 6th of December, '64 ; on the 7th, we started, and arrived at 4 P. M., at Lawrenceville, a distance of 17 miles ; after the enrolling-officer had taken our names, etc., we were turned over to the Sheriff, and locked up in the jail ; here we were insulted by very insolent language, from the young aristocracy. The Sheriff's wife paid us a visit, admitting, as a general thing, that the rebels were wrong, but complaining bitterly that they were robbed of their 'niggers.' After breakfast, we went by cars, and arrived at Newburry ; here we waited for the Greenville and Columbia train, during which time the negroes furnished us with cakes and pies ; at Columbia we arrived at 5 P. M., and were lodged in the jail, and marched next morning to Camp Sorghan again ; during our absence, one man had been brutally murdered ; on the 12th of December we encamped near the Lunatic Asylum : here tunnels were dug, through which to escape, but they were discovered ; General Winder directed that, if repeated, our shanties should be burned down, and we exposed to storm and weather; but this was his last order, as he died a few days later, of apoplexy, at Florence, S. C. When Sherman approached, we were taken to Charlotte, then to Greensboro', then to Raleigh and Goldsboro', where we were paroled on the last day of February, 1865. On the 1st of March we arrived in our lines, nine miles from Wilmington."

Quartered in churches and school-houses; sailing to Annapolis, Lieut. Peters obtained leave of absence to go to Washington and home to Elizabeth, N. J., arriving home on Sunday morning before breakfast, having heard nothing from his family in over ten months. Lieut. Peters was commissioned May 3d, 1864, when the regiment was at Yorktown; he could not be mustered while in the field, going into active service. Returning, the Lieut. requested to have his muster-in dated as far back as the day of his commission, having done duty as lieutenant from that day, and having been in command of the company at the time of his capture. The request repeated twice, it was approved by the Colonel commanding and other officers, but not granted, on account of the negligence or ignorance of company-officers and company-clerks not entering Lieut. Peters on the muster-rolls, for pay, as on duty with the company. Lieut. Peters could not be mustered back, by which he lost his pay. Officers have been mustered back for one year and over, who never were in active service, and never left the comforts of home or luxurious hotels, when Lieut. Peters never missed any duty, never failed in any engagement or battle, during service of over three years, and was captured while on duty, engaged in a bloody fight.

April 11th. Company H, Captain Pullen, was detailed on duty at General Cox's headquarters. It had rained all night and all day. Resumed march about 7 A. M., the Ninth guarding the wagon-train; halted at Mosgrove's plantation, near the Codfish Creek, where we took dinner; resumed march about 1 P. M.; passed William Atkinson's plantation, which is about ten miles from Goldsboro', where our forces on the previous day had had a heavy skirmish with about 1000 rebel cavalry and 500 infantry; passing Dr. J. W. Whitley's farm, we came to Thomas Atkinson's plantation. William and Thomas Atkinson were two brothers, and both arch traitors; the houses were burned down, and all furniture totally destroyed. The Doctor's house and property was left in good order, though his son was in the rebel army. Thomas Atkinson had been the late Sheriff; from his house rebels had fired on our worn-out and exhausted men, following in the rear; he had dragged and forced poor whites, who were of Union sentiments, into the rebel army; he had kept bloodhounds to hunt our men; it was also said that he ordered two of our men, who were captured while foraging, to be hung, which order was executed, near his house, but, by the revengeful hands of our Western men, his house was burned down, and everything else destroyed. Coming about sunset to Mrs. Mary Jane Smith's farm, we halted for supper; marched about two miles further, and bivouacked at 9 P. M. in open field.

April 12th. At the moment when the march was to be resumed a courier arrived from General Sherman, who, while riding along the whole line of about 100,000 troops, laying close together on both sides of the road, cried, to the utmost extent of his voice: " Gentlemen, General R. E. Lee has surrendered !" Newspapers may write about and the people of large cities may make large processions, hold meetings, pass resolutions, give dinners and suppers, arrange balls, have fireworks, etc., etc., at such a joyful event, but it cannot be compared with the pleasure—the deep-felt pleasure of an army receiving such great news. Hear the cheer of about 100,000 veteran soldiers, who have withstood the enemy's steel, and faced the cannon's mouth in many battles; hear the music of about thirty-five bands, who have played their martial-music in numberless attacks, joined by drums and fifes innumerable; see old, hard-looking warriors, who would not falter when their comrade and friend fell at their side; see these brave men, old and young, weep for joy, embrace and kiss each other; see how they carry regimental or Brigade officers on their shoulders, to have the news read again and again; see battle-worn and bullet-riddled flags waved and raised on highest poles;—see all that, and you may join in that noble feeling which, in procession, no newspaper report or description can awaken in your breast, and which it would be impossible to describe. This news very likely changed the plans of our Generals; the march was postponed till 11 A. M., when we passed Union, late Baptist meeting-house; found many houses burning, and nearly all property destroyed. The writer several times had occasion to convince himself that this setting fire to buildings was, in most instances, done by negroes, seeking revenge on their masters. Coming to Haw river, we found the bridges burned; crossed by pontoon, and bivouacked about four miles from Smithfield.

April 13th. Marched early in morning; marched the whole day, and bivouacked at 9 P. M., at Mrs. S. W. Allen's plantation,—a widow, whose husband had been shot in his own yard, on the previous day, by one of Kilpatrick's cavalry, who found him with a gun, and he not having come to a halt, when ordered to do so;— the corpse was attended to by one of the Ninth's hospital attendants. The country around here was in good order, and the land good.

April 14th. Marched about 6 A. M.; halted several times; bivouacked finally in open field, near Raleigh; the city had already been surrendered by the Mayor, Wm. H. Harrisson, Hon. Kenneth, Dr. McKee, and several others, to General Kilpatrick. After the surrender, a few of the rebel cavalry, who had remained as rear-guard, fired on some of Kilpatrick's men, of whom two were captured, and hung. Gov. Vance's dwelling was taken for General Sherman's headquarters, and the State-house used for Provost-Marshal and other offices.

April 15th. It had rained all night, and continued in the morning; the troops began to march about 7 A. M.: every one drenched to the skin; the Ninth and whole Brigade had already formed line, when the order was countermanded; the men, setting up their tents, again bivouacked as well as they could, in a most furious storm of rain.

April 17th. A negro-boy, servant of Lieut. Bryant, of Co. C, playing with a loaded musket, fired, as is believed, accidentally, the ball striking and bending Lieut. Applegate's sword and scabbard, cutting the upper-leather of his left boot, without doing any other injury. The circumstance would have led to more serious trouble, for several officers and men interfered, causing a great excitement, when Colonel Stewart appeared, and as coolly ordered the officers to go their quarters, and the men to their companies.

April 21st. Orderly Hulsart, Co. D, Serg't Wood, Co. A, Serg't Fatty, Co. G, Corporal Hill, Co. G, and many others, who had been from ten to eleven months in the numerous rebel prisons, seen their horrors and devilishly-designed tortures, joined the regiment again, all of them unfit for duty, suffering from scurvy, anasarca, and general debility, contracted and produced in the filthy dens of so-called chivalrous, but more properly hellish invention, to bolster up their traitorous cause, by slow starvation, poisonous vaccination, etc. They were in the prisons at Libby, Augusta, Camp Sumpter, Ga., Charleston, Florence, etc., etc. Their narratives differ but little from those already related. Hulsart reports nine deaths out of sixteen captured, belonging to his company (D). Hill reports twelve deaths out of sixteen captured, belonging to Co. G.

Lieut. General Grant, who had arrived on previous day, reviewed the troops : General Sherman on his right, and each Division-commander taking his position on the left, as troops arrived.

April 27th. Orders for a move ; moved southwest of camp ; this day the papers published the General Order of Johnston's surrender, but the excitement was not so much as had been expected.

April 29th. Thirteen guns were fired at sunrise, one every half-hour afterwards, and thirty-six at sun-down : one for each State, as ordered by the War Department, in memory of Abraham Lincoln. The regiment formed line at 10 A. M., to have the order referring to the assassination, read to the men.

April 30th. Regimental Inspection and muster ; Lieut. Col. Hufty, with forty men, went to Beaufort, after knapsacks and regimental luggage.

May 2d. Brigadier-General Ceasement resigned ; Brigadier-General G. W. Schoefield in command of Brigade. By this time, many reports and different rumors were in circulation, regarding the mustering-out and disbanding of regiments. All officers and privates were in a great state of excitement. Received order to move ; five Companies, A, B, C, F, and G, formed line ; left camp, and took at 3½ P. M. the cars for Greensboro'.

May 3d. Four companies, D, E, I, and K, formed line at 6 P. M. ; marched to railroad-depot, and took cars for the same place ; passed Morrisville, Durnham's, and Hillsboro' stations ; detained three hours ; passed then Mebane's, Haw river, Graham & Company's Shops stations : here we found a large stock of railroad-material, locomotives, cars, etc., etc. Complaints were also made by the citizens to Colonel James Stewart, Jr., that they were in daily and hourly danger of being robbed and even killed, by guerillas and desperate bushwhackers, lately belonging to Johnston's army. Five men, who had been arrested during the day, were put on our train, to be locked up for trial at Greensboro'. As the citizens at this station were not able to protect themselves, Col. James Stewart, Jr., ordered Lieut. Townley to remain with Co. K, at this place, on guard-duty, until relieved; passing Gibsonville and McLean's stations, we reached Greensboro' at 12, midnight; heard upon our arrival that many accidents had happened on previous day, because of men becoming drunk on whiskey found in Company Shop station, among which was that of a private of Co. A, who had been shot severely with a pistol, by a private of Co. G, the ball entering right eye; they had always been very good friends, and the accident was the result of carelessness alone. Another was slightly wounded in breast, by the accidental discharge of a musket.

May 4th. Having encamped near the depot, the commands reported in the morning to General Carter, commanding Division; were ordered to encamp on McCullough's plantation, west of Greensboro'. Lumber was very scarce; the men set up their tents, each company putting up bush-houses, to be protected from the rays of the sun. Rations were very small, and poor: smaller than ever before, because we shared with the whole of Johnston's army; it was very noble to feed and clothe our enemies, but our men suffered much, because it lasted so long before proper arrangements were made to have plenty of supplies. Again, our men had not been paid in from eight to ten and twelve months, and so they could not buy anything of the little that was for sale. The command received orders to send two companies, one to Charlotte, the other to Salisbury; Company G, under command of Captain Runyon, went to the first, and Co. I, under command of Lieut. Kille, to the second place. General Cox, commanding Corps, and Co. H, of the Ninth, which was still on duty at headquarters, arrived from Raleigh.

May 5th. Lieut. Colonel Hufty, with the detachment of men, arrived from Beaufort with knapsacks, regimental and hospital-luggage; the former were given out to the men.

May 6th. Upon our arrival, country-produce was very low: for instance, eggs ten cents per dozen; but our men were so much in need of nourishment, that the few who had a little money, were so eager to buy that the farmers, noticing their advantages, raised their prices to the sutler's standard, which is blood and fever-heat.

May 7th. At evening, Co. I returned from Salisbury, leaving camp on the afternoon of the 4th; taking cars at 4½ A. M. of the 5th; reaching Salisbury at 10½ A. M.; they halted, and took dinner near the so-called "Bull-pen," the place where our prisoners had been kept, when they moved into town, and quartered in houses. On Saturday, the 6th, a Confederate officer turned over all ordnances and stores to Lieut. Kille, of the Ninth, all of which was loaded on cars, and sent to Greensboro'; the loading was done by colored people; on the 8th, Colonel Strickland, with a full Brigade of the 2d Division arrived, to relieve Lieut. Kille and Co. I; they left at 10½ A. M., on the 9th, arriving at Lexington at 10½ P. M.; they were ordered to remain at this place, as guard for the night. Leaving Lexington at 2 P. M., on the 10th, they arrived in camp at Greensboro' again, at 7 P. M.

May 13th. Company G returned from Charlotte; Captain Runyon, commanding Co. G, made the following report :—

HEADQUARTERS CO. G, 9TH N. J. VOLS., }
Greensboro', N. C., May 13th, '65. }

SIR—I have the honor to submit the following report. In accordance with orders from Major-General Cox, I left Greensboro', N. C., with my company on May 5th, '65, and proceeded by railroad to Salisbury, N. C.; arrived there at 11 A. M.; I left Salisbury at 5 P. M., and was transported by rail to within five miles of Concord, a station 21 miles from Charlotte, N. C. The next morning, May 6th, I marched to Concord, and telegraphed to Charlotte, for a train. I received an answer, stating that an accident had happened to the downward train, and that no train would run for a day or so. I immediately took up line of march, and that evening encamped thirteen miles from Charlotte. The next morning I resumed the march, and arrived in Charlotte at 5½ P. M. I found the town filled with rebel soldiers; raids were made by mobs, on stores that had been left by the rebels. Drunkenness and disorder generally had been the order of the day. I immediately issued an order, assuming command of the post, also another, prohibiting the sale of all kinds of spirituous liquors. After my arrival, good order prevailed.

The following is the list of stores taken possession of, and guarded by my command : Medical Purveyor's establishment, containing a large quantity of medical stores; there being no Surgeon in my command, I had no means of determining the value of them. The rebel Navy Yard, containing a large amount of machinery, iron, etc., most of which had been taken from the

Portsmouth, Va., Navy Yard. A number of boxes, said to contain the records of the rebel War Department and all the archives of the so-called Southern Confederacy. Also boxes, said to contain all the colors and battle-flags captured from the National forces since the beginning of the war; a quantity of naval stores, and a quantity of commissary stores; a branch of the U. S. Mint was found, containing the machinery connected with it, all in good order. On Friday, the 12th, Brigadier-General Thomas, of the 1st Brigade, 1st Division, 23d Army Corps, arrived, relieving me of command of the post. On Friday, at 5 P. M., I received an order, by telegraph, to report to my regiment, without delay. The next day, the 13th, I had my command placed on cars, and reported at regimental headquarters, at Greensboro', N. C., at 4 P. M. the same day.

I am, Sir, very respectfully, your obedient servant,

M. C. RUNYON,
Captain Com'dg Co. G, 9th New Jersey Vols.

To E. W. WELSTEDT, Lieut. and Adjutant 9th New Jersey Vols., Greensboro', N. C.

Account of 2d Lieut. George Peters, of Co. G:—"As we approached the Yadkin river, on May 5th, we came up with the rear-column of Johnston's army, on their way home, numbering 8 to 10,000; a situation novel to us and all who witnessed it. For the first time we did come in contact with the rebels, without having to fight. To see them swarming around us, and to hear their expressions of friendship and good feeling, was, indeed, very strange to us, more so while they outnumbered us 100 to 1 : one-fifth of these being armed. One remarked that he had never before seen the Yankees, without being compelled to lay down, or without being ordered to do so. There were others who did not like the way pursued by their Generals; these would rather have fought on than to succumb, but the majority were tired of the war. Many stated that they would never have been in the rebel army, if they could have avoided it. The delay at Salisbury was very unpleasant, as, in case of any trouble, we would have been at their mercy, but everything passed off quietly, the troops being remarkably orderly. On the 7th, on our march to Charlotte, we met numbers of stragglers along the road : also citizen-stragglers, who were out to steal cotton, clothing, provisions,—in short, anything they could lay hands on and make use of. It is doubtful if there are many or any other company which has been situated as we were, surrounded and marching with our late ene-

mies, they outnumbering us, and that, too, when we were cut off
from all our forces by nearly one hundred miles of railroad, with
a break in it, so that trains could not run. The citizens of Charlotte we found very hospitable ; the rich and well-to-do class seemed
to be very well satisfied with the change ; the middle-class and the
poor spoke bitterly and with condemnation of Jefferson Davis and
his clique. The military institution, lately used for the medi-
cal-purveyor's office, was stored with great quantities of medicines,
some of which, such as morphine and nitre, were very valuable ;
all with English labels, and of English manufacture, which had
been procured by blockade-running. Among others, we found two
12-pound brass field pieces; two cannons ; about 900 small arms ;
400,000 percussion-caps ; 1400 pounds of powder; an immense
quantity of sabres, cutlasses, etc., cartridge-boxes, and other equipments. Out of a large number of flags and trophies, taken from our
forces during the whole of the war, Captain Runyon picked
the State-colors of the 33d New Jersey Reg't., intending to forward the same to the Adjutant-General of the State of New Jersey. The U. S. Branch Mint was found in good order, but no
specie or other valuables could be seen. Specie was plenty in the
hands of the citizens, and quantities of goods and arms were stored
away, which, by this time, have been found and taken care of, by
the Colonel who came to relieve us. As soon as Captain Runyon,
commanding post, put guards where the archives of the so-called
Confederacy (about 84 boxes) were stored, General Johnston, who
still remained at Charlotte, communicated the facts to General
Schofield, commanding Department of North Carolina, at Raleigh,
and a staff-officer was immediately despatched, and arrived at Charlotte, to take charge of the valuable documents, and to forward
the same to Raleigh. There was no opportunity left for Captain
Runyon to earn laurels, and it is very doubtful if General Johnston would have reported as he did, if no guards had been posted,
and chance had been left to him to burn or destroy the written and
printed proofs of their shameful treachery and rebellion. Thus,
we see, that to the gallant old Ninth is due the enviable credit
of having captured and preserved from harm all the archives of
the rebel government, their trophies, and many of their valuable
stores. Too much credit cannot be accorded to Captain Runyon
for the manner in which he performed his peculiar duties, and it

is doubtful if any one could more judiciously have comported himself, when, with only a small company of men, he was compelled to crowd his way through the thousands of rebel soldiers with whom he had, as it were, just been engaged in the fiercest fight. The records here obtained by Captain Runyon have been, are, and ever will be of so great value to the Government of the United States, that it is almost impossible to magnify the importance of the capture thus made. In less careful and scrupulous hands they might have been mutilated or lost. But in spite of the wishes and schemes of rebel officers, who were present, Capt. Runyon insisted that they should be ' severely let alone,' and in all their completeness succeeded in turning them over to the Government he served."

May 20th. Lieut. Bonham, of Co. A, was ordered to report with his command to Yanceyville, Caswell county ; Lieut. Bonham, with twenty men, went by railroad to Danville, Va., 48 miles ; marched 15 miles to Yanceyville, N. C., arriving on Sunday morning. Lieut. Henry Hopper, with 30 men, took the direct road, marching 42 miles, arriving at Yanceyville on the 22d.

May 22d. The object of this was to carry out General Orders No. 35, from the headquarters of North Carolina, to organize police-companies, and to elect twelve magistrates for the county : one for each district.

May 25th. Received notice of the resignation of General Heckmann ; the command was ordered to go to Deep Creek, to afford the men a chance to bathe ; this order could not be fulfilled, on account of heavy rain.

May 30th. Lieut. A. H. Evans, Co. E, was detached as Judge-Advocate, on court-martial. Lieut. Bonham, with command, left Yanceyville, and arrived in camp, at Greensboro', on the 31st.

June 5th. A large flag-pole was raised in front of Col. James Stewart, Jr.'s headquarters.

June 7th. When at Newport News, in 1863, men were detailed to form a new regimental-band, under the leadership of Gottlieb Hoyer, of Co. C ; the latter left, at the expiration of his time of service, in October, 1864, and other members of the band becoming sick, Lieut. Col. Hufty ordered the Quartermaster to take charge of the instruments, and the men to return to their companies.

June 8th. Lieut. J. W. Green, Co. D, with 45 men from the regiment, went by cars to Graham's Station, on guard.

June 14th. In compliance with General Order No. 73, dated Headquarters, Department of North Carolina, Army of the Ohio, Raleigh, N. C., June 2d, 1865, to discharge all men, 216 men of the Ninth were mustered out, of whom 191 were present in camp.

June 16th. The men mustered out on the 14th, under charge of Lieut. Cogan, of Co. B, left Greensboro', by cars, via Raleigh, Goldsboro', Kinston, and Newbern; embarking on the transport Pilot-Boy, sailing to Fortress Monroe; embarking on Louisiana, sailing for Baltimore; taking cars for Philadelphia and Trenton : arriving at the latter place at midnight, June 22d. This detachment was entertained on June 23d with a good, substantial breakfast, by the ladies of Trenton, belonging to the " Soldiers' Welcome Home," near the railroad-depot. At noon, they partook of a dinner in Bechtel's Hall, given by the city, on which occasion they were formally received and addressed by the Mayor of the city, to whom Lieut. Cogan responded. The writer, who was one of this detachment, and had been chosen by Captain Runyon as the bearer of the State-colors of the 33d Reg't New Jersey Vols. to the Adjutant-General of the State of New Jersey, delivered the same at the Adjutant-General's office, in Trenton. Said colors were captured by Private John E. Abernethy, in the fight of July 20, 1864, and retaken by Captain Runyon, at Charlotte, May, '65.

June 17th. A review of the Division took place, opposite the Court-house of Greensboro', by Major-General Cox ; troops passed in column by company : the Ninth New Jersey, under Lieut. Col. Hufty, in the right of the 2d Brigade.

June 21st. Surgeon F. B. Gillette, of the Ninth, appointed Acting Division-Surgeon of the 3d Division, 23d Army Corps, and Medical Director of the Post.

July 5th. Regiment paid off.

July 6th. Lieut. E. W. Green, with detachment on duty at Graham's Station, was relieved, returned to camp, and was paid off.

July 8th. The command received muster-out rolls, for the whole regiment to be mustered out. *Great joy among the men.*

July 9th. Surgeon F. B. Gillette received permission to go North, with the embalmed body of his child, which had died at Greensboro,' and to report within ten days at Trenton, by the commanding officer of his regiment.

July 12th. The regiment was mustered out at Greensboro', N. C. ;

all surplus ordnance, camp, and garrison-equipage was turned over.

July 13th. At 5 P. M. the regiment left for Danville, arriving at 10 P. M.

Colonel Stewart, for some time previous to the departure of the regiment from Greensboro', N. C., was in command of a Division, and recommended for a Brigadier. General Carter, commanding at Greensboro', addressed the following letter to Col. Stewart :—

> HEADQUARTERS 23D ARMY CORPS,
> DISTRICT OF GREENSBORO',
> GREENSBORO', N. C., July 13, 1865.

Col. James Stewart, Jr., 9th New Jersey Vet. Vol. Infantry :

My Dear Colonel :—While it may be that I can add but little to the well-earned reputation of the gallant officers and men of your veteran regiment,—a reputation made on many hard-fought fields, which have become matters of history,—still I cannot have you leave for your homes without joining my testimony to that of others, as to the discipline, drill, gallant conduct, soldierly-bearing, and efficiency of your noble regiment. On the march, in camp, under fire, and in the performance of all the duties of a soldier, the example of the Ninth New Jersey Vet. Vol. Infantry has been worthy of imitation, and entitles it to all praise and commendation.

With your regiment, my relations have never been other than the most pleasant, and I shall always cherish with the liveliest feelings of pleasure the fact that I have had the honor to command such men.

You return to your homes only after the rebellion has been crushed and peace restored, with the proud consciousness that you, as a regiment, did your part nobly and fully towards re-establishing the National authority, and securing the blessings which I trust you may, under God's good Providence, long live to enjoy. While I regret much the severance of the ties which have existed between us, I heartily congratulate you on a speedy return to the loved ones at home, who are, even now, so anxiously waiting to greet and crown you with the victor's wreath, and shower upon you the plaudits which are justly your due. With the best and kindest wishes for yourself, your officers, and men, and a " God-speed " you on your " homeward-bound " journey, I am, my dear Colonel, with feelings of attachment and respect, very truly, your friend,

(Signed)   S. J. CARTER,
Brigadier-General Comd'g.

July 14th. At 4½ A. M. the regiment left by cars for, and arrived at, Burkville, at 11 A. M.

July 15th. Took cars for City Point, at 2 P. M., where nine companies embarked upon the Nellie Pentz, Company B embarking on another steamer, starting for Baltimore.

July 17th. Arrived at Baltimore at 7 A. M.; took train for Philadelphia, at 11 A. M.; arrived at 9 P. M., where the regiment was sumptuously entertained by the Volunteer and Cooper-Shop Refreshment Saloon. "*God bless those noble men and women who have so untiringly labored to cheer the soldiers of their country upon their weary way to and from their homes. They have shed a lustre on the name of Philadelphia, which makes it shine pre-eminently as the loyal city of the Union.*"

July 18th. Tuesday; left Philadelphia, and took cars at Camden, at 2½ A. M., arriving at Trenton, at 6½ A. M. The Trenton *Daily State Gazette* said, among others, about each arrival :—

"The Ninth Regiment New Jersey Vols., Col. Stewart, arrived here yesterday morning, and were handsomely entertained at the Soldiers' Rest, the ladies having made abundant provision for their reception.

"The Ninth regiment was recruited in the fall of 1861, as a rifle regiment, consisting of twelve companies. The uniform differed from that ordinarily worn by infantry, the cords, stripes, shoulder-straps, &c., being of green instead of light-blue. * * * * * We ought to state that the Ninth, armed with Springfield rifles, had been frequently exercised in target-firing, and were expert marksmen. While encamped at Meridian Hill, some of the 'crack shots' of the Berdan sharpshooters challenged the Ninth. This was accepted, and the match to a trial of skill took place, resulting in the victory of the Ninth. * * * * It is remarkable that of the officers returning with the regiment, all except the Colonel and Lieut. Colonel originally joined the regiment as privates. This not only shows that the Ninth has seen hard service, and lost many officers, but that it was composed of a good class of men."

The regiment was furloughed until the following Tuesday, when the furlough was extended until Friday, the 28th.

July 28th. Major Samuel C. Harbert began to pay off the Ninth; enlisted men of Companies A, B, and C were paid, receiving their final discharge-papers.

July 29th. Enlisted men of Companies D, E, F, G, H, I, and non-commissioned and staff-officers, were paid off and finally discharged.

A meeting of the officers of the Ninth regiment was held at

the Trenton House, at 1 o'clock to-day, for the purpose of presenting to their Colonel—Col. James Stewart, Jr.,—a testimonial of the regard in which he is held by the officers associated with him. The testimonial—which was a badge embodying in small compass the various emblems appropriate to the regiment—was presented by Major T. B. Applegate, in a brief speech, recounting the high esteem and affection in which Colonel Stewart is held by his comrades, and the confidence which they have reposed in him in the positions in which the regiment has been placed, from the Carolinas to Coal Harbor and Petersburg: he dwelt upon the record of its Colonels, of whom the first, Col. Allen, was drowned at Hatteras; the second, Colonel Heckmann, promoted Brigadier-General; the third, Colonel Zabriskie, killed at Drury's Bluff: Colonel James Stewart succeeding. He concluded with recounting the cordial emotions of esteem and affection which had prevailed between the officers, and their confidence in their commander. Colonel Stewart responded in a brief but hearty and appreciative address, whose tone and its reception showed the feelings of mutual regard between the brethren at arms.

The badge, made by Tiffany, of New York, is one of the handsomest pieces of jewelry we have ever seen. Except the silver eagle which surmounted it in token of the rank of its recipient, it was of gold richly enameled:—its face uniting the following emblems: the Bastioned Fort of the 10th Corps, of red enamel; the Trefoil Cross of the 18th Corps, of white enamel; the Shield of Gold, with silver cannon and anchor, of the 9th Corps; the Quartered Shield, of blue enamel, 23d Corps; the Red Star of Heckmann's Brigade:—all which were combined, and surmounted by a silver eagle. Upon the gold back was the inscription: "Presented to Col. James Stewart, by the Officers of the Ninth Regiment, as a Token of Respect and Affection."

Noticing this presentation, the Trenton *Daily Monitor* remarks:

"This testimonial, coming as it does from the men who are best qualified to judge of the merits of the recipient, must be exceedingly gratifying to Colonel Stewart—a better officer and more thorough soldier than whom does not exist. His record is an exemplary one. Entering the service in the lower grades of office, he has, by a faithful discharge of duty in every position assigned him, worked his way upward step by step, winning (not stealing) his promotion as he advanced. During his last few months of service prior to the final struggle, Col. Stewart was placed in command of a brigade, and displayed an eminent degree of Generalship that should have gained for him the silver stars he so nobly earned. New Jersey has reason to be, and *is* proud of the old Ninth Regiment and its gallant commander, and the noblest tribute that a grateful people can pay to both (that of a lasting remembrance of their deeds and valor) is, and will ever be theirs."

Surgeon F. B. Gillette turns over to Surgeon in charge of U. S. General Hospital, at Trenton, all medicines and hospital-stores, forwarding to Surgeon-General at Washington hospital-records and books.

July 31st. Company K and all commissioned officers were paid off, and finally mustered out.

Brevet Brigadier-General Stewart, upon the strong recommendation of the various commanders under whom he had served, subsequently received an appointment as full Brigadier-General of Volunteers.

——o——

Thus ends the record of the Ninth New Jersey Vols. We have tried to be just and fair to all, and if any brave man fails to find notice of his own individual heroic deeds, he may be assured it was through no want of appreciation of the same, but because of its utter impossibility in such a work as this. Our time and space have been limited, and we have been compelled to omit many of the collateral events incident to the operations of the regiment, which, though they would have been interesting, must have swelled this record to an undue extent.

If any mistakes exist, they have been made unwittingly. Many blunders in composition and idiomatic delinquencies may doubtless be found, but it is hoped that the generous reader will attribute it, not to any wilful negligence, but to an imperfect knowledge with the language of the country of our adoption. Officers and men of the old Ninth! it is with pain we bid you farewell. Our task has been a pleasing one, and it has seemed as though we were still together around the camp-fire, on the bivouac, in the fight; but now we part. May the same kind Hand that has so long and so often protected us, be over and around us, and guide us in our journey through, and when we join the mighty multitude which at last must cross the deep River, may our record be pure, our "final statements" properly made out, and in order, and we all experience no difficulty in obtaining a " muster-in " into that great Army above, whose ranks have been swelled by the brave fallen ones of every battle-field that has been enriched by the warm blood of our brothers, shed in the glorious cause of " Liberty and the Right."

Principal Battles and Engagements.

Roanoke Island, N. C., February 8, 1862.
Newbern,   "   March 14,   "
Fort Macon,   "   April 25,   "
Young's Cross-road, N. C., July 27,   "
Rowell's Mill,   "   November 2, 1862.
Deep Creek,   "   December 12, "
Southwest Creek,   "   "   13, "
Before Kinston,   "   "   13, "
Kinston,   "   "   14, "
Whitehall,   "   "   16, "
Goldsboro',   "   "   17, "
Comfort,   "   July 6, 1863.
Near Winton,   "   " 26, 1863.
Deep Creek,   "   February 7, 1864.
Cherry Grove,   "   April 14,   "
Port Walthall, Virginia, May 6 and 7,   "
Swift Creek,   "   May 9 and 10, 1864.
Drury's Bluff, Va., May 12, 13, 14, 15, and 16, 1864, five days
    in succession.
Cold Harbor, Va., June 3, 4, 5, 6, 7, 8, 9, 10, 11, 12, 1864, ten
    days in succession.
Petersburg, Va., from June 20 to August 24, 1864.
Gardner's Bridge, N. C., December 9, 1864.
Foster's Bridge,   "   "   10, "
Butler's Bridge,   "   "   11, "
Near Southwest Creek, N. C., March 7, 1865.
Wise's Fork,   "   "   8, 9, 10, 1865.
Goldsboro',   "   "   21, 1865.

RECAPITULATION OF CHANGES, CASUALTIES, &c.

	Field and Staff	Non-Com. Officers	Musicians	Old A	B	C	D	E	F	G	H	I	K	L	Old M, New A	Total
Officers killed,	1					1					2					4
Men "				4	5	3	3	3	4	6	5	5	3		5	43
Officers wounded,	6	1		4	1	1	1	2	3	2	3	2	1	2		23
*Men "				4	33	28	28	40	34	29	49	62	41		27	376
Officers died from wounds,	1										1	1		1		3
Men "					4	2	4	4	6	4	1	4	4		5	43
Officers " disease,												1				1
Men "				1	4	6	8	8	10	4	12	6	6		10	75
Accidental Deaths,															1	7
Men discharged for wounds received,					6		2	8	2	2	4	5	3	1	1	41
Men " diseases produced in the service,				22	29	21	20	20	16	26	20	20	21		26	241
Officers resigned on Surgeon's certificate,	2				2	2				2		2	2		1	12
Officers resigned on expiration of time of service,	2								1							4
" " for personal reasons,					1	1		2	1				2	2	4	25
" dismissed the service,								1								1
" transferred to other commands,	2	1			1	1	2	1	1	2		2	1		1	7
Men transferred to other commands,				3	2	1	8	3		5	6	16	11	3	5	57
Officers mustered out,																6
Men mustered out, and discharged at expiration of time of service,			12		48	27	31	68	28	49	38	38	18	1	18	375
Men left behind,				5			1			1						5
†Men deserted,				8	28	3	6	12	4	9	10	9	13		17	120
Officers taken prisoners,							1	1	3	1	4		4			4
Men missing, and taken prisoners,					13	14	17	15	3	15	4	5	7		18	108
Died in rebel prison,						8	9	15	2	12	1	2	7		6	47

* Many of the wounded at Roanoke, Newbern, South-west Creek, Kinston, Whitehall, Goldsboro', 1862, are not included, because Medical Records were lost at the Goldsboro' expedition.

† Many deserted before leaving Camp Olden, some of whom were arrested; others voluntarily returned. The majority of the deserters were substitutes and drafted men, many of whom deserted when the regiment was paid off, shortly after Johnston's surrender.

Mile-Table.

1861.	FROM CAMP OLDEN, NEAR TRENTON,	Miles.
Dec. 4.	To Washington, D. C., by cars,	173
" 6.	" Bladensburg Camp, marched,	5
" 19.	" Meridian Hill,	7
1862.		
Jan. 4.	" Annapolis, Md., by cars,	50
" 13.	" Hatteras Inlet (sail),	275
Feb. 7.	" Roanoke, "	70
" 11.	" Hatteras Inlet, "	70
" 12.	" Slocum's Creek, "	70
" 13.	Marched,	14
" 14.	To Neuse and Trent Junction, marched on railroad,	6
Apr. 1.	Down Neuse river and up Slocum's Creek (sailed),	23
	To Newport Barracks, marched,	10
" 21.	Scout, marched,	20
June 12.	" "	19
" 14.	" "	28
" 24.	" "	21
" 25.	" "	12
" 26.	" "	12
" 29.	Marched home,	24
	Several other scouts during this month, marched,	50
July 26.	To Peltier's Mill, marched,	21
" 27.	" Young's Cross-road, marched,	10
	" Pollocksville, etc., "	20
	" Newbern, "	14
	Several other scouts during this month, marched,	150
Aug. 14 to 16.	Scout, to Cedar Point, and home, marched,	53
Sept. 4 to 11.	To Morehead City and Beaufort, cars and sail,	14
" 17.	To Adams' Creek,	20
" 18.	Marched,	5
	Return, marched,	25

Oct.	29.	To Newbern, by cars,	. . . .	41
"	30.	" Washington, N. C., sailed,	. .	. 185
Nov.	2.	Marched, ...		19
"	3.	" in 4 hours and 10 minutes,	.	. 14
"	4.	" . .	.	20
"	5.	"	.	. 16
"	6.	" . .	.	13
"	7.	" . . .	.	. 11
"	9.	" . . .	.	. 22
"	10.	To Plymouth, marched, .		. 30
		" Newbern, sailed, ...	.	250
"	12.	" Morehead City and Beaufort, cars and sailed,	.	41
Dec.	4.	" Newbern, cars, . . .	.	41
"	11.	Marched, ...	.	16
"	12.	"	.	12
"	13.	" . . .		9
"	14.	"	.	14
"	16.	" .	.	12
"	17.	" . .	.	13
"	18.	" . . .	.	. 17
"	19.	" . . .		15
"	20.	" . . .	.	. 32
1863.				
Jan.	13.	To Carolina City, by cars,	. . .	35
"	20.	" Morehead City, marched, .		. 4
"	29.	" St. Helena Island, S. C., sailed, .	.	. 250
April	5.	" North Edisto Inlet, "	.	40
"	10.	" Port Royal, " .	.	40
"	13.	" Beaufort, N. C., "		. 250
		" Newbern, " by cars, .	.	. 38
"	17.	Marched, ...	.	8
"	18.	" . .	.	15
"	19.	"	.	10
		To Washington, N. C., sailed, .	.	. 7
"	20.	" Newbern, " " .	.	. 185
"	25.	" Carolina City, by cars, .	.	. 35
June	26.	" Newbern, " . .	.	. 35
July	4.	" Pollocksville and further, marched,	.	20
"	5.	" Trenton and beyond, "	.	. 12

July   6. To Free Bridge and further, marched,   .   16
  "   7. " Newbern,   "   .   20
  "   13. " Newport Barracks, by cars, .   .   .   25
          Marched, ...   14
  "   14. To Cedar Point, marched,   .   6
  "   16. " Newport Barracks, marched, ...   18
           " Newbern, by cars, ...   25
  "   25. " Winton, sailed, ... 250
  "   26. " Hill's Bridge, marched, ...   7
  "   30. " Winton,   "   5
  "   31. " Newbern, sailed, ...   250
Aug. 26. " Carolina City, by cars, ... 35
Oct. 18. " Newbern,   "   .   .   .   35
  "   20. " Newport News, Va., sailed,   .   . 215
1864.
Jan. 31. To Jersey City, N. J., sailed, .   ·   275
Feb. 4. " Trenton,   " by cars,   .   . 55
Mar. 15. " Baltimore, Md.,   "   .   134
  "   16. " Portsmouth, Va., sailed, .   .   . 161
  "   17. " Getty's Station, by cars,   5
           " Julian's Creek, marched,   .   .   2
April 13. " Portsmouth,   "   .   .   5
  "   14. Up James river, sailed,   .   26
           " Chucktuck,   "   .   .   4
          Marched, ... 15
  "   15. To Portsmouth, sailed, ...   30
           " Julian's Creek, marched,   .   5
  "   26. " Portsmouth,   "   .   5
  "   "   " Yorktown, sailed,   .   .   .   56
  "   "   " Marched, ...   2
  "   29. Marched towards Williamsburg and return, .   . 20
May   4. To Yorktown wharf, marched, .   .   2
  "   "   " Bermuda Hundred, sailed,   . 133
  "   5. Marched, ...   1
  "   6. " Cobb's Hill, marched,   .   .   . 10
  "   7. Marched and returned to camp,   .   6
May   9 and 10. Marched and returned to camp, .   .   . 10
  "   12 and 16.   "   "   "   12
  "   26. Scout, marched,   .   .   .   7

May	27.	Scout, marched,	. . .	5
"	28.	To City Point, marched,	. . . .	10
"	29.	" Fort Monroe, sailed,	. . . .	90
June	1.	" White House landing, sailed,	. . . .	120
"	2.	" Masson's Mill, marched,	. . . .	10
"	3.	" Cold Harbor, "	. . . ,	5
"	12.	" White House landing,	. . . .	16
"	13.	" Bermuda Hundred, sailed,	. . . .	213
"	14.	Marched,	. . . .	4
"	15.	"	. . . . . .	16
"	16.	Skirmish, .	. . . . . .	35
"	21.	Marched,	. . . .	5
"	22.	To front of Petersburg, marched,	. . .	10
		In and out of rifle-pits, at the siege of Petersburg,		42
Aug.	21.	Marched,	. . . .	5
"	23.	"	. . . .	2
"	24.	" to near Battery No. 6,	. . .	6
Sept.	17.	To Bermuda Hundred, marched,	. . .	24
		" Norfolk and Portsmouth, sailed,	. . .	104
"	18.	" Fort Monroe, "	. . .	16
"	19.	" Morehead City, "	. . . .	260
"	21.	" Carolina City, marched,	. .	3
Dec.	5.	" Newbern, by cars, .	. . .	34
		" Plymouth, sailed,	. . . . .	250
"	9 and 10.	To Gardner's and Foster's Bridge, marched,	.	17
		To Asa Biggs' plantation, marched, .	. .	4
"	11.	" near Hamilton, "	. . . .	15
"	12.	" Asa Biggs' plantation, "	. .	10
"	13.	" Jameston, "	. .	9
"	15.	" Plymouth, sailed, .	. . .	24
"	22.	" above Williamston, sailed,	. . .	25
		" Jameston, "	.	11
"	24.	" Plymouth, "	. . .	24
"	29.	" Jameston, marched,	. . .	9
		" Plymouth, "	. . . .	9
1865.				
Jan.	7.	To Newbern, sailed, .	. . .	250
"	9.	" Carolina City, by cars, .	. . .	34
Feb.	1.	" Newport Barracks, by cars,	. . .	8

Feb.	2. To Adams' Creek, marched, . . .	31
"	3. Scout, marched, ...	20
"	4. To Newport Barracks, marched, . .	31
"	5. " Carolina City, "	8
March	4. " Batchelor's Creek, " .	41
"	5. " Cove Creek, " . .	13
"	6 and 7. To near Southwest Creek, marched, .	12
"	11. To Tilgham's Farm, " . .	11
"	14. " near Kinston, " .	12
"	15. " Kinston, "	2
"	20. Marched, ...	11
"	21. To Goldsboro', marched, ...	9
April	10 to 14. Marched to Raleigh, . .	58
May	2 and 3. To Greensboro', by cars, . .	82
July	13. To Danville, by cars, . . .	48
"	14. " Burkville, " .	50
"	15. " City Point, " . .	60
	" Baltimore, sailed, ...	265
"	17. " Philadelphia and Trenton,—home—by cars, .	134

Total, . . 7,652

Tabular List of Diseases.

[From April, 1862, when the records were commenced, to January 1, 1863, there occurred in camp three deaths, viz.: typhoid fever, 2; dysentery, 1. As the medical records were lost during the Goldsboro' Expedition, in 1862, no tabular list of diseases and no general summary can be made for that year.]

1863.	January.	February.	March.	April.	May.	June.	July.	August.	September.	October.	November.	December.	TOTAL.
Typhoid fever,		1						3	4			1	9
Remittent fever,							21	80	39	14	2		156
Intermittent quotidian,	20	31	7	15	41	39	5	110	42	50	17	22	399
" tertian,			2	3	3	2	40	20	88	42	50	47	297
" quartan,					1		4						5
Congestive fever,								2	1	3			6
Diarrhœa, acute,	24	9	3	15	36	35	60	15	30	26	19	16	288
" chronic,								2					2
Cholera Morbus,				1	3	4							8
Erysipelas,	1							2					3
Mumps,	2					1							3
Dysentery, acute,	3				5	3	4	2	10	6	3	3	39
" chronic,			1										1
Other miasmatic dis.,												12	12
Syphilis,		1			1					4	2		8
Gonorrhœa,	2			1	1		3		3	3		1	14
Orchitis,	1							2			1		4
Stricture of Urethra,											2		2
Rheumatism, acute,	10	6	2	1	2	1	3			5	2	9	41
" chronic,		4	1	3	1					4			13
Scrofula,										2			2
Epilepsy,								2	2	1		1	6
Headache,												8	8
Insanity,		1	1										2
Neuralgia,					2	1	5		4	2	4	2	20
Paralysis,					1								1
Sun-stroke,							13	3					16
Conjunctivitis,			3				3		4			4	14
Inflammation of the Iris,												1	1
Other dis. of the Eye,		2								1			3
Ear-ache,			1	1	2		6		3	2	1	2	18
Otorrhœa,			2		3		2	3					10
Other dis. of the Ear,							1						1
Asthma,					1								1
Bronchitis, acute,									10	26	26	11	73
" chronic,					1						3		4
Epitaxis,						4							4
Inflam. of the Lungs,								2		1	1	1	5
" " Pleura,		1						1	2		5	2	11
Catarrhus,												29	29
Colic,	1	2		10	2	5		1	12	7	5	3	48
Constipation,		2			1							3	6
Dyspepsia,			1		1				2	3			7
Fistula in ano,		1											1
Inguinal hernia,					1	1							2
Inflam. of the tonsils,	2	2	1	1	4		2		9		15	8	44
Acute inflam. of liver,								2			2	4	8

1863.	January.	February.	March.	April.	May.	June.	July.	August.	September.	October.	November.	December.	TOTAL.
Jaundice,..............	1	....	....	....	1	....	2	....	....	....	....	....	4
Piles, ...	....	2	....	2	1	....	2	....	2	1	2	....	12
Other digestive diseases,.	....	....	....	1	....	....	....	....	....	....	....	4	4
Incontinence of urine,..	....	....	....	1	2	....	....	2	....	....	....	....	5
Dislocations,..........	....	....	....	....	....	3	....	....	2	2	....	....	7
Abscess,..............	....	....	2	....	....	1	4	....	12	6	15	6	46
Boil,.................	....	1	2	....	....	....	....	....	....	....	1	....	4
Carbuncle,...........	....	....	....	1	1	1	2	....	1	....	....	....	6
Whitlow,.............	....	....	1	....	3	....	10	2	1	1	3	....	21
Skin diseases,........	....	....	....	....	2	....	2	2	4	4	1	....	15
Burns,...............	....	....	....	1	....	....	....	....	....	....	....	....	1
Contusion,...........	....	1	....	....	2	9	3	....	....	....	....	2	17
Gunshot wounds,......	1	1	1	1	1	....	....	....	1	1	....	1	8
Punctured wounds, ...	....	....	....	....	....	....	....	....	....	1	....	....	1
Poison,..............	....	....	....	....	1	....	....	....	....	....	....	....	1
Sprains,.............	....	....	....	....	....	....	....	....	....	....	....	7	7
Incised wounds,......	....	....	....	....	6	....	....	....	....	3	....	....	9
Drowning,...........	....	....	....	....	....	....	1	....	....	....	....	....	1
Other accidents and injuries,..............	....	....	....	....	2	....	3	....	....	....	....	....	5
SUMMARY.													
Taken sick & wound'd,.	68	66	30	60	135	110	212	249	276	230	183	210	1829
Returned to duty,......	107	20	8	65	110	75	196	43	339	229	222	223	1637
Sent to general hospital,	58	....	....	11	5	6	20	75	8	15	....	....	198
Discharged,...........	....	....	10	....	16	....	....	....	....	....	7	....	33
Died of disease,......	....	....	....	....	....	1	1	....	1	....	....	....	3*
Mean strength of com'd,	921	726	715	717	687	704	684	612	651	712	710	824	
Ave. num. sick daily rep.,	75	54	66	50	54	82	77	208	136	110	95	64	
1864.													
Typhoid fever, ...	....	....	2	5	....	....	....	1	....	....	....	....	8
Yellow fever, ...	....	....	....	....	....	....	....	....	1	....	....	....	1
Remittent fever,......	1	....	....	....	....	4	....	2	2	22	8	6	45
Intermit. " quot.,..	9	3	25	54	....	14	4	23	29	31	33	20	245
" " tert.,...	31	10	75	201	35	5	13	61	84	110	44	75	744
Congestive "	....	....	....	2	....	....	....	....	....	1	1	....	4
Diarrhœa, acute,.......	8	6	17	15	51	156	124	149	141	64	18	31	780
" chronic,......	....	....	....	....	....	4	....	....	....	....	....	....	4
Dysentery, acute,......	....	....	5	7	7	4	....	4	1	....	....	....	28
Measles,..............	....	4	4	6	....	....	....	....	....	....	....	....	14
Mumps,..............	....	1	1	3	....	....	....	....	....	....	1	....	6
Debility,.............	....	....	....	....	....	5	1	7	5	....	....	....	18
Syphilis,.............	....	4	25	1	....	....	....	3	3	1	3	....	40
Gonorrhœa, ...	1	3	15	3	1	....	....	1	....	5	1	....	30
Orchitis,.............	....	....	5	2	....	....	....	....	....	....	1	....	8
Stricture of urethra,....	1	....	....	....	....	....	....	....	....	....	....	....	1
Rheumatism, acute,....	5	2	8	7	3	2	1	5	2	....	1	2	38
" chronic,..	....	....	15	9	....	....	....	1	....	....	....	....	25
Scrofula,.............	....	....	....	....	....	....	....	1	....	....	....	....	1
Itch,.................	....	....	....	....	....	1	....	....	....	....	....	....	1
Epilepsy,.............	....	....	2	....	1	....	....	....	....	....	....	....	3
Headache, ...	1	....	7	....	12	....	2	....	....	....	2	5	29
Neuralgia, ...	....	....	....	....	....	....	4	....	....	....	....	....	4
Sun-stroke, ...	....	....	....	....	19	....	....	....	....	....	....	....	19
Other nervous diseases,.	....	....	....	....	....	....	....	....	1	....	....	....	1
Inflam. of Conjunctiva..,	2	1	....	....	1	1	....	1	....	....	....	2	8
Inflam. of the iris,.....	....	1	....	....	....	....	....	1	....	....	....	....	2
Night blindness,......	....	....	....	....	....	....	7	6	2	....	....	....	15
Inflam. of internal ear,..	....	....	1	....	....	....	....	....	....	....	....	....	1
Otorrhœa,............	....	....	....	2	....	....	....	....	....	....	....	....	2
Varicocele, ...	....	....	5	....	....	1	....	....	....	....	....	....	6
Bronchitis, acute,......	5	....	....	10	....	....	....	1	1	1	4	7	29
Inflammation of lungs,..	....	....	2	6	1	....	....	....	....	....	....	....	9
" pleura,.	2	....	4	....	....	....	....	....	....	....	....	....	6
Hemorrhage of lungs,..	....	....	....	....	....	....	....	....	....	....	1	....	2
Catarrh,..............	13	10	41	....	....	....	....	....	....	....	3	5	64
Colic, ...	....	....	4	....	1	....	3	4	....	....	8	5	20
Constipation,..........	1	1	4	....	....	....	4	1	1	3	8	4	27

* Disease of heart, 1; drowned, 1; typhoid fever, 1.

1864.	January.	February.	March.	April.	May.	June.	July.	August.	September.	October.	November.	December.	TOTAL.
Cholera morbus,										1			1
Dyspepsia,							1						1
Inguinal hernia,	1		7		2		19		2			2	33
Inflam. of the tonsils,	4	3	6	4	2			5			2	2	28
Acute inflam. of liver,	2	4	6		9								21
Chronic " "		2											2
Jaundice,					4			2	4	2	1		13
Piles,			1	2			2	6				2	13
Dropsy from renal dis							1		2				3
Inflam. of the Kidney,						1	2	1	1				5
Incontinence of urine,							1	1					2
Abscess,	1	1	3							1	1		7
Boil,	6		6					1	7	5	3	8	36
Carbuncle,							2	1					3
Ulcers,		1		2	2	1							6
Whitlow,		1	4	4						1	1		11
Skin diseases,												63	63
Burns and Scalds,	1												1
Contusions,	1						1		5		2	2	11
Sprains,	2									1	3	4	10
Frost-bite,	2		2									22	26
Simple fractures,			1	1		1							3
Gunshot wounds,			2		157	40	15	16				2	233
Incised wounds,	2				1					2	3		8
Lacerated wounds,												2	2
Punctured "	2												2
Convalescents,										10		2	12
SUMMARY.													
Taken sick & wound'd,	105	58	305	347	309	236	212	305	303	251	147	266	2844
Returned to duty,	120	18	215	323	199	39	154	179	291	267	147	270	2222
Sent to general hospital,			4	69	131	128	71	123	9	1	3	8	447
Transf. to Res've Corps,	41			36									77
Discharged,	1												1
Died of disease,								1		1	1		3*
Killed in action,			1	1	15	7	2						26
Mean strength of com'd,	569	393	875	875	469	507	514	446	492	538	528	555	
Ave. num. sick daily rep.	41	23	91	136	62	46	47	33	77	55	44	23	

1865.	January.	February.	March.	April.	May.	June.	Total.
Intermittent quotidian,	11	16	6	18	47	48	146
" tertian,	35	49	22	39	119	95	359
Remittent fever,	1		1	2		2	6
Typhoid "					1		1
Rubeola,				1			1
Other eruptive fevers,	1	11	2	6			20
Colic,	1			6		1	8
Constipation,	5			14		6	26
Diarrhœa, acute,	20	43	25	49	186	69	392
" chronic,				2	1		3
Dyspepsia,					1		1
Hepatitis, chronic,					1		1
Tonsilitis,	3	1			4		8
Asthma,		1					1
Bronchitis,	5	37	4	5	8		59
Catarrhus epidem.,		15		16			31
Catarrh,			1				1
Phthisis pulmonalis,		1	1	2		1	5
Pneumonia,		2					2
Other respiratory dis.,	1						1
Phlebitis,					2		2
Cephalalgia,	1	1			21	6	29
Epilepsia,		1	1	1	1		4
Neuralgia,		1					1
Enuresis,					1		1
Gonorrhœa,	1	2		2		6	11
Syphilis primitive,	1		1			3	5
" consecutive,				1	5		6
Hydrocele,				1			1

* Congestive fever, 2; yellow fever, 1.

1865.	January.	February.	March.	April.	May.	June.	TOTAL.
Rheumatism, acute,....	7	15	1	5	8	....	36
" chronic,..	....	..	...	2	1	....	3
Abscess,........	..	....	...	2	....	....	2
Boil,.................	....	....	...	....	....	4	4
Anthrax,..............	9	12	1	....	....	....	22
Fistula,..............	....	....	....	....	1	....	1
Paronychia,...........	1	....	....	....	....	....	1
Ulcer,................	2	....	3	9	8	....	22
Ambustio,.............	....	1	1	....	8	2	12
Contusions,...........	1	1	3	6	1	1	13
Fractures,............	....	....	....	....	1	....	1
Gelatio,..............	....	1	....	....	....	....	1
Hernia,...............	..	1	1	5	4	....	11
Luxatio,..............	....	....	....	....	2	....	2
Sub-Luxatio,..........	2	5	1	....	....	1	9
Vulnus inscisum,......	1	1	2	2	2	1	9
" laceratum,......	....	2	2	....	....	....	4
" punctum,.......	....	1	....	....	....	....	1
" sclopeticum,....	....	....	10	....	2	....	12
Other injuries,.......	....	....	3	....	1	....	4
Opthalmia, ...	1	1	1	....	3	2	8
Otorrhœa,.............	....	2	...	1	....	1	4
Deafness,.............	....	....	....	....	....	1	1
Other diseases of Ear,.	....	....	....	....	2	....	2
Debilitas, ...	....	....	1	2	....	....	3
Hemorrhois,...........	2	6	....	4	5	....	17
Convalescent,.........	....	....	2	....	16	1	19
SUMMARY.							
Taken sick & wounded,.	112	230	97	203	478	245	1365
Returned to duty,......	112	205	78	159	422	251	1227
Sent to general hospital,.	4	11	31	18	5	13	82
Discharged,...........	....	....	....	....	2	....	2
Died,.................	....	....	....	....	2	....	2*
Mean strength of com'd.,	580	611	618	634	698	599	
Ave. num. sick daily rep.	24	43	9	47	92	84	

*Typhoid fever, 1; dysentery, 1.